NIGHTS IN GOLD SATIN

JAKE PERRY

NIGHTS IN GOLD SATIN

WHEN WOLVERHAMPTON WANDERERS
RULED THE WORLD

FOREWORD BY PETER CRUMP

pitch

First published by Pitch Publishing, 2025

1

(pitch)

Pitch Publishing
9 Donnington Park,
85 Birdham Road,
Chichester, West Sussex,
PO20 7AJ
www.pitchpublishing.co.uk
info@pitchpublishing.co.uk

A CIP catalogue record is available for this book
from the British Library.

ISBN 978 1 80150 964 0

Typesetting and origination by Pitch Publishing

MIX
Paper | Supporting
responsible forestry
FSC
www.fsc.org   FSC™ C016779

Printed and bound on FSC® certified paper in line with
our continuing commitment to ethical business practices,
sustainability and the environment.

Printed and bound in India by Replika Press Pvt. Ltd.

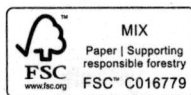

Contents

For Tony and Keith, who were in the crowd for several floodlit friendlies and, two decades later, took me to my first games at Molineux.

With much love.

Acknowledgements

MY GRATEFUL thanks go, first of all, to Jane Camillin and all the team at Pitch Publishing. Working with you is a huge pleasure: thank you for giving me the chance to tell this special story.

Setting out on the project was not a little daunting – adding something new to the litany of books on my hometown team written by so many truly great historians of the club – but the way in which I have been not only inspired but supported by them is something for which I will always be grateful. Steve Gordos, as kind a man as he is distinguished a writer, has given me unfailing support and encouragement, always there with extra details and an expert proofreading eye. My sincerest thanks, too, go to Mike Crump, whose advice and generosity in sharing the fruits of his research for the *Champions of the World* project has been incredible. Launched in 2014 to coincide with the 60th anniversary of Wolves' victory over Honvéd, financed by the Heritage Lottery Fund and supported by the Wolves Museum and the National Football Museum, a newspaper campaign encouraged members of the public to share their memories of the match and the other floodlit friendlies of the time. Alongside the set of DVDs that were subsequently produced, the resulting archive of personal accounts provides a precious insight into the experience through the eyes of the fans themselves. I am enormously grateful to Mike, who has given me permission to quote from the interviews he conducted and the letters he also received.

There are many others without whom this book would not have been possible: Kev Baker, Paul Berry, Martin Brodetsky and Oxford United FC, Paul Butler, Phil Clayton, Clive Corbett, Peter Cullen, Andrew Cullis, Christopher Evans, Mel Eves, Ted Farmer, Gaizka Garamendi, Tim Gibbons, Paul Godfrey and Cheltenham Town FC, Robert Goggins and Shamrock Rovers FC, Yvonne Grieve, Alan Haynes, Kenny Hibbitt, Harry Hunt, Simon Inglis, David Instone, Dr Alexander Jackson, Dave Jones, Frank Lockley, Steve Long, Jim McCalliog, Graeme Nicholson, Neil Pennington, Brian Punter, John Richards, Robyn Spence, Michael Taylor, Tania Taylor, Sam Warrington, Jonathan Wilson, Graham Winwood and, of course, Wolverhampton Wanderers Football Club. Thank you all. My love and gratitude to Mum and Dad, Lin, Keith, Francesca and Tom, and to Susan, Emma, Douglas and Alfie: this, as always, is for you.

My thanks also go to the English Football League, the National Football Museum Archive, the Lancashire Archives, the Oxfordshire History Centre and the wonderful staff of the Wolverhampton City Archive, who were so welcoming on my many visits there. While my trawls through the British Newspaper Archive and the website of the RSSSF supplied much valuable information too, I am deeply indebted to the newspaper I grew up with, the *Express & Star*: the story of Wolves in the 50s was told primarily through the eyes of the paper's dedicated correspondent 'Commentator', the eminent Phil Morgan, and I am hugely grateful to have been granted permission to quote from his priceless body of work.

And to have been given access to a similarly precious source. The minutes of the club's board meetings shone new light, appropriately, on the background to the games, and in that the role of Wolves Museum and club historian Peter Crump was key. Pete's passion for the club and its story – as shines through in the foreword he has so generously written – is as limitless as the time and support he gave me, helping me find my way through its archives and unearthing so many extra gems I would never otherwise have found. Wolves are very lucky to have such a tireless champion, and I am very proud to call him my friend.

On the wall in Pete's office in the Stan Cullis Stand is a famous quote from another distinguished English manager, which caught my eye more than once as I worked. 'What is a club in any case?' Sir Bobby Robson asked. 'Not the buildings or the directors or the people who are paid to represent it. It's not the television contracts, get-out clauses, marketing departments or executive boxes. It's the noise, the passion, the feeling of belonging, the pride in your city.

'It's a small boy clambering up stadium steps for the very first time, gripping his father's hand, gawping at that hallowed stretch of turf beneath him and, without being able to do a thing about it, falling in love.'

Writing this book took me back to being that small boy, to the first times I experienced that thrill: an excitement rekindled every time I visit Molineux today. And, yes, to falling in love: with the present, of course, and the heroes of the day, but with the past as well.

If fans are the heart of a football club, then history is its soul. I have loved every minute of working on *Nights in Gold Satin*. If it brings you just a little of that pleasure, I shall be very happy indeed.

Jake Perry

Summer 2025

Note: Various sources give different spellings of the visiting players' names. Each has been researched individually to arrive at what I believe to be the correct one: any errors are mine.

Other floodlit matches are also referenced in the text: the details of those involving Wolves, including the competitive European ties they played over the period – together with a collation of the player-by-player data from the 16 Molineux floodlit friendlies – are included as appendices to the book.

Foreword by Peter Crump

THE STORY of Wolverhampton Wanderers began in 1877; maybe even as early as 1875. By 1888 they were founder members of the Football League. Twelve clubs began the oldest football league in the world and to be a part of that is something incredible. It's a history that is told at Wolves Museum and to visitors on our stadium tours and the other events we hold here at the museum.

The floodlit friendlies are a huge part of that story, and I have been honoured and privileged to help in a small way with this fantastic piece of work that commemorates that vital and special time.

From the first floodlit friendly in September 1953, the journey the Wolves players and supporters went on was quite incredible. The famous rayon shirts, the iconic players, the huge attendances, the amazing sides that visited: it's all part of the traditions of Wolverhampton Wanderers and of why they are where they are today.

The Honvéd game stands out, of course, as the most famous floodlit match. It is arguably the most important in our history, and certainly the most important as far as the history of European club football and competition is concerned. It was Wolves against Honvéd, England against Hungary and Wright against Puskás as well. The match also took place on 13 December 1954, my dad's tenth birthday: it's a night that isn't just part of Wolves' history, but my family's history, too. But there were many other iconic games that took place in this series: against Celtic, Valencia, Real Madrid and MTK, not to mention many other big names, like Spartak and Moscow Dynamo too. It must have been an incredible experience to be at those games and so special for the supporters of the time.

Watching football under floodlights is still very special. I love Saturdays, of course, but there is something about a game at night that still excites people today: I always look forward to the fixtures coming out and checking who is travelling to Molineux for our evening matches. But the excitement and anticipation in the 50s and 60s must have been something else, both in the build-up and the game. Football under lights in those days was not the norm. I can only imagine what the supporters must have thought when this new concept arrived.

I'm really pleased that my friend Jake has written this book. It is an excellent piece of work and another tool we now have to allow us to tell this story. His passion, commitment and sheer dedication to the project has been incredible. Right from the first email we shared, it was clear that Jake is a passionate Wolves supporter with a huge interest in our history. He grew up in Wolverhampton – in Compton to be precise, not far from where our training ground is today – but now lives in Edinburgh, so researching it wasn't easy at times, but his many hours in the museum office or at the Wolverhampton City Archives going through old newspapers and minutes have paid off, as you shall see. Considering Jake was teaching full-time in a high school in Scotland as well, this truly is an amazing achievement.

I'm very proud that Wolves Museum could help facilitate this project. Please also come and visit us to see some of the artefacts we have on show. The rayon silk shirt, for example, is one of the finest pieces in the museum: I was lucky to be involved in finding it along with my brother Michael back in 2014. This piece is very personal to me for this reason, and I'm extremely proud to see it on display. We are lucky to have many other original items from the games as well.

I will finish by sharing one of my favourite stories to come out of those famous floodlit games. A youngster was born in Belfast in 1946: on 13 December 1954, the date of the Honvéd game, he was eight years old. He would go round to his neighbour Mr Harrison's house to watch the second half live on BBC Television. His name? George Best.

'I was mesmerised by those games,' he later wrote. 'The football was fantastic and there were 55,000 fans locked inside Molineux for every one of them. But it was the floodlights which made them magical for me, made football into theatre. I had already begun a scrapbook on Glentoran, in which I pasted all the match reports from the *Belfast Telegraph*. Now I turned the book upside down, and in the back I began pasting in reports of Wolves.'

George Best is arguably the most talented footballer ever born. The fact he was a Wolves supporter as a boy makes us very proud. His favourite player was Peter Broadbent, arguably the greatest Wolves player of all time, and the company Broadbent shared in that era at our club makes that an amazing accolade.

Enjoy reading!

Up the Wolves,

Peter Crump

Club historian, Wolverhampton Wanderers FC

Prologue

Those Were the Days, My Friend

Molineux: Tuesday, 8 August 1989

HIS FAMOUS trilby was missing, but the gentleman walking towards me was no less recognisable. In suit and tie, a raincoat draped over his arm, he made his way along Waterloo Road towards the North Bank, the old terraced area of the ground that would one day bear his name. He chuckled as I excused myself, my voice trembling a little as I asked for an autograph: surprised, I thought, that this youngster should have wanted it. But this was a man whose reputation went before him, whose influence on this place had been both lasting and profound. His greatest days had come a decade before I was born, but I knew of their legend all the same. Through the long and eventful history of Wolverhampton Wanderers Football Club, there had never been anyone quite like Stan Cullis.

The feats of Cullis and the team he shaped are woven through the fabric of the city. Growing up there through the 70s and 80s, I watched a club still inspired by those glories: one that twice added to them, but never matched their scale. The FA Cup wins of 1949 and 1960 had bookended a decade of dominance in the league, with a maiden First Division title in 1954 followed by back-to-back championships in 1958 and 1959. But it was the story of the team's success on a different stage that really fired my imagination. In the days before formally organised European football, the role of the club in paving the way for what is now the Champions League always gave me an extra surge of pride.

The floodlit friendlies. For a Wolves fan, there is no more evocative phrase. The pioneering series of weeknight games brought the biggest names in Europe to the Black Country, ready to do battle with Cullis's men under the brand-new Molineux lights. Moscow Spartak, Dynamo, Real Madrid and, most famously, Honvéd were beaten, underlining Wolves' status as one of the best teams in the world. Those watching on never lost their sense of awe.

'It was the sort of experience you never forget. It was Molineux, our pitch, but everything else was totally different. The lights, the teams: even the little things, like the captains exchanging pennants before kick-off, I'd never seen before. I just stood there, taking it all in: mesmerised, really.'

The years have rolled by, but the superlatives are no easier to find. My uncle Keith was 11 in 1954, five years younger than Tony, my dad, who stood on the South Bank beside him. The passage of time takes the edge off the sharpest of memories: the emotion that accompanies them, though, stays fresh.

'It took your breath away,' Keith continued. 'Suddenly we'd got European football, and we just didn't know what to expect. These were players we'd only ever read about – Hidegkuti, Puskás, Kocsis, Di Stéfano – footballing gods, really, and now they were here, in the flesh, running out at Molineux in front of us.

'I can't tell you what that was like. It was something else, it really was.'

As was the mood on the terraces. 'Like a cup final,' my dad recalled. With 55,000 crammed in to watch Wolves play Honvéd, the excitement was palpable.

'It was electric,' said Keith. 'Where we stood on the South Bank, I could've taken my feet off the ground and been carried out, it was that much of a crush. But my abiding memory of the Honvéd game is of the luminous shirts Wolves were wearing. I'll always remember them coming out, glowing under the lights. They looked fantastic.

'But it was all so new. Everything was fantastic. Floodlit matches are as common as anything these days and they aren't as special as a result, but back then it was the start of a whole new era. It was fresh, it was exciting: it was the beginning of everything, really.'

Like all those born under a Wanderers scarf, I was brought up on such stories: the tales that added the colour to the grainy black and white footage of that legendary team in action.

Once I was old enough to join Dad and Keith on the South Bank, perched on the wooden stool they carried in for me – old enough, yes, tall enough, nowhere near – I could start collecting memories of my own: of King John and Waggy, Kenny Hibbitt and the Doog, of the side that, in 1974, brought the League Cup back to Molineux, the first major silverware of the post-Cullis era. Saturday afternoons were treasured, but most precious of all were the midweek trips into town after the long school day had ended. An evening game under those famous lights was something very special indeed.

I remember a relegation four-pointer (only two points for a win in those days, of course) against Derby County in April 1979. I can still picture the crowds as we queued at the turnstile, still see those flaming gold shirts from our place on the terrace and feel its surge forward as Billy Rafferty and George Berry – what a goal that was – put us two ahead. And, most of all, I can hear the noise: the chants, the roar, the razor-sharp wit that always surrounded us, win, lose or draw. Wolves – and, indeed, Derby – stayed up that season, but darker clouds were already gathering. The new Molineux Stand would open four months later: the financial fallout from its construction would very nearly put the lights out for good.

Yet Wolves survived, and Molineux too: battered, bruised, with the decaying North Bank and Waterloo Road Stand shut to spectators, but it was picked up, dusted off and started all over again. The South Bank sang the praises of a new idol as Steve Bull wove his magic, the most tumultuous decade in the club's history ending with back-to-back promotions and the Sherpa Van Trophy: not the biggest of the honours Wolves had won over the years, but, without doubt, one of the most meaningful. 'We're back' sang the squad on a seven-inch single released to mark the occasion. So was the buzz that had long been missing from the town.

But when it came to commemorating the centenary of Molineux in 1989, there was only one way to do it: with a new floodlit friendly, a chance for Wolves' latest generation to test themselves against a familiar foe again. It was a very different atmosphere from the one that had greeted

Moscow Dynamo on their first visit to Wolverhampton in 1955: a different sort of team as well, one that had, two seasons earlier, been playing in the bottom tier of the English league. But Wolves rose once more to the occasion, Robbie Dennison and Steve Bull trading strikes with Andrey Kobelev and Andrei Novgorodov before Bull took the roof off with the winner. Another floodlit thriller: the Wanderers greats watching from the stand most certainly approved.

My programme from the evening, Stan Cullis's signature on its cover, still sits on my desk today, a reminder of that game and all it represented. By 2003, when Wolves finally returned to the top flight, their recovery was complete: Sir Jack Hayward had brought stability as well as investment, laying the foundation on which the club of today has been built. My life, too, had changed, as the study that had taken me to Edinburgh became the work, wife and family that kept me there: my trips to Molineux became less frequent than they once were. But my love for my hometown team never wavered, nor my fascination with what will always be the most iconic part of its history.

Echoes of that past still surround the club today. Statues of Cullis and his captain Billy Wright (along with one of Sir Jack) watch over the modern Molineux, redeveloped and officially reopened – with a game against Honvéd, naturally – in 1993. Visitors to the Wolves Museum, located inside the Stan Cullis Stand, can see the relics of those days: the cups, medals, shirts and souvenirs that bring them to vivid life again. They are its motivation and, at times, its burden, a reminder of where the club has been and where its sights are set again for the future.

This, then, is that story: of Cullis, his players and the matches that defined them. The 16 floodlit friendlies are as much a part of their legend as the clutch of trophies that burnished it: games that, seven decades on, are revered by supporters as much as ever. 'Hail Wolves champions of the world now,' said the *Daily Mail* after Honvéd were defeated, words that summed up the magnitude of the achievement: words that ushered in a new age of European competition as well. Ah yes, as Molineux sings, those were the days, my friend: the days when football broke new ground.

When Wolverhampton Wanderers ruled the world.

1

Cullis's Wolves

'IT WASN'T that Wolves at that time were a "better" team [than Honvéd]: it was that they had more determination jointly. It's not always the better team that wins a game, and the reason is something which is emotional and difficult to translate into words.'

Amid all the praise that was lavished on his team after its most celebrated and momentous win, Stan Cullis would have been pleased with that more level-headed assessment of what it was that lay behind its success. Plenty of clubs had talent – and fight to go with it, too – but supporter Percy Young, quoted in Taylor and Ward's *Kicking and Screaming: An Oral History of Football in England*, got to the nub of the elusive extra something that put Wolves in a class of their own. 'We didn't think we were ever going to get beaten,' said Peter Broadbent, one of the heroes of that night, in an interview featured in *The Official Video History of Wolverhampton Wanderers*. 'That was the relationship amongst the players: we just thought, we're going to win today. We knew it before we went out. It was lovely to play in a team like that, where everybody knew what they were doing and why they were there. The atmosphere in the changing room was marvellous.'

They were already the side to beat in the First Division: the team that had shaken off its tag of 'nearly men' to become English football's premier force[1]. They did it through a combination of sweat and toil and a perfectly executed tactical plan: one that upset the purists, to be sure, but gave the public the goals and excitement they craved. 'I had to endure the arrows that were hurled at me for our so-called long-ball game,' said Cullis in 1992, when the phrase carried even more loaded connotations. 'But it was a bit naughty to suggest we were a kick-and-rush side because we had players in the England team for so many years.' Billy Wright, Jimmy Mullen, Ron Flowers and Bert Williams were just a few of those to wear the three lions in that time: Wolves played direct football, it's true, but there was much more to them than that.

Cullis hadn't inherited the style when he was appointed manager of the club in the summer of 1948; nor, indeed, had he been drawn to it by the way he played the game himself. He was, in his decade as Wolves captain under the formidable Major Frank Buckley, a tough but cultured number 5, not afraid to take a risk, described by Ferenc Puskás as the most classical of his time, but all in the team's

---

1   A 2014 study – led by Dr Ian McHale, then director of the Centre for Sports Business at the Salford Business School – named Cullis's Wolves as the third-most successful English side of all time. Every league and cup match from the foundation of the Football League in 1888 to the end of the 2011/12 season had been analysed using a mathematical formula that took into account the relative performance of each team against the quality of opposition they faced. When assessing ten-year dominance rather than single-season strength, only Manchester United (1992–2002) and Liverpool (1979–1989) fared better than Wolves in the years between 1951 and 1961.

orthodox W-M formation[2] and approach that, in practice, had little to differentiate it from half a dozen of its peers. But the influence of the Major could be seen in the way Cullis set about devising a method that put efficiency, not aesthetics, at its core: Buckley had never liked 'no conclusion' flourishes on the field, but Cullis would make an even greater virtue of substance over style.

A kindred spirit in the uncompromising attitude he brought to the role, Cullis's experience with the Major had taught him to think beyond the norm. One of the more adventurous managers of his time, Buckley had brought several innovations into his players' daily routine: rowing machines for fitness, a ball-dispenser for training and, in the dressing room at Molineux, equipment to deliver the very latest in electrical therapies for recovery and conditioning. He was among the first to recognise the value of what we now call sports psychology, employing a counsellor to work with the team more than two decades before Brazil more famously did the same. There were more radical interventions, too, most notoriously the so-called 'animal secretion' injections he introduced to Molineux in the summer of 1937: a monkey-gland extraction, it was reported, though Cullis later shared his belief that it had been a ruse, designed to give the players a psychological rather than chemical edge on the field. 'The Major ... did not lack a sense of publicity at this time,' he wrote in

---

2   Created by Herbert Chapman at Arsenal in the mid-1920s, the W-M formation consisted of four lines: a right-back (wearing the number 2 shirt), centre-back (5) and left-back (3) behind two half-backs (4 and 6) and a pair of inside-forwards (8 and 10) supporting the front three – the outside-right (7), centre-forward (9) and outside-left (11) – making a 3-2-2-3 shape overall.

his 1960 autobiography *All For The Wolves*, 'or, for that matter, at any other time. The injections ... were nothing more potent than an immunisation against the common cold, and certainly I do not think they ever helped or hindered me.'

But where Buckley had delighted in his place in football's avant garde, Cullis, on becoming manager, went back to basics instead. 'There is no substitute for hard work,' he declared, gathering the playing staff together to spell out exactly what that meant. 'I want – and I am going to get – 100 per cent effort from you all both on and off the field,' he said. 'If I get this support, you can take it from me that I will be 100 per cent behind you. Nothing else is going to be enough.' He could forgive a shortcoming or a mistake honestly made, but woe betide anyone giving less than his best. 'Never did I know him verbally lash a player whose skill had broken down in a game,' remembered Dennis Wilshaw in an interview quoted in Jim Holden's fine book *The Iron Manager*, 'but I did hear him give some tremendous lashings to players who did not give everything they had when it came to effort.'

Cullis's motto – painted in block capitals on a board fixed to the dressing room door – became Wolves' mantra. As a PT instructor during the war, he had seen the transformative effect of physical training on the stamina of new soldiers for himself, and, with trainer Joe Gardiner at his side, he was determined to bring similar rigour to Wolves' fitness regime. Former Amateur Athletic Association (AAA) champion Frank Morris was employed to lead the squad in twice-weekly track sessions at nearby Aldersley Stadium, while a further hour was set aside for weight training when that, too, was a novelty. 'At Molineux, we strive to make the abnormal an everyday achievement,' said the manager in *All For The Wolves*. 'I tell my players that they must train until it hurts because it makes them better players on Saturday.'

'We trained very, very hard,' Billy Wright told the BBC's Gerald Sinstadt. 'We'd open up on Tuesday morning by running about three miles: then we'd go down to a mile, then 800 [yards], then 200, and then the sprints. [We saw the ball] for about five minutes afterwards, that's all we got! But the number of times we won our matches in the latter stages of the game purely and simply [because] we were the fitter side, [was enormous].'

'Our main [advantage] was our fitness,' said Ted Farmer, who made his first-team debut in 1960. 'We had the athletics sessions, but the big secret was the pre-season training. At a little village called Brocton there was a three-mile cross-country course which we had to go round twice every Tuesday for the month before the season started. And if I tell you it was a killer: well, it was a real, real killer.' The military-style circuit over the heathland of Cannock Chase took in three hills, each to be scaled at speed. 'By the time the season opens, the players are as hard as nails,' Cullis proudly said in his autobiography, 'able to play at a cracking pace not only for 90 minutes but for 120 if necessary.'

There were minimum targets to be reached – 100 yards in 10.5 seconds, 220 yards in 24 seconds, 440 yards in 55 seconds, 880 yards in two minutes five seconds, one mile in four minutes 50 seconds, three miles in 15 minutes 45 seconds, six miles in 34 minutes, and, in the high jump, 4ft 9in – all to be achieved within 18 months of arriving at Molineux, while further drills addressed identified flaws in individual skill or technique: for Eddie Clamp, his running posture; for Jimmy Murray, his balance; and for Ted, a customised piece of agility to enhance his natural eye for a goal.

'They knew I'd always give a hundred per cent, was quick in the penalty area and would score goals,' he told me, 'but they saw straight away that when I was left up front on my own, I didn't have any tricks. I didn't have the skills of a Peter Broadbent or a Denis Law or Bobby Charlton, so if my speed and strength was matched by the defenders I couldn't keep the ball long enough for people to come up [and support].

'So they had me back in the afternoon with a goalkeeper – Bert Williams, it was, he had retired by then but he still came down to help with training – and a corner stick, which they put on the edge of the penalty area in line with the middle of the goal. They would hit balls up to me on the halfway line, and I would control them, turn and run towards the corner stick then feint to the right by moving my right foot over the top of the ball then collect it with my left and go the other way. The stick beat me nine times out of ten to begin with, but I slowly got the hang of it. The first time I did it in a practice match I sent the centre-half the wrong way, which helped my confidence a lot.'

'I could quote many instances of the dividends Wolves have drawn from the work of our trainers and coaches,' Cullis wrote. 'Often I tell my players that there is no substitute for hard work, although hard work in itself is not enough. It must be work designed specifically to bring every footballer on to the field in a state of perfect mental and physical fitness.'

The value of the training programme, fuelled by the sense of unity and common purpose that had been instilled in the team from the start, could be seen in the execution of a strategy that was a good deal more sophisticated than the manager was often given credit for. Far from crude or obvious, charges that were routinely laid at his door by journalists comparing his approach with that of Matt Busby, whose multi-passing style had made Manchester United the darlings of the press and crowds, Wolves' 'so-called' long-ball game, as Cullis pointedly put it, was the result of countless hours of careful deliberation and equally scrupulous research. Always thirsty for information (and meticulous in the way he collected it: as a player, he had kept a diary in which he recorded his post-match appraisal of every centre-forward he faced) Cullis had analysed the tactical approach of every other First Division side, factoring in the issues that were affecting the wider game in England as well: the general dip in quality that the post-war years had brought, the effect of heavy pitches on particular styles of play and, far from least in those days of economic hardship, the need to provide the paying public with as much value for money as possible. The result was a system tailor-made to Wolves' strengths: direct, fast-moving, and full of goals for the fans.

'Basically, we rely on a framework of tactics which gives ample scope to the operation of the law of averages in football,' he explained. 'The number of scoring chances which will arrive during the course of a match is in direct proportion to the amount of time which the ball spends in front of goal. If the defenders in the Wolves team delay their clearances, the ball will be in front of our goal for too long a period and the scoring chances will go to the other team.

'If too much time is spent building up our own attacks, the ball will spend less of the game in the other team's goal-area. Then the chances of our own forwards to score will become substantially fewer and, of course, we shall score fewer goals.'

'He used to say: "Cut [the pitch] into three,"' Ron Flowers told Mike Crump in an interview for *Champions of the World*. '"That third, we're attacking, we're going to score in that third: get it in there as quick as you can. That third, we're defending: get it out of there as quick as you can. And I'm not interested in the middle one." It was attack all the time.'

But it was never 'hit and hope' with Cullis: the booming kick from goalkeeper to target man that characterised the 'route one' football of the 80s and early 90s. Wolves played, instead, a long-passing game, designed to turn defence into attack with precision as well as speed. In Johnny Hancocks and Jimmy Mullen they had one of the greatest wing pairings of any club and any era: as the attack began with a ball from the back, their role in leading it was key.

'On many occasions I pushed the ball up to Mullen and then watched as he moved smoothly into our opponents' half,' wrote Billy Wright in *One Hundred Caps and All That*, 'waited until their defence started pivoting and then switched the focal point of attack with a long diagonal pass to Hancocks, who, more often than not, was standing quite unmarked. If the left-back was slow to move there would be a thunderbolt of a shot from Johnny's little right foot [not much more than five feet tall, Hancocks wore boots that were around size four and a half]. If the full-back was in position there would be a finely controlled ball to the head of Roy Swinbourne or Jesse Pye or even another cross-field pass, shorter this time, to Mullen, who by now was streaking in hungrily from the left in the hope of snatching a goal.' The addition of Peter Broadbent, signed from Brentford in 1950, brought a further variation to the routine: used as an advanced winger lying 20 or so yards ahead of Hancocks on the right, he would often find himself in the clear when Hancocks chipped the ball on to him having just received it out of defence. The opposing full-back, caught between the two, was played out of the game.

'The Wolves' strength of those days lay in a number of things,' *The Times*'s Geoffrey Green later wrote in *Soccer in the Fifties*. 'The penetration of Hancocks and Mullen down the wings; the goalscoring of Swinbourne, Wilshaw, and, later, Murray through the middle; the subtle prompting from inside-forward by Broadbent; but most of all the power and grit generated by a succession of fine half-backs from Billy Wright ... Flowers, Slater and Clamp, all of them internationals. The half-back lines of those years were the backbone of the side: long, swift passing, the avoidance of unnecessary frills and first-time shooting gave the whole machine its teeth.

'There was a hunger about those Wolves.'

That appetite was sharpened when Europe's best came to town. But the story of the floodlit friendlies is about more than the matches alone: it charts, from Wolves' perspective, a period that forever changed our national game.

Because floodlighting is so integral to the sport as we know it today, it is easy to forget that there was a time when it was not only discouraged but resisted. When league and cup football restarted after the war, playing under lights was banned, the result of a ruling by the Football Association dating back to August 1930. 'Attention having been called to the fact that the playing of matches under artificial light is being organised,' it had said, 'the council express their opinion that the playing of such matches is undesirable, and that clubs are prohibited from taking part.' FA Cup holders Arsenal had wanted to play Scottish Cup winners Rangers in challenge matches at Wembley and Ibrox Park. 'It is understood,' reported the *Dundee Courier* in August 1930, 'that the Association [has] come to this decision on the grounds it would tend to commercialise the game.'

But by the start of the 50s things were changing: not through any sudden shift in the FA's position on the subject, but because of the initiative clubs were now taking for themselves. Several had already lit their practice facilities – Manchester United's junior sides were playing floodlit football at The Cliff, their training ground in Salford, for example, long before lights were installed at Old Trafford – while the growing number of foreign tours to Europe and North America had opened eyes to the opportunities lighting stadia, too, could bring. In January 1951 the governing body finally gave some ground, passing an amendment permitting floodlighting 'under certain circumstances': it was still forbidden for competitive matches – unless special permission had been given – but clubs could now play friendlies, at least, without the need for prior approval.

It would do – for the moment – but the chance to prove the worth of floodlit football was there. What happened next would make sure it was taken.

2

Out of Darkness: Wolves v.
South Africa, 30 September 1953

'THE EVENING will stay with me forever. Everything looked different: the pitch, the stands, the crowd. It was a very colourful scene.'

For Eddie Stuart, the honour of being the first to lead Wolves on to a floodlit Molineux pitch was doubly special. Sidelined for months by an illness that had threatened far more than his career, his comeback game against the national side of his native South Africa marked the end of a personal journey as well as the beginning of a new one for his team. No one could have imagined how influential the series of matches that would grow out of that night would be, but the excitement that surrounded them was already very real. A new age was dawning, and Wolves were ready to make the most of it.

They hadn't been the first to install floodlights: not even in the Midlands[3], though the club had played a part

---

3 The region's first competitive floodlit game had been played at Aggborough Stadium, home of Kidderminster Harriers, on 17 December 1951. A crowd of 4,000 turned out to see Aston Villa snatch a late 2-1 win in the Birmingham League, lit by 32 1,500-watt lamps arranged on either side of the pitch. Special consent to play the game had been given at a meeting of the Worcestershire FA 12 days before.

in one of the first floodlit matches to be staged there. On the evening of 27 February 1952, the works team of the Revo Electric Company – manufacturers of streetlights and traffic signals at their 60-acre factory in Tipton – had welcomed Wolves' Worcestershire Combination side to their ground beside the Birmingham New Road at Tividale. Five down within half an hour – another ten Wolves goals would follow – they had been hopelessly outclassed on the field, but their success in showing a watching group of league and club officials what could be achieved off it was the real talking point of the night. 'Last night's game proved … that the 40,000 wattage installed on the ground is adequate both for the spectators and players,' reported the *Birmingham Gazette* the next day, 'although whether [other] junior clubs consider the expense involved [to] be a practicable proposition remains to be seen.'

Wolves' decision to make the necessary investment, though, had already been made. The match at Tividale had not been their first under lights: that had come four months earlier, on 17 October 1951, when a Wolves XI had travelled to Gloucestershire to take up Cheltenham Town's invitation to christen their new floodlights at Whaddon Road. Championed by manager George Summerbee – the father of Mike, Manchester City's captain against Wolves in the 1974 League Cup Final – and funded by the club's supporters' association, the stadium's setup featured 20[4] large electric

---

4 As relayed by Phil Morgan in the *Express & Star* match report on 18 October. The *Robins Review*, a supporters' newsletter published in the 1960s, gave the number as 112. Taking the two sources into account, similar installations elsewhere and the time that had elapsed when the second piece was printed, I have taken the number quoted in Morgan's report as the more likely figure.

lamps, each mounted on a wooden pole: an arrangement not without its snags – with the lights only 20 or so feet off the ground, the ball was lost in the darkness of the night sky if kicked too high in the air, while nearby residents complained that their house lights and television sets were affected every time the system was switched on (the Midlands Electricity Board, which had assisted with Cheltenham's installation, opened a new substation at Whaddon Road to rectify the problem shortly after). However, with a bit of pre-game razzmatazz adding some extra glitz to the occasion, it made for a memorable evening's entertainment all the same. 'The match was staged with a real sense of showmanship,' the *Cheltenham Chronicle*'s 'Soccerates' enthused. 'As a prelude, the Cheltenham Spa Prize Band played a selection of music in the full glare of the floodlights. Then, as they left the field, the lights went out and a spotlight came on, focusing on the players as they paraded on to the field, to be introduced to the mayor before the kick-off.'

Ready to greet him was some established Wanderers talent: Roy Pritchard, Angus McLean, Roy Swinbourne and goalkeeper Dennis Parsons, later of Aston Villa, who would make 11 league appearances that season as cover for England's Bert Williams. But all but one of their team-mates would play First Division football too[5]: three within

---

5   The exception was Arthur Wainwright, brought in to the side when Les Smith, who had been named in the original starting eleven, was unable to play. Another who would appear – and score – in the match against Revo, research by Steve Gordos shows that most of his games were at centre- or right-half in Wolves' A side, which played in the Birmingham League: he does not appear to have graduated to the reserves, and by early 1954 had moved on to Bromsgrove Rovers, who competed in the same division. A tall, powerful-looking player, a photograph of the team gives an indication of Wainwright's size: he stands well clear of Dick Neal, who was 6ft 1in.

six months, the 20-year-old Stuart, who had joined from Johannesburg club Rangers in January, among them. Ken Whitfield was another – he would mark the second of his ten senior call-ups with a hat-trick against Blackpool in December – while Ocker Hill-born winger Malcolm 'Maxie' Clews, a key member of the reserve team that was in the midst of winning the Central League title for the second of three years in a row, would play in Wolves' 1-1 draw with Liverpool on 5 January. That it turned out to be his only first-team appearance was no reflection on his ability – 'Clews, making his senior debut ... was prominent with a succession of good centres and some strong shots,' the *Birmingham Gazette* reported – but on the abundance that lay elsewhere: with Johnny Hancocks and Jimmy Mullen at the club as well as a more than capable deputy in Les Smith, only injury to two of the three could bring Clews into contention. Their consistency was Maxie's misfortune. Mullen returned next game, recovered from the ankle knock that had kept him out at Anfield, and Clews dropped back to the second string once more.

Others had a bit longer to wait for their big chance to arrive. Sixteen-year-old inside-forward Colin Booth, who had joined Wolves after turning down an approach from Manchester United, would make 82 senior appearances between 1955 and 1959, while wing-half Dick Neal, 18 at the start of the month, would find success in the first team too: not in Wolverhampton, as it turned out, but at Lincoln City – where Clews also relocated in 1954 – then Birmingham, for whom he would play 197 times. But the final member of the Whaddon Road eleven had the brightest of the futures ahead: Ron Flowers, not long signed from Wolves' nursery club Wath Wanderers after an impressive three-game trial. The terms of his contract agreed – £7 a week in the winter, £6 in the summer, plus bonuses – he had played his first game in a Wolves shirt on 18 August, a 4-1 win over Jack Moulds Athletic in the Worcestershire Combination League.

It wasn't quite so straightforward a start for the 17-year-old in Cheltenham, however, as, 11 minutes in, he gave away the penalty that allowed the hosts to take the lead. The stage was set for a thrilling game: Wolves hit back, Neal cracking home from 25 yards before two more in a minute, the first an own goal by Frank Allcock, the second scored by Swinbourne, put them 3-1 ahead 11 minutes into the second half. But the real fireworks, as 'Soccerates' put it, were yet to come, as Cheltenham not only weathered the storm but, through Cyril Dean and Eddie Cowley, got themselves back on level terms. A breathless finale followed – 'seldom has a Cheltenham soccer crowd been roused to such a pitch of excitement as it now was', the *Chronicle* correspondent declared – but neither team could find a winner before the final whistle blew. 'Over 4,500 paid for admittance, and what they saw was worth 18 pence of anyone's money,' he concluded. Hundreds more had scrambled over the walls and into the ground for free: conscious of the lost revenue, Wolves returned their half-share of the gate money, minus expenses, to ensure the Southern League club didn't miss out.

But their trip to Whaddon Road had been valuable in other ways. 'Wolverhampton Wanderers see immense possibilities in floodlighting … and their first move will probably be the lighting of the club's new training ground at Castlecroft,' the *Sports Argus* reported that weekend. 'The first reaction of Wolves coach George Poyser after the match [was], "What a wonderful thing floodlighting is from a training point of view." And this is what he was getting at, "Playing under floodlights made the boys move in double-quick time. [They] had to move their feet quickly because when the ball came to them it seemed further away than it really was. Then at the last split-second they would realise it was right on top of them, and speed in action was the result."'

Lighting Castlecroft, Wolves' venue for senior training and Worcestershire Combination matches as well as youth coaching, would not only allow work to take place through the winter evenings but expand the scope of the club's entire junior programme, the paper said. 'As yet, Wolves have not discussed the question of installing floodlighting at Molineux,' the article added, 'but they are certainly interested.'

They were: and thanks, in equal part, to another floodlit match being played the same night. While Poyser was with Wolves in Cheltenham, Stan Cullis was in north London watching Arsenal take on Rangers in the first official game at the fully floodlit Highbury[6]. A crowd of

---

6 Arsenal had already played twice under their new lights before their formal inauguration: against Hapoel Tel Aviv on 19 September and non-league Hendon in the London Challenge Cup the following month. While the Israelis were beaten 6-1, the amateur team from the Athenian League (which would nowadays lie below the National League South) became the first to defeat Arsenal in a Highbury floodlit match, winning 1-0 on 8 October in front of a crowd of 13,458: inside-right Arthur Phebey scored two minutes from time after a concussion injury and a suspected broken leg had reduced Arsenal to nine men for the last 38 minutes. Hendon had discarded their usual green and white strip in favour of white shirts and black shorts for the occasion.

over 60,000 – many more were left outside – had enjoyed an equally exhilarating contest, settled by a brace from Doug Lishman as the Gunners won 3-2. For the *Daily Herald* and its reporter Clifford Webb, it was a taste of what was now inevitably going to come. 'The future of floodlit football in this country was decided last night by the 62,012 spectators who packed Arsenal Stadium ... and by the thousands who were locked out,' he wrote the next day. 'This overwhelming demonstration in favour of top-class evening football staggered even the most enthusiastic sponsors of soccer-under-lamps.'

The reaction of the Wolves manager was, sadly, unrecorded, but we can be sure that the experience had given him plenty of food for thought. Cullis had long seen the value of floodlighting for practice, but his approach to the idea of lighting competitive games had always been more cautious. In that he was not alone: just two weeks earlier, the Wolverhampton-published *Express & Star* had spoken to the managers of every senior club in the area and concluded that, despite the growing popularity of floodlighting in the south, there was little to no chance of it catching on in the Midlands for anything other than coaching. Lighting training grounds would save wear and tear on first-team pitches, they agreed, but the standard of light required for senior matches – not to mention the discomfort spectators would likely experience standing in freezing temperatures watching them – meant its use in actual games was likely to be limited. 'From all the clubs there was agreement that floodlighting might be found useful in helping with congested fixture lists for their junior matches towards the end of the season,' the *Star*'s report went on, 'but none went so far as to visualise full-scale football under these conditions. As one of them put it, "the thing is still in its infancy".' But the success of the game at Highbury had proved that the technology to support it was there: Cullis had arrived in the capital with questions, but he left with a clear picture of what Molineux's future could be.

And so, tucked away in club secretary Jack Howley's minutes of the board meeting held back at the ground on 18 October – the day after the games in Cheltenham and London had been played – is a short but significant line. 'Reports were given of the flood-lit [sic] matches, Arsenal v. Glasgow [sic] Rangers and Cheltenham Town,' it reads, 'and it was decided to investigate the possibilities of floodlit installation at Molineux.' We can only speculate as to what those summaries may have been – no further detail is given – but a hint of the manager's likely input could be found alongside George Poyser's quotes in the *Argus*. 'I have been thinking about it for a long time,' he told the paper, 'and I think it has great possibilities, particularly from the "spectacle" point of view.'

So began the journey by which Wolves joined the floodlit revolution, one in which both manager and board were determined to take the time to look at every available option along the way. The Simplex Electrical Company in Birmingham was among their first ports of call – 'The sample floodlights having been inspected, it was decided to purchase from Simplex Limited [sic] 90 floodlights, suggested as sufficient to floodlight Molineux for matches,' the minutes of 10 November record – while Archibald Kent Leitch, son of the architect behind Molineux's original development in the 20s and 30s[7], was also contacted as they weighed how best to proceed. But though that enquiry appears to have gone no further, the next 14 months saw a range of individuals and businesses consulted and the submission of several quotes: one, of £4,850 from British Building and Engineering Appliances for a framework of tubular scaffolding by which lights could be mounted on the stands – a setup not dissimilar to the one at Highbury – was received and considered the following July. But Cullis is sure to have noted the same flaw in Arsenal's system as Clifford Webb, who, while full of praise for its effect as a whole in his report of its inauguration on 17 October, had observed that pylon lighting behind the goals was needed to perfect it. Barnet Saidman's famous photograph of the Arsenal–Rangers match for the London-based *News Chronicle* shows exactly what he meant: while the central strip of pitch is brightly lit, its touchlines and corners are in comparative darkness.

It was the plan put forward by France's Electric Limited of Darlaston, then, which got the final nod. 'Mr W.G. France [William George France, born in Wednesbury; the company's managing director] ... attended the meeting [on

---

7   Although described as a 'consulting engineer and factory architect' on the letterhead of the company his son had since inherited, Archibald Leitch (1865–1939) was the foremost designer of football stadia in the early part of the 20th century. Between 1900 and his retirement in 1936, his client list included Manchester United, Liverpool, Everton, Blackpool, Tottenham, Arsenal, Chelsea, Fulham, Millwall, Crystal Palace, Charlton, Southampton, Portsmouth, Aston Villa, Derby, Sunderland, Middlesbrough, Huddersfield, both Sheffield clubs and both Bradford clubs (City and Park Avenue) as well as Wolves. At the peak of his career in the 1920s, 16 of the 22 First Division clubs had paid for his services at one time or another.

29 January 1953] and explained his scheme for floodlighting Molineux Grounds from steel towers at the four corners of the field,' wrote Howley. With post-war construction work still restricted in favour of factories and housing, Cullis travelled down to London himself to ask for permission to proceed.

By the time the board next met, on 5 February, the official go-ahead had been given. 'It was reported that the Ministry of Works [has] granted a licence for our application to install floodlighting at Molineux Grounds,' the secretary minuted. 'It was decided to apply to the Town and Country Planning Department of Wolverhampton Corporation for permission to [begin]. On receipt of this[8] [it is then agreed] to purchase the towers from Horsley Bridge and Thomas Piggott Ltd.[9], [with the building] work to be done by A.M. Griffiths and Son Ltd. and the electrical installation by France's Electric Ltd., Darlaston. Samples of the leading makes of projectors [are also] to be obtained and chosen after being tested.'[10]

That the club ended up with the system it did – 'Britain's brightest,' the *Express & Star* proudly claimed – was entirely down to the industry and ingenuity of William France. The initial details of his design had been worked out on

---

8 Final permission was given at a meeting of the Wolverhampton planning committee on 23 March. Work began at Molineux as soon as the 1952/53 season was over.

9 As it turned out, Wilfred Robbins Ltd. of Great Bridge was awarded the final contract instead.

10 'After consideration of the report by Mr W.G. France on the test carried out at Molineux with floodlights of GEC, Simplex, Phillips and Hollophane [sic],' the board minutes of 28 February record, 'it was decided to purchase [Holophane] floodlights [at] £38 10s. each.' The lights purchased from Simplex in November 1951 were returned to the company in 1954, the club being credited with the amount it had paid against any future purchases of electrical equipment from the business, according to the board minutes of 1 April 1954.

the dining table of his Bilston home using model towers and a scale map of the Molineux pitch: calculations that had even extended to its likely running costs, estimated at seven shillings and sixpence per hour. He had visited every club in the country with floodlighting equipment and sourced additional information from abroad, gaining valuable insight into the systems in use on the continent and in the USA: that of New York's Yankee Stadium was particularly influential as he revised and refined his idea. Wolves' directors had asked for the best, and France was making sure that they got it.

Taking his work from tabletop to reality was a no less thorough process. The construction at Molineux began with the towers, each of galvanised steel, anchored in concrete and topped by a platform and a series of 14ft beams. Next came the lights, 15 to each pylon (with space left on each for five more): twelve 1,500-watt lamps and three 1,000-watt projectors, set to illuminate the goalmouth at the opposite end of the ground. The reflective effect of grass made wet by rain or dew was considered in determining their angle, as was the maximum height to which a ball could be kicked to ensure it could always be seen. A diesel-powered generator was also installed to provide emergency lighting for the stands, passageways, bars and offices in the event of a power cut in the area. 'In other words,' said the *Express & Star*, 'almost every contingency has been anticipated and covered as far as is humanly and scientifically possible, and Wolves may feel they have got what they wanted: the best floodlighting system it is possible to have for their particular needs.'

All at a cost of £10,000. Nearly 20 tons of steel, 270 tons of concrete and around 6,000 yards of electrical cabling had gone into the development: by September, seven months after France had first presented his idea, the lighting of Molineux was complete.

In the meantime, Wolves had been welcomed to four more newly floodlit venues, one of them two days before the initial meeting between engineer and board had taken place. On 27 January – a week later than intended, the original game having been postponed because of fog – Bristol City had been beaten 4-1 in the first evening match at Ashton Gate. Then, on 2 March, came a shock, as Hull City inflicted a 3-1 defeat – Wolves' first under floodlights – at Boothferry Park, which had already hosted three floodlit matches, including one during which a floodlight had fallen on to the pitch, leading to play being held up for a couple of minutes while broken glass was cleared. Eight days later, at Queen Street, Johnny Hancocks led a more youthful Wanderers eleven to a 4-2 win over non-league Bilston before finally, on 24 March, First Division rivals West Bromwich Albion fell to a similar scoreline at Cross Keys, home of Hednesford Town.

In the middle of the sequence, on 23 February, there had been another game, too: against the Southern League semi-professionals of Headington (later Oxford) United. Managed by former Wolves forward Harry Thompson, Headington had been one of floodlit football's original pioneers[11]: on 18 December 1950, near-neighbours Banbury

---

11 The Manor Ground's first setup consisted of 16 pole-mounted lights – borrowed from college buildings usually illuminated at night – arranged on either side of the pitch with another immediately behind each goal. '[The] players afterwards said it was not too bad at all, except in the middle of the field,' reported the *Banbury Guardian* after the home side's 3-0 win over Banbury Spencer.

Spencer had visited the Manor Ground to play an evening match just 48 days after Southampton had switched on England's first set of permanent floodlights with a friendly against Bournemouth and Boscombe Athletic at The Dell. 'Floodlit football is tremendously popular at Headington, and games of this quality should help make it more so,' said the *Express & Star* the day after Wolves' entertaining 3-2 win: Bill Guttridge (leading the attack rather than in his more familiar place at left-back), Johnny Hancocks and Eddie Stuart got the goals, but Headington pushed them all the way. Thompson's men would win the Southern League and cup double at the end of the season; the bumper gate provided by the 10,000-plus crowd added some extra gloss to their year, too.

But it was to Molineux's grand opening that Wolves' attention had now turned, and in that, the prompt conclusion of the building work had given some flexibility as to when, and against whom, it might be.

Wolves had already made arrangements with a potential first opponent, pencilling in a match with Celtic on 14 October as their inaugural floodlit night. But a second, earlier friendly was in the diary as well: against South Africa, due to arrive in the UK on 4 September to begin an eight-week tour. A year beforehand – on 3 September 1952 – an invitation from the Football Association to host the team on 30 September had been received and accepted by the board: then, a few weeks before the game, its kick-off time was confirmed as 3pm.

A month later, however, all that had changed. 'At the request of the South African FA,' Jack Howley minuted on 10 September, 'it was decided to play the match with them ... under floodlights.'

The South Africans' appeal for an evening game had gone to Celtic, too: assistant tour manager Doolan Hosking had written to the Scottish club directly to explain just what a switch would mean. 'Our share of the receipts will amount to over £1,000 thanks to Celtic's generosity,' he told the *Daily Mirror* after their consent was given: 'As we must make £13,000 to break even on this tour, you can see just how much this floodlit match will help us.'

The *Express & Star* relayed a slightly different version of the story – 'When the date of the match with the South Africans became known, it was immediately realised that a floodlit game would probably draw a bigger gate than an afternoon fixture at a time when so many people would be working. Wolves put the position to Celtic, who readily agreed to the South Africans taking first place on the floodlit list' – but its upshot was the same. 'Incidentally,' the paper added, 'the date with Celtic, which had been provisional, has now become definite, so that Wolverhampton will have two first class floodlit games in a fortnight to test reaction to this most attractive form of exhibition football.'

But in that, Wolves had something else in store. Molineux's lights were not going to be the only thing the first-night crowd would remember.

* * *

Back at Whaddon Road in 1951 – the starting point, in many ways, of the path that had brought Wolves here – the *Star*'s Phil Morgan had made a telling observation. 'Because there has to be a first time,' he had begun, writing under his familiar byline of 'Commentator', 'I went with Wolves on this goodwill trip and returned to Wolverhampton convinced that here is an idea with a future. I can visualise the effect of floodlights at Molineux where the resources of a wealthy first-class club could produce something better than the commendable initial effort by hard-up Cheltenham.

'One thing that was plain, however: Wolves' old gold strip is not the thing for floodlights, Cheltenham's red and white showing up much more plainly.'

Wolves' traditional playing shirt had already been the subject of discussion. It had, ironically, once been red and white too[12], but old gold and black – said to have been inspired by Wolverhampton's coat of arms and its motto, Out Of Darkness Cometh Light – had been the club's official colours since 1890, when they were registered as such with the Football League. But the chosen shade of gold had its issues: in the rapidly darkening afternoons of winter especially, the rich but hardly vibrant colour had never been easy to pick out. A brighter alternative, then, had been mooted, one that would be clearly visible to players and fans whatever the state of the light may be. The result of that debate would become the defining image of the floodlit friendlies: its original objective, though, was to solve the team's problem in the daytime game.

---

12 St Luke's FC, the team founded by John Baynton and John Brodie in 1877 – which merged with cricket club Blakenhall Wanderers to form Wolverhampton Wanderers two years later – played in blue and white hoops. The switch to red and white stripes had been made by 1883. In 1889, old gold and black was adopted, becoming official a year later to avoid a clash with the red and white of Sunderland in the newly formed Football League.

On the afternoon of 24 November 1951, as Wolves tried to turn around a run of form that had brought them just one point from their last five games – Cullis's future had even been discussed, but, on 10 November, he had received a unanimous vote of confidence from the board – an unsuspecting Molineux was given its first sight of a striking new look. 'Spectators in Wolverhampton gasped when, in the second half, the Wolves [playing Charlton] turned out in bright yellow luminous shirts that gave them the appearance of dancing flames,' the *Weekly Despatch* reported. 'Mr J.T. Howley, Wolverhampton Wanderers secretary, said afterwards, "We had the shirts in stock for two weeks, just waiting for a suitably dull day."' They had certainly got that: rain had been falling steadily throughout the first half.

Made of rayon, a soft, shiny, semi-artificial silk, its bagginess accentuated by an elasticated waistband – a feature that would make it doubly unpopular with the players thanks to its tendency to ride upwards as well as trap in sweat – the new shirt was very different from anything the supporters had seen before. While details of its origins are sketchy, Stan Cullis was very much at the centre of its development, overseeing the trial of the prototype in several training games: one back at the Revo Electric ground, where youth team left-winger Brian Punter wore it in a match against Birmingham County FA. 'This was a sort of practice game, I presume to check their floodlighting system out, because Revo Electric were experimenting with floodlights at the time[13],' he told me. 'There was just

---

13 Revo had installed a small number of floodlights for training purposes the previous season, but, by November 1951, had begun the process of upgrading their system to allow the playing of full-scale floodlit matches.

one shirt[14], which I wore because I was a winger and the manager wanted to see how it looked from the other side of the pitch.' While Wolves failed to sparkle in its first official outing – 'If their play had shone like the fluorescent yellow shirts they wore for the first time in the second half against Charlton Athletic, the Wolves could have claimed as their own the town's motto,' said the *Birmingham Gazette*, not the only paper to make use of the analogy in its report of the 2-2 draw – the impact they were looking for was there. 'To the white ball and the floodlit pitch has been added the luminous "strip" as a means of brightening the gloom that so often pervades winter soccer,' the *Birmingham Mail* remarked. 'If the Wolves failed to find their old form … they certainly made a hit sartorially.' There was one catch, as club director Arthur Oakley explained – 'the Charlton players could see Wolves better than Wolves could see them' – but 'it was a good day to try them out', nonetheless. 'I think fluorescent shirts are bound to come for midwinter games,' he said, 'but for full effect, both sides should wear them.'[15]

---

14 This could be the shirt – a distinctive golden peach in colour (to these eyes, anyway; others have described it as pink) – that is now housed in the Wolves Museum. It had been retrieved from a pile destined for a skip at Castlecroft following its sale at the height of Wolves' financial troubles in 1986.

15 It can only be speculation in the absence of definitive proof, but Oakley may well have been the source of the suggestion to look at new materials, not just colours, for the shirt. In 1950, as vice-president of the Football League, he had been involved in meetings at which the introduction of fluorescent linesmen's flags was discussed; inspecting different samples of fabric had presumably been part of that process as the various options were explored. 'Coloured red and yellow, they have been issued by the Football League to all league clubs and have to be used in all the club's matches in the future,' the *Grimsby Daily Telegraph* reported on 6 September after the final decision was made. 'The fluorescent quality in the flags will make them show up better in bad light.' The cloth the league chose was unspecified, but it is from here, a year earlier, that the idea for Wolves' shirts possibly came.

Wolves changed into the same shirts at the halfway point of their next two home games, on 8 and 15 December. They may have helped in the 4-0 win over Middlesbrough, Jesse Pye (twice) and Roy Swinbourne finding the net after the interval, but there was no such magic on show seven days later when former Wolves hero Dennis Westcott scored the only goal of the second half to salvage a 2-2 draw for Manchester City. But then, without warning, the experiment was suddenly shelved: perhaps, as Steve Gordos and Clive Corbett have suggested, the club agreed with Arthur Oakley and decided that the opposition had been handed too much of an advantage; maybe the Football League had let it be known that the shirt didn't conform to its regulations. I can find no record of the definitive reason why[16]. But either way, its suitability for floodlit football was clear: it had been dropped for the league, but Wolves' rayon kit – its brightness enhanced by the reflectiveness of the fabric that would so often be described as 'fluorescent' or 'luminous' at the time – was still very much in their plans for the new night-time game[17].

---

16 This fact alone makes the first suggestion the more likely. There is no mention of the shirt, let alone of it breaching regulations, in the minutes of the Football League management committee (held in the Lancashire Archives in Preston) or, as far as I have been able to ascertain, in the press. Had the league, presumably through Oakley, made a more informal representation, it is still likely to have been reported by the newspapers.

17 Other clubs followed Wolves' lead in experimenting with rayon – some, like Manchester United, under lights. In November 1952, The Cliff hosted an FA Youth Cup tie between United and Nantwich that featured both sides in 'luminous' shirts. According to unitedkits.com – its information confirmed by youth football historian Tony Parks – United owned both sets (one in their traditional red, the other in bright amber), having purchased them on their close-season tour of North America earlier in the year. They were clearly happy with the results: the practice of offering the 'away' set to the visitors for floodlit games at The Cliff continued for the next three years.

Two months later, on 27 February, the shirts made their first appearance under lights in the 15-1 win at Revo – 'In their other floodlit experience at Cheltenham last autumn Wolves wore their normal club strip, and the difference last night, when the team turned out in the new luminous shirts, was 100 per cent improvement,' Phil Morgan was happy to report – before they surfaced again in the friendlies Wolves played at the start of 1953 as their own lighting system was being developed. 'The game will have much to commend it as a spectacle under floodlight for there will be the sharp colour contrast between Wolves' new luminous gold strip and the bright green shirts of the South Africans,' said the *Express & Star* on the eve of its unveiling. A brand new strip? No it wasn't, but after their early false start, Wolves' gleaming golden shirts would give Molineux's floodlit matches a look all of their own.

* * *

As the fans took their places on the terraces and in the stands – many taking advantage of the 'bob' gate offer that gave entry to the North and South Banks for a shilling – the players in both dressing rooms readied themselves for the game. Wolves were no strangers to South Africa or its football having toured there in 1951, and though the Springboks were still an amateur side – the National Professional Football League, the first such setup in the country, wasn't established until 1959 – they had already shown the talent that was present in their ranks. Their best performances had come in the capital, where, after a 4-0 demolition of England's Amateur XI at Selhurst Park on 19 September, they had held Arsenal to a 2-2 draw under the Highbury lights four days later. With a record of three wins and only one defeat in their six tour games so far, the Springboks were not a side to be taken lightly, no matter what their status might imply.

Not that, for Wolves, that was ever going to be the case. Cullis announced only two changes to the previous weekend's team: one precautionary, the other for different reasons. Ronnie Stockin came in for Dennis Wilshaw, his workload being managed as he recovered from recent injury. Bill Shorthouse, meanwhile, chose to stand down to allow Eddie Stuart to not only play against his fellow countrymen, but, with the blessing of Cullis, captain the team as well.

Never a man much given to sentiment in his professional life, the manager's gesture towards his young centre-half was about more than that alone. Stuart's Wolves career had started brightly: after a spell in the reserves he had made his league debut on 15 April 1952, marking it with a goal against West Bromwich Albion in front of 48,000 at Molineux. But his return to South Africa on a post-season scouting visit nearly ended in tragedy as, on his way back to England to prepare for the next, he picked up a rare, malaria-like infection during a stop-off in Egypt: gravely ill by the time he arrived in Wolverhampton, he was rushed to the town's Queen Victoria Nursing Institution as a specialist was hurried from London to treat him.

'Of the details I remember very little,' he said in an interview published in *Charles Buchan's Football Monthly* in 1954. 'They tell me I was given the slenderest chance of survival. [But Mr Cullis] then did something for which I and my family ... will always be grateful. He sent for my mother, who made the long trip to my bedside by Comet[18]. She stayed as a guest of the club until I was out of danger.

'The cause of the illness is still something of a mystery, but it was mastered by a combination of medical skill and a tremendous religious faith on the part of my mother and myself.' The danger passed, but it was several months before he could play again: after making his reserve team comeback in the 4-2 defeat at Derby County on 23 January, he featured and scored in Wolves' games against Headington United and Bilston – perhaps significantly in the context of his recuperation, Wolves' only non-league opponents in the five floodlit matches they played at the start of the year – before appearing at centre-half for the Whites against the Colours in the traditional intra-squad pre-season game at Molineux on 15 August. His long-awaited return to first-team action, then, was full of extra emotion.

The strength of the team he led into the Molineux lights was mirrored by that of the South Africans, who fielded their first-choice side. Two key players were back from injury: Ross Dow, the Springboks' skipper, now recovered from the ligament damage that had kept him out for three games, and Les Salton, the 20-year-old centre-forward from Northern Transvaal, who had already scored five times. Three of the team that had played alongside Dow for the national side in the two 'test matches' that concluded Wolves' trip in 1951 – Johnny Claassens, Wally

---

18 The Comet, manufactured by de Havilland and introduced the year before, was the world's first commercial jet airliner, flying between London and Johannesburg. A bank draft of £316 16s. (the equivalent of about £10,000 today) was sent to the South African FA to cover the cost of Mrs Stuart's return ticket.

Warren (who Wolves had previously tried to sign along with fellow tourist Charlie Hurly, who was not selected for the Molineux game) and Cliff Jacques, Stuart's former Rangers team-mate – lined up to face them again, while Doug Rudham, Southern Transvaal's goalkeeper in the opening game of the tour two years earlier, looked to add to the burgeoning reputation that had already brought Chelsea to his door. The 24-year-old would return to England the following October to sign amateur forms with Liverpool: in August 1955, having served the FA's mandatory two-year qualifying period as an overseas player, he signed the professional deal that would keep him at the club for another five years.

As the match got under way Rudham's class was soon clear, while the skill of inside-forwards Gibson and Warren was also warmly acknowledged by the fans, but the difference in the speed of thought and movement of the men in gold, however, was what quickly set its tone. The previous Saturday, Chelsea had been run ragged by Hancocks and Mullen – the former scored a hat-trick in the 8-1 win that remains the Blues' record loss to this day – and the wingers were soon at it again as the hosts settled into their stride. Billy Wright and Bill Slater (playing his second match against the tourists, having captained England's amateurs in London 11 days before) were equally prominent at wing-half, and while Wolves didn't show the same ruthlessness that had undone Chelsea so spectacularly, the barrage of cross-field passes between the four was more than the visitors could contain.

It was Mullen who opened the scoring on 32 minutes after an exchange of passes with Hancocks then Swinbourne and a drive that went in off the post. Two minutes later it was two as Peter Broadbent finished superbly, beating right-back Ben Machanik before lashing a cross-shot home. Gibson's header pulled one back three minutes into the second half as the home defence looked in vain for a flag, but Wolves put the game beyond doubt four minutes from time when Swinbourne deflected Hancocks's cross into the net for the third. They could, probably should, have had more – '[Wolves] tackled the tourists so politely and with such holiday-like spirit that it seemed nothing could persuade them to be so ill-mannered as to score,' said the *Birmingham Gazette* – but it was the spectacle of it all that the fans would remember: of a different Molineux and a different game.

But while the write-ups in the morning focused mainly on that, Wolves' opponents, too, were roundly praised. The quality of their football had improved – by about 75 per cent, in Stan Cullis's very precise assessment – since the Midlanders' tour of the country: both he and Fred Fell, the London-born president of the South African FA, agreed it was obvious how beneficial the club's visit had been.

The Springboks went on to play another 13 matches before their departure on 12 November, winning two, drawing two and losing nine: one to an Anglo-South African XI at Highbury, where Eddie Stuart was among the scorers in the expats' 6-1 win. Their travels had taken them to Anfield, Dens Park, St James' Park, Hillsborough and, for a third floodlit encounter, The Dell, but it was the memory of their night at Molineux that would linger. They each took away two mementoes of the area – a Walsall-made leather wallet and a Brierley Hill-crafted glass bowl, presented at the mayoral reception that preceded the lunch with the club directors that had welcomed them to the town – but not before one last battle with Wolves had been waged: on the golf course, where both sets of players met the day after the game.

'Call it what you will, football in fairyland, football in Technicolor or just plain football by floodlight … it all adds up to the fact that last night's inauguration of Wolves' new lighting system at Molineux was one of the most illustrious occasions in the club's long history,' wrote Phil Morgan in the *Express & Star*. 'The 33,681 spectators went to see the floodlighting out of curiosity and, with all due respect, the South African tourists … out of courtesy. They stayed to be fascinated by the lights and full of admiration for the South Africans' football.

'We may take it, I think, that the South Africans will never forget the welcome they received in Wolverhampton, and it was to the credit of the town's football followers that they provided the biggest crowd yet to watch the tourists in this country, despite the fact that the evening weather was anything but ideal. It is doubtful if the Springboks will play before a bigger gate during their tour, and if they like to feel that this shows how much Wolverhampton admired them and the way they recently entertained Wolves, we shall be quite happy.

'After all, we can now say that they helped to entertain us, on an occasion that few who were there will readily forget.'

Wednesday, 30 September 1953: Wolves 3 South Africa 1

Wolves: Williams; Short, Pritchard; Slater, Stuart, Wright; Hancocks, Broadbent, Swinbourne, Stockin, Mullen.

South Africa: Rudham (Germiston Callies); Machanik (Marist Brothers), Jacobsen (Johannesburg Rangers); Dow, Naish (both Berea Park), Jacques (Johannesburg Rangers); Claassens (Garrison [Pretoria]), Warren (Marist Brothers), Salton (Berea Park), Gibson (Balfour Park), le Roux (Queen's Park).

Goalscorers: Wolves – Mullen (32), Broadbent (34), Swinbourne (87); South Africa – Gibson (48).

Referee: F. Read (Willenhall).

Attendance: 33,681.

3

Battle of Britain: Wolves v. Celtic, 14 October 1953

THE MORNING after Molineux's night before, excitement still crackled in the air. 'Let nobody have any doubts,' said Phil Morgan. 'Floodlit football sold itself to the local following at the first attempt last night. In as many [enquiries] as I could make among all sorts and conditions of people, from the captains of the teams to the newest woman onlooker, I found nothing but praise for the system or the setup.' Ross Dow, he wrote, found the lighting to be first class, while Billy Wright considered it the best he had played under in England. Stan Cullis, too, was delighted, declaring that the quality of the system more than justified the wait for its completion. 'There is no [doubting] the wisdom of the Wolves directors in making careful [enquiries] before rushing in with a scheme without counting the possibilities of even partial failure,' said Morgan; the meticulous efforts of the past two years had paid off in spades.

The *Express & Star*'s coverage of the evening extended into its centre pages, with a photographic spread shining a 'spotlight on [a] brilliant game'. While one of its reporters hadn't made it in the end – 'After a rather dreary afternoon plodding about in the pouring rain [enquiring] into readers' complaints of inconvenience on revised bus routes,' the unnamed correspondent grumbled, he had been left stranded at a bus stop on his way to the ground after falling victim to them himself – the celebratory mood of the local paper was echoed in the nationals as well. 'It was carnival night at Molineux,' the *Daily Mirror*'s Tom Lyons proclaimed. 'Thirty-five thousand fans, all in amiable mood, enjoyed the newly installed floodlights. Wolves wore brand new [sic] short-sleeved luminous shirts for the occasion, and the football was fast, open and thrilling.' The success of Molineux's 'Technicolor friendly', as the *Birmingham Gazette* dubbed it, was complete.

Wolves returned to league business at Bramall Lane three days later, where Roy Swinbourne's 84th-minute strike earned the 3-3 draw with Sheffield United that kept them third, a point behind Huddersfield and three adrift of leaders West Bromwich Albion. With seven wins and two defeats from their 12 First Division matches so far, it had been a promising start for Cullis's side. The rout of Chelsea stood out, but victories at Maine Road and Highbury as well as over Cardiff City, Sunderland, Liverpool and Portsmouth had put them in a strong position in their bid for what would be the club's first top-flight title. The 2-1 win at St James' Park that then consolidated it on 10 October – Wolves' first victory on Tyneside since February 1903 – showed their strength in depth too, as Ron Flowers, Les Smith and Ronnie Stockin all impressed in the absence of Wright, Mullen and Wilshaw, called up by England for their match against Wales the same afternoon. 'Take away Billy Wright, Jimmy Mullen and Denis [sic] Wilshaw from Wolves and what is left?' asked the *Mirror*. 'Newcastle United found the answer on Saturday ... still a fine fighting force, full of ideas and the will to win.' Wolves left it late to respond to Tommy Mulgrew's early opener, Smith driving in an 81st-minute equaliser before Swinbourne applied the *coup de grâce* in the 88th, but it was a pleasant journey home all the same. Five more wins from their next seven games, including a 1-0 victory over Albion, moved Wolves into second, now just a point behind their local rivals.

In between their trips to Sheffield and Newcastle, Wolves had played under Bilston's lights again – drawing 0-0 on 5 October in the first round of the Staffordshire Senior Cup – and then, the following day, at the inauguration of another floodlit ground: one at which their league form counted for little as Second Division Bury (captained by former Wanderer Angus McLean) won 3-1 at Gigg Lane. A second defeat followed three weeks later, this time at Highfield Road, where Ian Jamieson's second-half penalty gave third-tier Coventry City a 1-0 win to go with the 1-1 draw they had earned against Queen of the South in the ground's first floodlit game a week earlier[19]. 'Opinions differ regarding the permanency of floodlit football,' a note in the programme for the opening match had said, 'but we believe there is a great future in this type of entertainment. And why not? Does it not give us

---

19 Wolves turned down two further invitations to play floodlit games in London: against Queens Park Rangers on 5 October and Millwall on 9 November (board minutes, 29 May 1953).

the opportunity of allowing our supporters to see the best teams, not only in Great Britain, but also continental teams of repute?'

It did, and Wolves had, by then, given their own fans the chance to watch the next of them. The visit of Celtic on Wednesday, 14 October attracted Molineux's biggest crowd of the season so far: it was rewarded with a game to remember as both teams went all-out for the win.

Though Celtic's supporters had another six years to wait for some floodlit football of their own, the team from the green half of Glasgow were no strangers to the night-time game. On 25 February they had played Newcastle in the first floodlit match at St James' Park, going down to a brace from George Robledo despite the long spells of pressure they applied. It had been, in many ways, the story of their season: at times brilliant, beating Arsenal, Manchester United and Hibernian on their way to lifting the one-off Coronation Cup, but lacking the consistency and ruthlessness to mount a sustained challenge in the league. Injury had played its part in that campaign: eight players had been tried at both centre-forward and left-half as Celtic slipped further down the table, eventually finishing in eighth, a distant 14 points behind Rangers, who denied Hibernian a hat-trick of First Division titles on goal average after tying with them on points at the top of the league.

But the chopping and changing of Celtic's eleven was also symptomatic of the way the club was being run at the time. The team was picked by chairman Robert Kelly, its tactics left up to the players: uppermost in Kelly's mind was for them to play with sportsmanship, to uphold the spirit of a bygone, amateur age. '[The captain] has no decisions to take about [the] team ... or tactical changes,' centre-half Bobby Evans complained, as reported in Frank Rafter's book *Standing on the Shoulders of Giants*. 'The answers to these problems come from the directors' box to the track, and are passed to the field by the trainer.' Manager Jimmy McGrory was little more than a figurehead; the contrast with the Wolves of Stan Cullis, who took personal charge of every footballing matter from the youth team to the first, was stark.

But after a sluggish start to the current season, a more settled side had emerged: one more representative of the array of talent the club had always had on its books. Six of the Scottish Cup-winning team of 1951 (Scotland internationals Evans, Bobby Collins and John McPhail, Ireland caps Sean Fallon and Bertie Peacock and goalkeeper George Hunter, back in the line-up after current number one John Bonnar and his understudy Andy Bell had both been injured) formed the spine of the eleven named for Molineux, with Mike Haughney and Jimmy McIlroy strengthening the defence and midfield and Jimmy Walsh, Willie Fernie and Neil Mochan adding extra pace and power in attack.

Though centre-half Jock Stein was missing – he was part of the travelling squad, but left out of the final team – the game 'should provide an example of the best in both English and Scottish football', declared the *Express & Star*. With Celtic lying third in the Scottish First Division, the match had, as Phil Morgan remarked in his piece for the evening's programme, been eagerly awaited ever since it had been confirmed. 'We owe [the visitors] our thanks because they so sportingly stood down from their claim to be our first opponents under the lights so that we could pass that honour on to and assist financially our recent visitors from South Africa,' he said in his guise of 'Wanderer', his second *nom de plume*. 'Let our reception therefore be such that Celtic will have no reason to regret their splendid gesture.'

For Wolves, Wright, Wilshaw and Mullen all returned, but several further changes to the eleven that had beaten Newcastle had to be made elsewhere. With Roy Pritchard unfit and Bert Williams unwell, Bill Guttridge stepped up to partner Jack Short at full-back, while Nigel Sims – who, with Williams dropped, had played the first five league games of the season – was in goal. Bill Slater was a later withdrawal, bringing Bill Baxter into the team, but it was Cullis's final selection that made the headlines in the paper that afternoon. 'Tipton boy plays for Wolves against Celtic tonight' read the *Star*'s back page. Local lad Bobby Mason had earned his maiden first-team start.

Born in Great Bridge and schooled at Park Lane Secondary Modern, the 17-year-old's journey to the senior side had begun two years earlier, at a game that had already played its part in Wolves' early floodlit story. Mason was part of the Birmingham County FA youth eleven that faced the Wolves youth team – complete with Brian Punter in the club's prototype rayon shirt – at the Revo Electric ground. '[The manager] spotted him in that game,' Brian recalled, 'and not long after – it might only have been a couple of weeks – he signed for the Wolves.' Now on professional terms, Peter Broadbent's absence, released to play for the RAF at White Hart Lane as he came to the end of his national service[20], had given the youngster his chance.

He would duly shine, as would Molineux once again. While the match against South Africa had been everything Wolves had hoped for, the game against Celtic put the final seal on their success. The crowd – 8,000 bigger than a fortnight earlier – allied to a dry night and the all-round quality of the football on display ensured Molineux's second floodlit friendly would be even better received than its first. 'The football, for me, was some of the best and certainly some of the most exhilarating we have seen on the ground for a long time,' wrote Phil Morgan the next day. 'It was in keeping with the brilliance of the lights, which have caught on like few local developments in football history.' There was something extra to enhance their brightness, too: white goal nets, an idea borrowed from Bury, who had used them to great effect in their game at Gigg Lane the week before. 'White Nets – What Next?' asked the *Express & Star*. It wouldn't be the only such innovation the floodlit friendlies would see.

A friendly by name, the clash with Celtic was anything but in practice, as keenly contested as any league or cup encounter with points or trophies on the line. The Scots began superbly, thrilling the crowd with their speed of movement and the crisp precision of their passing: Bobby Evans was pivotal, the wing-half quickly endearing himself to the home supporters with his skilful, intelligent play. But

20 Tottenham's ground had hosted its first floodlit fixture on 29 September – the day before Wolves met South Africa – Spurs beating Racing Club de Paris 5-3. On the same night as Wolves played Celtic, Broadbent's RAF team lost 4-0 to an FA XI, for whom Bristol Rovers' Geoff Bradford scored three.

for all Celtic's attacking prowess, Wolves' defence was equal to it. The interval arrived with the game still goalless and everything to play for in the second half.

And, as the match restarted, it was the hosts who had the upper hand. On the right, Bobby Mason's influence was growing, while Johnny Hancocks, too, was threatening, the winger firing a shot just over the bar before another effort, on target this time, knocked George Hunter off his feet; full-back Alex Rollo took over in goal for the five minutes he was receiving treatment off the field. But just as it looked as if the deadlock wouldn't be broken, two Wolves goals in as many minutes decisively settled the game.

The first, in the 86th minute, was not without controversy: Dennis Wilshaw had, the visitors insisted, used a hand as he took Roy Swinbourne's pass past three defenders and fired it into the net. There was no doubting the second, however, as, from a free kick given away by the still unhappy Scots two minutes later, the two combined again, Wilshaw hooking the ball in from his team-mate's backward header to double Wanderers' lead. There was nearly time for a third, Hunter producing the save of the match to deny Mason a fairy-tale finish to his night, but 2-0 it remained: harsh on Celtic, perhaps, but Wolves' greater all-round strength had prevailed.

Alongside the impressive Mason and the ever-dependable Nigel Sims, Wolves' two other reserve players had performed with distinction too. The transfer-listed Bill Baxter – watched by scouts from Middlesbrough as the Teesside club pondered a deal – did his reputation no harm, forcing another fine stop from Hunter with a flashing, long-range drive. Meanwhile, Bill Guttridge (known to the fans as 'Chopper', for all-too-imaginable reasons), had shown admirable restraint in curbing his natural instincts and been all the more effective as a result. But Celtic, like South Africa, had more than earned the acclaim that also came their way. 'Nobody would have had any complaints if Celtic had drawn,' wrote Phil Morgan in the *Express & Star*, 'but ... they left behind them a high regard for their particular brand of Scottish football along with the hope that, through floodlight, we may be able to see some more of it.'

The enthusiasm of the home supporters was carried into the following weekend, when just over 40,000 watched goals from Hancocks, Broadbent and Swinbourne secure a 3-1 victory over Manchester United. By the time Molineux hosted its next floodlit friendly, Wolves and Albion would be moving into the final stages of their battle for the league. What was already a ground-breaking season was fast becoming an historic one.

Wednesday, 14 October 1953: Wolves 2 Celtic 0

Wolves: Sims; Short, Guttridge; Baxter, Shorthouse, Wright; Hancocks, Mason, Swinbourne, Wilshaw, Mullen.

Celtic: Hunter*; Haughney, Fallon; Evans, McIlroy, Peacock; Collins, Fernie, McPhail, Walsh, Mochan.

*Temporarily replaced by Rollo while receiving treatment in the second half.

Goalscorer: Wilshaw (86, 88).

Referee: R.J. Leafe (Nottingham).

Attendance: 41,820.

4

From the New World: Wolves v. Racing Club de Avellaneda, 10 March 1954

THOUGH THE lights had shone on Molineux twice in the space of a fortnight, it would be a while before they were powered up again. 'We feel this sort of football entertainment has a future of its own and we are anxious to have a part in its development,' a note in the Celtic programme had said, '[but] at the same time we are sure that it is something which ought not to be overdone.' That the Wolverhampton public had to wait nearly five months for their next fix of floodlit football, then, was quite deliberate: Wolves were keen to protect the health of their new old-golden goose.

But there was plenty going on behind the scenes to bring the next top-class team to town. Hajduk Split were approached in early December: due in the UK in the new year (halfway through their domestic season's winter break) the Yugoslav champions had already arranged floodlit matches with Hull, Bristol City, Watford and Coventry and an afternoon game with either Blackpool or Luton Town. Wolves' suggestion was for a daytime match, too, on Saturday, 30 January, the day of the FA Cup fourth round –

their third-round defeat to Birmingham City subsequently ensured they were free – offering the tourists half of the gate receipts or £500, whichever was the greater. But Blackpool and Luton had got in first, securing an agreement for Split to meet the loser of their third-round tie (Luton would eventually face Split after losing to Blackpool in a third replay, which coincidentally took place at Molineux): Wolves travelled north to play Aberdeen instead, going down 5-3 at a snowy Pittodrie in front of 14,000 hardy fans.

But other clubs were also being contacted as Wolves looked to organise a floodlit game for the spring. Neither Barcelona nor Rangers were free in March or April, it was reported to the board, while Eintracht Frankfurt's offer to visit Wolverhampton on 25 March was declined as Bolton Wanderers were due at Molineux the afternoon before to play a rescheduled game in the league. Potential dates suggested by two more teams from what was then Yugoslavia, Lokomotiva Zagreb and Partizan Belgrade, also had to be turned down.

The latter was with good reason. Partizan's offer of a game on 10 March, discussed by the directors on 24 February, was deemed too close to another proposal to which they had just agreed. 'It was resolved,' Jack Howley had minuted on 11 February, 'to accept the invitation of the Football Association to play a floodlit match with [either] Fluminense FC or Racing Club [de Avellaneda] at Molineux on Saturday, 13 March if we have no league match on that date, or on Monday, 15 March or Wednesday, 17 March if we [do].' Confirmation of which it would be came three weeks later, the wording of the secretary's minutes implying that a game with the team from Rio had been expected. '[It was reported that] Fluminense ... had decided not to visit England and that a floodlight match with Racing Club ... had been arranged instead,' he wrote, confirming that return tickets from London and a night of hotel accommodation would be provided as well as a half-share of the gate. Wolves were, as it happened, free on the 13th[21], but as Racing were already committed to playing Chelsea at Stamford Bridge that day, the 10th – a Wednesday – was nominated instead. The 12-time Primera División champions would be coming to the Midlands as 'representatives of the New World in association football' said journalist Ivan Sharpe[22]. As England was fast discovering, that world was new in more ways than one.

* * *

---

21 This was the original date of the game against Bolton that was rearranged for Wednesday, 24 March because of the latter's match against Sheffield Wednesday in the FA Cup sixth round. 'What a lot of consequences would be eased if Wolves and Bolton Wanderers could play their league game under the Molineux floodlights, but it cannot be,' the *Express & Star* complained. 'The Football League, powerful and autocratic, have ruled against floodlit league games for the present. There is no uniformity for lighting systems, they say: indeed, there are many Division One clubs who have no floodlighting. What a pity! Perhaps it will come one of these days, but if the League are going to wait for standard forms of lighting, they will be waiting a long time ... Could [they] not ... relent to the extent of leaving the clubs concerned to decide for themselves, in matches such as that at Molineux next Wednesday, to play or not to play under floodlight? How well such a commonsense decision would be received by the football-loving public.'

22 The *Sunday Chronicle*'s Ivan Sharpe wrote a weekly column – 'Today's Topical Talk' – for the centre pages of Wolves' matchday programme until 1967, alternating between the publications for the club's first and reserve team games. The board minutes of 2 July 1952 reveal that in 1952/53 he was paid £10 10s for each piece, on the condition he did not write for any other Midlands team. By way of context, the half-dozen on Wolves' highest players' wage – Billy Wright among them – received £14 a week (£10 in the summer) over the same period.

After the relative familiarity of their first and second floodlit visitors, neither Wolves nor their fans knew quite what to expect from their third. 'England, Scotland, Italy: these, hitherto, have been the hotbeds of the game,' Sharpe wrote in the match programme. 'Now Argentina, Brazil, Uruguay and other South American countries are equally fanatical and sometimes, possibly, more so. Amid this enthusiasm and excitement has grown a love for stylish, scientific, even showy football. I don't know quite what calibre of play you're going to see tonight because I only know the Racing Club of Buenos Aires [sic] by reputation … [but] I hope the pitch is fast enough for the Racing Club lads to do some racing: to play fast, clever, individual, combined football of the kind that's bred in them.'

Wolves' international players already had some experience of what it was that he meant. Billy Wright, Bert Williams and Jimmy Mullen had been with the rest of the national squad at the Maracanã when Brazil thrashed Mexico 4-0 in the opening match of England's first World Cup in 1950, a tournament that the Football Association had expected to underline English football's superiority but which had shown just how the established order of the game had changed around it instead. By the time Brazil lost to Uruguay in the decisive match of its final round, England were already home, their defeats to Spain and, notoriously, the USA the reward for the combination of under-preparation and over-confidence that had doomed their campaign from the start. Even their departure was hopelessly tin-eared, as the chance to see more of the teams that were, ironically, the ones leaving them behind, passed by. 'I felt much could be learned from them,' wrote

Stanley Matthews, a late arrival in Brazil after being sent on the goodwill tour to Canada that had, bizarrely, been organised by the FA to run simultaneously instead, in his autobiography *The Way It Was*. 'Tom Finney quite fancied the idea [of staying] as well, but we were tied to travelling home with the England party. It is one thing for players to return home, but neither [FA chairman of selectors] Arthur Drewry nor [manager] Walter Winterbottom stayed on to study how the teams who had reached the next stage were applying themselves to the tournament.

'All the English sports journalists were also recalled by their newspapers, so while the game of football continued to develop with new ideas being put into practice, we all went home and, to all intents and purposes, buried our heads in the sand.'

And there, by and large, they had stayed, a 2-1 win over Argentina in May 1951 – England's first match against South American opposition on home soil – marking the start of a two-year unbeaten run that further reinforced their self-belief. England were, after all, the mothers of the game, the team that had been welcomed to Rio with the headline 'The kings of football are here!' But while the defeat to the USA could be explained away as the result-in-a-million it undoubtedly was, the effect of that complacency would soon be even more dramatically exposed.

Through the 150-year history of England's national team, no result resonates more deeply than the country's 6-3 loss to Hungary on 25 November 1953. It wasn't just the magnitude of the scoreline, the brilliance of the visitors' display or the fact that it was England's first home defeat to opposition from outside the British Isles that made its impact so profound. It was the sense of utter shock that swept over a nation that genuinely hadn't seen it coming. '[When we arrived in England, we] were welcomed with a friendliness that touched us deeply,' Hungary captain Ferenc Puskás later wrote in *Captain of Hungary*, 'but the press left no doubt that we were regarded as England's victims.'

The warning signs, though, had been there. In their match against the Rest of the World on 21 October – a scratch team (assembled to commemorate the FA's 90th anniversary) that had been together for less than a day – England had struggled, only holding on to their unbeaten home record through a dubious last-minute penalty that tied the score at 4-4. 'Fan me with a corner flag!' Clifford Webb exclaimed in the *Daily Herald*. 'That proud soccer record of ours, which has been intact for 90 years, was only 30 seconds from disaster!' But where the Rest left off, the Hungarians then began, pulling England apart with almost nonchalant ease. 'We thought we would demolish this team,' Bobby Robson, then of Fulham, who was watching the game from the stand, later told the BBC. 'England at Wembley: we are the masters, they are the pupils. It was absolutely the other way [round].'

Outclassed in technique – 'My goodness, if he can turn on tricks like this we ought to have him on the music hall,' Kenneth Wolstenholme told the BBC television audience after Puskás's drag-back-and-shot in the 24th minute left Billy Wright tackling shadows and Gil Merrick retrieving the ball from his net for the third time – England had no answers to the tactical questions the Olympic champions also posed. Hungary's 3-2-3-2 formation, with its inversion of the forward half of the standard W-M, was, in practice, a shade away from 4-2-4, tearing up the rulebook to which the English still adhered. 'We constantly changed positions, so where we lined up at kick-off was irrelevant,' forward Nándor Hidegkuti later said. 'We concentrated on creating the maximum confusion in our opponents' defence.'

This was Total Football, two decades before the term was coined. It was a rout in every sense, led by the 31-year-old Hidegkuti, who tormented England from the deeplying role he adopted in spite of the number nine on his back. He scored three, the free-roaming Puskás two. 'They beat us, in goals, by a ratio of two to one,' wrote Leslie Edwards in the *Liverpool Daily Post* the next day, '[but] they were so much better that had we lost 14-3 no one could have complained.'

The roots of Hungary's system lay in the tactical experiments of Márton Bukovi at Budapest side MTK (or Vörös Lobogó – Red Banner – as they became known), and it was from their own club game that England were now urged to learn. 'Albion and Wolves have the idea,' said Charles Harrold in his column in the *Sports Argus*. '[They] are the only two clubs I have seen whose wingers are unorthodox in the sense that they vary the heights of their centres. They ... play with thought and precision, and where are they? First and second in the league!' Racing Club, reported the *Express & Star*, 'play the type of game favoured by the Hungarians'. With the memory of Wembley still fresh, there was an extra layer of interest in how Wolves' approach would fare.

* * *

The South American party arrived in Wolverhampton on the afternoon of the game, three days after travelling to London from Belgium, where they had played the latest match of their two-month European tour. After opening with a goalless draw against AS Roma on 24 January, the Argentines had visited Zagreb, Belgrade, Bilbao, Barcelona, Seville and, on 6 March, Brussels, where they had lost 3-2 to Anderlecht at the Stade Émile Versé. Their gruelling schedule had taken its toll – the day after their arrival in the capital, several players were treated by Chelsea's medical staff at Stamford Bridge for the knocks they had picked up along the way – but manager Guillermo Stábile was still able to name a team containing several full internationals. One of them was Norberto 'Tucho' Méndez, a veteran of the loss to England three years earlier and a key member of the Racing side that had won a hat-trick of league titles between 1949 and 1951.

It was on the Wolves eleven, though, that the newspapers were focused. With Roy Swinbourne injured, Ron Flowers had worn the number 9 shirt in the league game at Old Trafford the previous weekend, with 19-year-old Eddie Clamp, in turn, given his senior debut at left-half. As national servicemen the two were now unavailable, however, having being called up by the RAF for an inter-forces game against the Royal Navy being played the same day. Norman Deeley came in for Flowers in midfield, while reserve striker Doug Taylor was named centre-forward in an otherwise first-choice front five.

The 22-year-old Taylor had played in the senior side once before, scoring Wolves' opener in January's friendly in

Aberdeen, but he hadn't yet made the step up to a full debut despite some good performances in the Central League. That he had been in his manager's thoughts, though, was clear: he had led the line for the Whites against the Colours at the start of the season, and he now had a chance to prove he could do the same for the first eleven again in one of its highest-profile games of the year.

And, in the 16th minute, it was Taylor who opened the scoring, set up by a downward header from Dennis Wilshaw that left a tap-in at the end. But the lead lasted for less than a minute: straight from the restart Racing swept upfield and Juan José Pizzuti, latching on to a ball slipped through the middle by Méndez, levelled the score with a powerful left-footed drive.

It was no more than they had deserved. Ivan Sharpe had hoped for some 'racing', and the visitors had certainly obliged, moving the ball with short, sharp passes – 'apart from the free and goal-kicks,' said Phil Morgan, '[they] did not hit the ball more than 15 yards' – in their skilful build-up play. 'Nor [should] their sportsmanship [be] allowed to pass unrecognised,' the *Star*'s correspondent added, 'perhaps because it was a little out of keeping with some of the things we had heard about the Latin temperament and all that sort of thing. These fellows would fetch a ball for their opponents, a courtesy beyond the comprehension of many a Football League player; they almost hugged the men who charged them, and, above all, there was never a semblance of tantrums.' Racing Club had won 40,000 new friends, said the *Daily Mirror*, by the time the interval arrived.

But even though they had found a way to unlock the home defence, the tourists then decided that their tactics had to change. Méndez's attempts to play the same through ball again had often ended with a forward caught offside, and so, for the second half, the ploy was abandoned in favour of a tighter possession game. The decision proved costly: their tendency to over-elaborate played straight into Wolves' hands, and, quick to regain the ball then move it into attack, Cullis's men took control of the game.

That Racing kept the score level for as long as they did was down to goalkeeper Rogelio Domínguez, but even he could do nothing about Wolves' second, a 25-yard piledriver from Deeley that was in the net before he could react. In the 71st minute Jimmy Mullen's cross-shot made it three: the agile Domínguez kept the score respectable, but there was no way back from there.

Racing had impressed, but the hosts were simply better. Billy Wright (playing, as he had for Wolves' last three First Division matches, at centre- rather than left-half) was imperious, using all his experience to keep the dangerous Pizzuti at bay – '[He] showed us tonight he is ready to take over the … position in England's team,' Charles Buchan wrote in the *News Chronicle*. 'I have never seen him so dominating' – while Deeley, even without his wonder goal, had done enough to book his seat on the train to Preston for Wanderers' next league game. But the following day's coverage was quick to draw wider messages from Wolves' victory as well. With just one win from their 11 matches Racing had, in truth, been second best all trip, but after all the soul-searching of recent weeks, English football was glad to wake up to some much-needed good news.

'WOLVES strike a blow for ENGLAND' read the headline in the *Express & Star*, the capitals leaving no doubt as to its interpretation of the night. 'As I saw it, this was not so much Wolves v. Racing Club as England v. Argentine, or any other foreign short-passing, ball-controlling specialists,' wrote Phil Morgan. 'And, from the purely selfish point of view, I was delighted to see demonstrated my own contention that quick tackling and direct methods can master ultra-short passing.' Rex Bellamy, in the *Birmingham Gazette*, agreed. 'In recent years it has become fashionable to compare English football unfavourably with that of some of our foreign competitors,' he said, 'and last night's game was a most refreshing reminder that our game is not in the parlous state some people would have us believe.'

The reaction to Racing's performance back in Argentina was less amiable. After Wolves' win was 'dismissed briefly' by the country's newspapers, President Perón's National Sports Council decreed that only teams able to 'ensure compliance with the sporting objects of the nation' would be allowed to travel abroad in the future. 'Argentine clubs are expected to be able to uphold the honour of the flag,' the *News Chronicle* reported, 'to conduct themselves decently and, above all, to win.' For a country desperate to prove itself on the world stage, Racing Club's defeat had not been part of the script.

But they could at least console themselves with the thought that they had lost to England's best. Wolves' single-goal victory at The Hawthorns on 3 April drew them level with West Bromwich Albion at the top of the First Division, then a 5-0 thrashing of Charlton put them two points clear. It was a lead they wouldn't relinquish. Roy Swinbourne's 23rd and 24th goals of the season sealed Wanderers' maiden league title against Tottenham Hotspur on an unforgettable final day, one of glory for Wolves, and vindication for their manager too.

'This is a triumph for all that is right and proper in our football,' the *Chronicle*'s John Camkin reflected. 'Cullis, the modern soccer crusader, has staked his faith and his reputation in ideals. First is that football is an attacking game. Second is that football should be a clean game. And thirdly, he flies proudly the flag of youth.

'So this championship is a blow against everything evil in our winter game. For Cullis, it is his life's ambition achieved before he is 40.'

'I am going to make the shortest speech on record,' said the manager as he received the famous silver trophy from Arthur Drewry. 'I am going to say to the supporters, thank you very much for your support. I hope we shall still merit it next season.'

Albion would make up for some of their disappointment by beating Preston in the final of the FA Cup. Wolves, though, had written a new chapter in their history, and more – so much more – was to come.

Wednesday, 10 March 1954: Wolves 3 Racing Club de Avellaneda 1

Wolves: Williams; Stuart, Shorthouse; Slater, Wright, Deeley; Hancocks, Broadbent, Taylor, Wilshaw, Mullen.

Racing Club: Domínguez; Dellacha, Fernandez; Giménez, Balay, Alvarez; Cupo, Méndez, Pizzuti, Simes, Sued.

Goalscorers: Wolves – Taylor (16), Deeley (60), Mullen (71); Racing – Pizzuti (17).

Referee: J.H. Clough (Bolton).

Attendance: 37,122.

5

Cup-Tied: Wolves v. First Vienna, 13 October 1954

WOLVES BEGAN their first season as English champions with a suitably celebratory new look. Three years after they had first discussed brightening the colour of their famous old gold shirt, it was finally and permanently changed, from its original shade, closer to brown, to gold, nearer yellow. 'With their merry marigold shirts reflecting something surprisingly like summer sunshine, Wolves made everything lovely in the Molineux garden on Saturday,' wrote Phil Morgan in the *Express & Star* after the title holders beat Sheffield Wednesday 4-2. 'Here were champions playing like champions ... a bright team in a bright strip.' It was the club's special rayon kit that would soon be dazzling again, however, as Wolves' programme of floodlit fixtures resumed with three games in less than a month.

Their first opponents didn't have far to travel. On Wednesday, 29 September – nine days after Wolves had drawn 3-3 in a return match with Celtic, who had lost only six of the 31 games they had played after their defeat at Molineux in winning their fourth domestic double – West Bromwich Albion came to Wolverhampton to play for the FA Charity Shield. After their nip-and-tuck battle for the title the previous year, a crowd of 45,000 turned out, eager for more of the same.

Now settled in its place as the curtain-raiser to the English season[23], the annual meeting between the winners of the league and FA Cup was, in those days, a far more moveable feast. The First Division was already ten games old by the time the date of the match arrived – the previous year's contest, between Arsenal and Blackpool, hadn't been played until 12 October – while its venue, too, was unfixed: it wasn't until 1974 that Wembley became its permanent home. That same flexibility extended to its playing conditions as well. Not only was the match allowed to be played under floodlights – still banned for competitive games – but substitutes could also be used, a full four years before they were formally permitted by a change to the Laws of the Game.

The latter was a novelty West Brom would happily embrace, but the thoughts of the club on floodlit football provided an interesting contrast to those of their neighbours. Wolves had made £13,551 from their three games at Molineux, Albion's shareholders were told at their August AGM, but chairman Major Henry Wilson Keys still believed that evening matches were a fashion that would pass. 'You may remember that last year I said we would be prepared to install floodlighting when we could see that the Football League were ready to recognise floodlit matches in the league championship,' his address to the meeting, as reported in the *Express & Star*, had

---

23 Wolves created the precedent for the Charity Shield being played at the start of the season when, as league champions, they hosted Nottingham Forest on 15 August 1959.

said. 'They have taken no step in that direction, and your directors will not rush into spending £10,000.' Without that competitive edge, he insisted, floodlit football was doomed to fail: friendlies between First Division clubs wouldn't interest the public when they could watch them play real 'blood matches' already. But the clash with Wolves might bring the Major round, the *Express & Star* suggested: with a sell-out guaranteed and more gala nights to come, even the biggest of sceptics would surely be given cause to pause for thought.

The paper had promised an exhibition piece, and so it proved: 'easily the most exciting floodlit match yet seen on Wolves' ground, and that is saying something', Phil Morgan enthused. The hosts twice took a two-goal lead only for Albion to peg them back to 4-4. It was a 'thriller of thrillers', said Morgan, '[a game] which was almost a complete answer to those who see no future in English soccer'.

Such a match had seemed unlikely when Wolves' team for the night was announced. Both Billy Wright and Bill Slater were absent – they, along with West Brom's Ray Barlow, were en route to Belfast with England, who were playing Northern Ireland at Windsor Park that weekend – as were Eddie Stuart, Roy Pritchard and Jimmy Mullen, all injured. It meant that only six of the side that had faced Huddersfield Town the previous Saturday were still available, two of whom – Ron Flowers and Dennis Wilshaw – had to be switched from their usual positions to cover at right-half and outside-left. Eddie Clamp, Bill Guttridge, Bill Shorthouse and Norman Deeley came in, as, for Les Smith, did Johnny Hancocks, now recovered from the ankle injury that had kept him out of first-team action for most of the month. But the manager's biggest call came at the back, where 19-year-old debutant Peter Russell was given the task of deputising for Wright, whose previous switch from midfield to centre-half had been made permanent three games into the new campaign.

It was the youngster's opposite number who was first under pressure, however, as, in the 12th minute, Roy Swinbourne nipped past Joe Kennedy to score the opening goal. It drew first blood in what was another fascinating clash of styles – Wolves with a high tempo, quick-tackling and direct; West Brom playing a more patient game as they passed their way upfield. Flowers and Deeley stood out for the hosts – the latter especially, who combined with Wilshaw to make a highly effective Wolves left wing – while Russell, too, impressed in his duel with Albion's Ronnie Allen, who also looked lively from the start.

But it was after the interval that the match really came to life, as both sides moved up a gear. After Deeley had doubled Wolves' advantage in the first minute of the half with a header from Hancocks's free kick, the visitors struck back, a two-goal burst from Allen in the 55th and 57th minutes bringing the score back to 2-2. Wanderers came again, Swinbourne bagging his second from a great ball by Deeley before turning provider himself, setting up Hancocks for Wolves' fourth of the night and with it, seemingly, the win. Albion, though, weren't finished, as Paddy Ryan and a third from Allen ensured the Charity Shield would be shared. 'What a match!' gasped Clifford Webb. In the long history of the Black Country derby, there has never been another quite the same.

It was quite a way to open Molineux's second floodlit season, and there was plenty more excitement at the news of who else was coming, too. 'Russian team will play the Wolves at Molineux' announced the *Express & Star*'s front page, revealing that a tour by an as yet unnamed Soviet side – likely to be Moscow Spartak or Dynamo, the paper said – would include a floodlit game in Wolverhampton on 16 November. 'Interest in the match is certain to outshine even the Charity Shield,' the report went on. 'And Wolves [still hope] to persuade the crack Hungarian side Honvéd to pay them a visit in November.' A letter inviting the country's star-studded champions-elect to Molineux had been provisionally accepted back in August, but a final date for that even more tantalising prospect was proving difficult to pin down.

That of Wolves' next floodlit match, though, was already set, and with another familiar team. First Vienna had drawn 2-2 with Cullis's men at the Hohe Warte Stadium on 15 August in a pre-season game arranged to commemorate the Austrians' 60th anniversary; now, on 13 October, the sides met at Molineux for the return.

Wolves had had the better of their first meeting, played in relentless, driving rain. Wearing their white change strip – they had packed their new gold kit, but Vienna asked to play in their usual yellow shirt instead – they had thrilled the 15,000 who braved the terrible weather, particularly in a second half they dominated despite falling briefly behind. Dennis Wilshaw had put Wolves into a 35th-minute lead only for Otto Walzhofer and Hermann Sühs to score either side of half-time. Roy Swinbourne's deft finish restored parity just before the hour, but no amount of further pressure could find Wolves a winner as the hosts held out determinedly to the end. 'Wolves are the best English team [to have visited] Vienna since the war,' goalkeeper Kurt Schmied later told the *Express & Star*, just one of the accolades the Englishmen received after the game. They were given an impressive golden trophy, too, which the Association of Vienna Friends had commissioned to commemorate the day.

The plan had been to play for it again in Wolverhampton on 22 September, but four midweek matches in the opening month of the season had prompted Wolves to ask for the later date instead. The Austrian party flew in to Elmdon (later Birmingham) Airport, then, on the afternoon of the 12th, where they were welcomed by Wolves director James Marshall and taken to a dinner with the playing squad and board that also featured the presentation of a benefit cheque for £750 to Billy Wright, now in his 16th year at the club. Stan Cullis had brought Nigel Sims in to a 14-man group that featured two more changes from the one that had travelled to Vienna. Johnny Hancocks – whose fear of flying kept him at home for most of Wolves' foreign trips – and Eddie Clamp were also added, while Dennis Wilshaw, Roy Pritchard and Tommy McDonald dropped out; Les Smith – who had replaced McDonald at outside-right for the second half at the Hohe Warte – was another inclusion, giving Cullis six forwards from whom to choose. A training injury to Roy Swinbourne then meant a seventh had to be found: Bill Slater was moved from left-half to number 9, with Clamp given the number 6 shirt in his place.

After a morning of training on one of the pitches at a factory sports ground in the town (where the Austrians' light blue, canary-trimmed tracksuits and matching knitted hats were noted with approval by the press) and a reception at the Town Hall, First Vienna manager Leopold Hofmann had had a similar, if more straightforward, decision to make. With his first-choice striker Herbert Grohs also injured, reserve centre-forward Karl Jericha was drafted in to an eleven otherwise unchanged from the one that had played Wolves in August. Among its five Austrian internationals, two – Schmied and half-back Karl Koller, Vienna's other standout player in the clubs' earlier meeting – had been part of the team that had finished third in the World Cup in Switzerland the previous summer.

The Austrians had scored 14 goals in that tournament – half of them in an epic 7-5 victory over the host nation in the quarter-final in Lausanne – but, at Molineux, it was their compatriots' defensive skills that were put to the test again. And, once more, First Vienna stood firm against all that Wolves could throw at them: for the second time, Hofmann's team battled their way to a draw.

It didn't have the thrills and spills of the Charity Shield, but the crowd of nearly 40,000 still had plenty of entertainment nonetheless. Kurt Schmied was again the visitors' hero, making brilliant saves from Slater, Clamp, Flowers, Hancocks and Deeley and a particularly spectacular effort to keep out a rasping Broadbent drive, safely gathering the loose ball at the second attempt. Whenever the keeper was beaten, a team-mate was there to support, Julius Schweiger then Alfred Umgeher denying Deeley and Flowers on the line, while fortune, too, was on his side, Bill Slater watching a seemingly goal-bound header bounce down off the underside of the bar for a defender to gratefully clear. 'It was almost worth the money to see Schmied,' said Phil Morgan in the *Express & Star*, '… but let us give credit to [those] who played in front of [him, too]: to Röckl, one of the Austrian team who held England 2-2 at Wembley a year or two ago; to the cool Koller, also a World Cup player; and to the sturdy Umgeher and Nickerl, who performed to a nicety the overhead scissors clearance much favoured by the famous [Carlo] Parola of Italy. That, and Wolves' inability to finish, was the reason why First Vienna escaped the defeat which had looked absolutely inevitable.'

An escape it was, as the Austrian front line struggled to make any sort of impression themselves. Hans Menasse – a player with English connections, having begun his career in Luton Town's academy after being evacuated from Austria on the Kindertransport before the war – came closest, cutting in from the right wing and past three defenders before Wright blocked the resulting shot from Peyerl, but such moments were few and far between in a game in which the visitors' backs were almost always to the wall. Hofmann made changes, replacing Jericha with Erich Medveth and switching Schweiger to outside-left, but to little effect; with Wright seemingly everywhere with timely tackles and interceptions, Bert Williams's goal remained largely unthreatened.

But even though they had failed to turn their dominance into victory – 'If football matches were decided by points, Wolves would have won with plenty to spare,' said Rex Bellamy in the *Birmingham Gazette*. 'Seldom, if ever, can they have exerted such persistent pressure with no material reward' – Wolves got to keep the cup. '[It] will remain here [for the moment],' club chairman James Baker told the *Evening Despatch*. 'We shall play two other games for it, but I don't think they will be this season.' He was right. More than seven decades on, that rematch is still to be arranged: the elegant, two-and-a-half-foot-tall trophy – its gilding largely faded now, but dedication from the *Vereinigung Der Vienna-Freunde* still clear – can today be seen in the Wolves Museum.

The board minutes of 23 May 1957 record that an invitation from First Vienna to play a floodlit game in the Austrian capital on 10 August – four days before the start of the 1957/58 season – had been received. Wolves were touring South Africa at the time, and it was decided to postpone any decision on acceptance until the manager had returned. Unfortunately, the result of that conversation does not appear in any of the minutes that followed. The fixture, though, wasn't played.

First Vienna would claim a more precious prize at the end of their anniversary season: their sixth Staatsliga title, won on goal difference over city rivals Sport-Club after one of the closest-run championships in years. They would follow it up with five top-three finishes over the next six seasons and, in 1961, an appearance in the final of the ÖFB-Cup, the country's premier knockout competition, where they lost 3-1 to Rapid Wien. A slow decline, however, was beginning, a fall from grace that, in 2017, would culminate in near-bankruptcy and relegation to the Vienna conference of the Landesliga, the fifth tier of the Austrian game. But while more recent seasons have been less than kind to the nation's oldest club – its anglicised name a legacy of the Englishmen who founded it back in 1896 – First Vienna will always have a special place in the history of the floodlit friendlies. Wolves' first visitors from the continent were the first to leave unbeaten as well: it would be another two years before another team could say the same.

Two very different draws, then, kicked off Molineux's new floodlit season, the 85,000 fans who paid to watch them proving just how popular evening football had become. A year had passed since that memorable night against South Africa – the perfect time, thought Ivan Sharpe, to take stock of just how far the club had travelled since then. Wolves' matchday programme columnist summed up the thoughts of many who had followed the growth of weeknight football at Molineux and elsewhere: excitement in what had already been seen, and in the future, too.

'When the light went on at Football League grounds I was apprehensive,' he admitted. 'I had a feeling it would be artificial football: too commercial, like playing cricket under a glass roof. Then I watched the Wolves' displays and changed my mind.

'In fact, I came away from the [First Vienna] match wondering whether it wasn't better than daylight play. The spectacle is sharper; the colour is more vivid; the ball and the movements of the players are easier to see. The whole picture is more impressive.

'The new football, as staged at Wolverhampton, tempts me to compare the floodlit match [to] the colour film. Undoubtedly there's a big future in it, given new, fresh, novel opponents.

'Are new leagues, new competitive links with foreign countries on the way? I shan't be at all surprised.'

Wednesday, 13 October 1954: Wolves 0 First Vienna 0

Wolves: Williams; Stuart, Shorthouse; Flowers, Wright, Clamp; Hancocks, Broadbent, Slater, Deeley, Mullen.

First Vienna: Schmied; Röckl, Nickerl; Umgeher, Koller, Schweiger; Menasse, Walzhofer, Jericha (Medveth 63)*, Sühs, Peyerl.

*As reported by Rex Bellamy in his write-up of the match in the *Birmingham Gazette*; the team listing in the *Express & Star* names the replaced player as Sühs.

Referee: B.M. Griffiths (Newport).

Attendance: 39,969.

6

Avalanche: Wolves v. Maccabi Tel Aviv, 28 October 1954

THOUGH WOLVES' first floodlit friendly of the season had ended goalless, their supporters' appetite had certainly been whetted for what was about to come. On 2 October, Moscow Spartak had been confirmed as the team visiting England in November: they would be playing at Molineux exactly a week after meeting Arsenal in what would be the ground's first all-ticket floodlit game.

But before that was the third evening instalment of Wanderers' seven-match month, a sequence that had continued with another four-goal showing after their draw in the Charity Shield. On 2 October, Manchester United had been beaten 4-2 at Molineux thanks to a late Johnny Hancocks brace, Swinbourne and Broadbent scoring the earlier goals after United had twice gone into the lead. Draws with Manchester City and Cardiff then followed either side of First Vienna, but a 4-0 drubbing of West Brom got Wolves back to winning ways on the 23rd, Hancocks and Swinbourne sharing the goals that saw them jump from seventh to second in the league. Maccabi Tel Aviv would be on the receiving end of an even bigger thrashing as they flexed those muscles again: after the frustration of First

Vienna, their forwards showed little mercy as the Israeli champions were overwhelmed.

With other plans also brewing, though, the game very nearly wasn't played. It had first been proposed in July, at a board meeting that suggested arranging it for 27 October, but with talks to bring a prized Hungarian side to Molineux also just beginning, it was then agreed to offer the date as part of those negotiations instead. 'As no definite arrangement [has yet] been made with Maccabi Tel Aviv, it was decided [to] not now fix a game with them,' Jack Howley minuted on 18 August. 'In reply to a letter received from the Hungarian Football Federation in which was stated they were considering accepting our invitation for one of their clubs to play a floodlight match at Molineux, it was resolved to request them to come at the end of October or up to [the] middle [of] November, not the end of November as suggested by them, and that for preference we would like the Honvéd club.' By September, however, the Maccabi match was back on: the Hungarians 'could not consider sending a team before 4 December', the directors were told, and the previous minute was withdrawn.

Although Maccabi, like South Africa, were an amateur side, they brought with them a glowing domestic reputation and a growing one beyond. Winners of the national league for four seasons in a row and featuring four of the Israel team that had lost by just a single goal to Yugoslavia in a World Cup qualifier 11 months earlier – matching England's result against the Slavs in a friendly on 16 May – they had already undertaken several foreign tours, most recently to Italy and France, where, after a goalless draw with Lazio and a 7-1 defeat to Napoli, they had come within two minutes of a win over Racing Club de Paris before conceding an equalising goal. They would be facing two Second Division opponents in England, Hull City and Notts County, after meeting first Arsenal then Wolves: matches they were approaching with varying degrees of confidence, as goalkeeper Avraham Bendori disclosed. 'For the Arsenal, 25-year-old Ben-Dori [sic] was prepared to concede the possibility of a draw,' the *Express & Star* revealed. 'Hull City and Notts County, might do better. But the Wolves? Alas! Only an avalanche of goals did he expect.'

If his team was to have any chance of finding some in return, much would depend on three of the eight internationals in the side. Outside-right Shmuel Israeli arrived as the latest 'Stanley Matthews' of his country – 'How the maestro's reputation gets around!' Ivan Sharpe exclaimed in his matchday programme column. 'When the Austrians were here the other night, they fielded [in Hans Menasse] the "Stanley Matthews of Vienna"!' – while Yosef Merimovich, the captain of the team, was known for his goals and guile on the left wing. The star turn, though, was Yehoshua 'Shaya' Glazer, who had shared with Merimovich the unusual distinction of scoring every goal in Israel's recent tour of South Africa, a trip that had ended with seven wins and only two defeats from their 11 games in April and May. Quick and two-footed – 'a centre-forward of the alert, attacking type' in the words of Sharpe – Glazer would score 130 goals for the club, for many years a Maccabi record; already a national celebrity, he would be voted Israel's Player of the Decade in a 1960 poll.

That Maccabi had skill was apparent – 'The amateurs from Israel put up a remarkably fine show against Arsenal's first team at Highbury last night,' Charles Buchan wrote in the *News Chronicle* after the opening game of the tour. 'Even on a soft surface [it had rained for hours before the match] they produced a brand of football that matched a lot of the continental teams I have seen' – but their 4-1 defeat in north London also highlighted some tactical flaws in the side. 'The Wolves backs should have a good game if, like the Arsenal men, they get in quick to the tackle,' said a piece in the *Express & Star*. 'The Tel Aviv players tend to hold the ball just that second too long and appear slow-moving. Their centre-half, [Itzhak] Schneur [sic], is a thorough "policeman", but his wing-halves play so much in the middle that opposing wingers are given plenty of room. [Arsenal's Arthur] Milton and [Don] Roper made the most of their chances, and [Cliff] Holton, in the middle, did the rest. [But] Wolves should keep a close watch on Israeli and Merimovitz [sic],' the unnamed correspondent cautioned, 'who are excellent ball players and good shots.'

Many English eyes were on a different forward, however, who had found himself in the news. Three days after they played First Vienna, Wolves confirmed that Dennis Wilshaw's absence from the team had been through suspension, imposed for an unspecified breach of club discipline that had taken place the week before. 'At the moment I have no comment to make,' Wilshaw told an *Evening Despatch* reporter at his home. 'According to the terms of my contract with Wolves, I cannot make any statement which has not previously been authorised. Something will certainly come from this matter, however, but when it will I cannot say at the moment.' Though the reason behind it was implied – 'last Saturday I was unfit to play,' he insisted – the board minutes of 14 October made it clear, 'The manager reported that [Wilshaw] had refused to play in the reserve team on 9 October, and it was decided to suspend [him] for 14 days.'

But a week later, the situation was resolved. '[Wilshaw] attended the meeting and, after discussion and consideration, it was decided to withdraw the suspension,' noted Howley on the 21st, as well as the wording of a statement to that effect for the press. The England man was back for the visit of West Brom that weekend, and kept his place in the side to face Maccabi. Nigel Sims and Tommy McDonald also came in for the friendly, Bert Williams and Les Smith making way. They were the only two reserves in an otherwise full-strength Wolves eleven, one with far too much quality for the tourists, as it turned out, who were never remotely in the game.

Maccabi lined up with five defenders strung across the pitch – one of them Glazer, preferred in his one-time position of left-back to Israel Ben Dror – but it was soon clear that they would need more than that to keep the English champions contained. The match was all but over before a quarter of it was played, Flowers, Swinbourne and Broadbent putting Wolves three up before Sims had had that many touches of the ball. Broadbent's 19th-minute goal delivered a further blow, too, as Bendori, in trying to prevent it, was left with a damaged hand. Haim Buch – who, like Ben Dror and striker Eliezer Spiegel, was playing under the Tel Aviv banner as a guest from league runners-up Maccabi Petah-Tikva – came on as his replacement, but the writing was already on the wall. Long before Johnny Hancocks added his name to the scoresheet, pushing the ball past Glazer then screwing it high into the net four minutes before half-time, Wolves were in total control.

Maccabi coach 'Jerry' Beit Halevi rang the changes, moving Glazer to centre-forward and Ben Dror off the bench to left-back – replicating the team he had selected at Highbury – but the outcome was the same: a surge from the striker forced a corner, but McDonald then set another Wolves attack in motion that ended in goal number five, Swinbourne pulling the ball back from the byline for Wilshaw to slot home. Three more in four minutes continued the rout: a header from Swinbourne, a cross-shot from Hancocks that sailed in from 40 yards and a goal from McDonald that meant that all of Wolves' forwards had now scored. Broadbent and Swinbourne – completing his hat-trick – took the final tally to ten: '[It] was a "maccabre" night for Maccabi,' wrote Phil Morgan in the *Express & Star*, '[and] they were lucky it was not even greater, for Wolves just toyed with them for nine-tenths of the game.' The tourists never gave up, even mounting a late rally as injury forced Broadbent from the field, but the gap, in all senses, remained: had it not been for some terrific saves from Buch, too, Maccabi's evening would have been a lot worse.

The visitors took it well, said Morgan, but the result had been as Bendori had feared. '[But] how can a team of amateurs like ourselves hope to compete with your league champions?' team-mate Itzhak Schneor had also wondered when the squad first got off the plane. 'I work as a bus driver: others are bankers, foundrymen and shopkeepers. We may possibly extend the Wolves, but we will never beat them unless they have changed since I saw them'. In October 1948, he had been in the crowd at Molineux when Wolves beat Huddersfield Town 7-1, a performance he described as the greatest he had ever seen. Since those early days under Cullis, however, Wolves had only got better, as Schneor and his colleagues had found.

It seems strange to suggest that a 10-0 drubbing should count as one of the 'least-worst' results of a tour, but Maccabi would have been more disappointed by the last two games that they played. There was no disgrace in losing to two of England's top-flight teams, but that Hull and Notts County then beat them comfortably as well – 4-0 and 4-2 respectively – was a blow the Israeli press was less inclined to excuse. But while it had been a chastening experience for the country's premier side – one that had seen them concede exactly twice as many goals in total as they had through their entire domestic league campaign – the players were keen to draw the positives from their visit all the same. One of the first things they would do on their arrival home would be to follow up on the tactics they had learned, Israeli FA president Samuel Stahl declared, adding that he hoped to welcome British teams to similar tours of Israel soon.

Souvenirs had been exchanged prior to their departure, Maccabi receiving cut-glass bowls from Wolves and gifting engraved cigarette lighters in return. But every one of the fans that had seen them at Molineux had been given an even better memento of the game: a voucher, guaranteeing priority for what was now the hottest ticket in town.

Moscow Spartak were coming, and the whole country would be watching.

Thursday, 28 October 1954: Wolves 10 Maccabi Tel Aviv 0

Wolves: Sims; Stuart, Shorthouse; Slater, Wright, Flowers; Hancocks, Broadbent, Swinbourne, Wilshaw, McDonald.

Maccabi: Bendori (Buch 20); Reznik, Glazer; Halivner, Schneor, Turika; Israeli, Goldstein, Spiegel (Ben Dror HT), Studinski, Merimovich.

Goalscorers: Flowers (11), Swinbourne (16, 64, 80), Broadbent (19, 78*), Hancocks (41, 66), Wilshaw (50), McDonald (68).

*Various newspaper reports name Wolves' penultimate scorer as Slater. The club's contemporary record, however, confirms that Broadbent got the goal.

Referee: A. Murdoch (Sheffield).

Attendance: 26,901.

7

The Fog of War: Wolves v. Moscow Spartak, 16 November 1954

WHILE MACCABI'S tour had been covered with interest by the English press, there was no mistaking the elephant that was also in the room. The name of Moscow Spartak was never far from the headlines, even as the Israelis arrived: the visit of the 'People's Team', as the Soviets were known, was always going to be different from those that had gone before.

Ever since the Iron Curtain had been drawn across Europe in the wake of the Second World War, tensions between East and West had dominated the political scene. To one side, the United States and its allies; to the other, the Communist Bloc, locked in a struggle for the hearts and minds of the other half of the divide. This was another kind of conflict: a new, cold war, a clash of ideology where every victory, however small, was one for the greater cause. 'Both the United States and the Soviet Union had been born in revolution,' wrote John Lewis Gaddis in *The Cold War: A New History*. 'Both embraced ideologies with global aspirations. What worked at home, their leaders assumed, would also do so for the rest of the world.' Proving it was everything, and any way was fair game.

Aside from the race for nuclear arms and the surrogate 'proxy wars', it was a battle fought more implicitly – through espionage, embargoes and the pursuit of technological goals, as seen in the rush to develop satellites that began the space race in 1955. And, of course, through sport: for many, the only way to get a glimpse of the real men and women behind all the politics as well. 'To see people coming from behind the Iron Curtain, it was like seeing people from the moon,' said Wolves fan Bob Bannister on the *Champions of the World* documentary. 'Almost impossible.'

After years of isolation – the USSR didn't enter any major sporting events until the Olympics of 1952 – football in the Soviet Union was a similarly closed book. The only Russian team to have ever visited Britain had been Moscow Dynamo, who, in the spirit of Allied solidarity in the immediate aftermath of the war, had played in London, Cardiff and Glasgow in November 1945. They had amazed and delighted the crowds with their speed and ingenuity as they drew 3-3 with Chelsea then thumped Cardiff City 10-1 – *passovotchka*, as the style became known, an early taste of the bigger schooling English football had in store – but the mood had soured in a chaotic 4-3 win over Arsenal played, with Highbury unavailable, at White Hart Lane, a match marred by mutual allegations of sharp practice, some dubious decisions from Russian referee Nicolay Latyshev and the thickest of pea-soup fog. Dynamo headed home to a heroes' welcome after a 2-2 draw with Rangers kept their unbeaten record intact. Reinforcing the bonds of friendship had been important, for sure, but showing the supremacy of the communist state had been the biggest objective of all.

'Now that the brief visit of the Dynamo football team has come to an end, it is possible to say publicly what many thinking people were saying privately before the Dynamos ever arrived,' wrote George Orwell in *Tribune* once they were safely on the plane. 'That if such a visit as this had any effect at all on Anglo-Soviet relations, it could only be to make them slightly worse than before.' The gathering winds of the Cold War blew any chance of a rematch away. Mindful of the risk of handing the USSR another propaganda coup, an invitation to the Football Association to make a reciprocal tour the following year was politely, but firmly, turned down.

But with the Soviets' new willingness to join the international sporting fold had come the chance to build bridges again, and first thoughts naturally turned to the unfinished business of the Dynamo tour. A delegation from Moscow had been invited to the FA's anniversary celebrations in October 1953, and after watching Arsenal beat Charlton and England's 4-4 draw with the Rest of the World, the previous offer was extended again. 'Remember the Dynamos, the Russian football team that beat the Arsenal eight years ago?' asked the *News Chronicle*'s Michael Moynihan. 'Well, they want a return game. And more than that: the representatives of Russia's soccer-fan millions are hoping that an exchange of top teams will become an annual event between the two countries.'

Arsenal would be playing Dynamo and Spartak on 5 and 8 October, Reuters reported when the details of the visit were finally announced the following May, before they and another, still to be nominated, English side faced one of the two Moscow teams in return. The start of the

English season added the first missing name to the plan – and brought a change to it, too: whereas Wolves, as league champions, were confirmed as hosts of the second 'home' game, the match against Spartak had to be scrapped after the Football League refused Arsenal permission to postpone their league fixture on the 9th – while a first international fixture between the two nations was also enthusiastically proposed. It was in a spirit of growing cooperation, then, that Arsenal began their journey east: ready, they hoped, to answer a question left hanging in the air for nine years. 'Like the FA, the average Englishman has always wanted to see us have another crack at the Russians,' wrote Eric Stanger in the *Yorkshire Post & Leeds Mercury*. 'Not because he has any animosity towards them engendered by political differences ... but because he really wants to know if [they] are as good at soccer as they appeared to be in 1945.'

Not everyone shared that sentiment, however, as the political concerns that had scuppered any chance of an earlier visit came bubbling to the surface again. The USSR had made its performance at the Helsinki Olympic Games a matter of national honour – an intensive effort to prepare for the competition had been launched after the IOC's invitation to compete at the 1948 Games in London was refused (on the direct orders, it is believed, of Joseph Stalin himself, who felt the Union's athletes were not yet up to world standard) – and though international relations had undoubtedly improved since the death of the Soviet leader in 1953, Embassy and Foreign Office officials in Moscow and London still believed that Arsenal had only been invited to Russia because they were likely to lose. Lying 15th in the First Division – the three consecutive defeats with which their season had begun would remain the club's worst start to a league campaign for another 67 years – and with an ageing squad, the team that had won the title in 1952/53 was far from the side it once was. 'Don't go to Russia, Arsenal!' Charles Buchan, writing in the *News Chronicle*, had implored back in February after a struggling Cardiff City had held the then-champions to a draw. 'Slow on the ball, slower still in recovery and hopelessly amiss in front of goal … [The Russians'] quick-moving style, on the Hungarian pattern, [will] carve [you] to pieces!'

And, under the lights of the Dynamo Stadium, it duly did, five unanswered goals leaving no doubt as to the gulf in quality between the teams. 'Arsenal were crushed … by a more skilful and better-balanced side and were so outplayed in the last half-hour that the Dynamos made the crowd laugh with a series of exhibition moves,' Buchan reported. 'The Russians were superior in every respect. They were magnificent.' Out-run as well as out-thought – 'Arsenal faded badly in the later stages,' wrote Clifford Webb in the *Daily Herald*. 'So badly, in fact, that play dwindled down to a fiasco, and when the fifth goal went in just before the finish, the spectators were streaming out giggling' – the visitors were, indeed, sliced apart. The Soviet newspapers were magnanimous, even praising the Englishmen for their 'fine passing and good stopping' according to the *Express & Star* – they could afford, after all, to be kind – but the result was taken as yet more evidence of just how far behind the times they were. '[It] proved what we have known for many months,' said the *Nation Belge*. 'That an excellent continental style is superior to the football produced by the English.'

It was with a touch of trepidation, then, that the papers tracked Spartak's progress through Europe as they made the opposite journey at the end of the month. On 27 October, ten days after the last game of the Soviet season – they had missed out on a third consecutive Top League title after finishing four points behind Dynamo, who claimed their first in five years – Spartak played the first of two matches in Belgium, thrashing league champions Anderlecht 7-0. Five days later it was the turn of Standard Liège, who, defending deep and breaking fast, did a little better in keeping their loss down to 5-2, though Arsenal manager Tom Whittaker, who was present at the game, had his thoughts as to why else that might have been. 'I think Spartak were keeping something in hand,' he told the *Western Mail*. 'Mr Whittaker would say nothing about [his side's] prospects at Highbury next week,' the paper added, 'but he rated Spartak on a par with Moscow Dynamo, who beat Arsenal 5-0.'

And so it was on to England, where a 3-2 win over Newcastle had just put Wolves top of the league, ahead of Sunderland, also on 20 points but with a marginally inferior goal average. While the focus had been on the Londoners, Stan Cullis and his men had been quietly watching on, mindful of their own game with Spartak, of course, but with an eye on a sequel as well. 'If Wolves are asked to play in Russia in the near future, as seems highly probable, they will ask for much better travelling arrangements than those made for Arsenal,' the *Express & Star* reported on 6 October, quoting the manager's thoughts on the Gunners' experience in the USSR. 'Agreeing that the journey exacted its toll of Arsenal and there was no possibility of them being at their best [they had arrived in Moscow only a day before the game after an 11-hour fog delay in Minsk], [Cullis] said that if his club do go to Russia they would want more time than Arsenal were given ... "It will be very interesting to see how much time the Russians allow themselves in England before they play the return match at Highbury," [he added, recalling] that when the Dynamo team came to England in 1945, they arrived more than a week before their first match.'

The answer to that question turned out to be five days, as Spartak flew in to London Airport on the morning of 4 November. The 'team of all the talents', as the *Star* had hailed them the day before, had plenty of time to rest and train, then, as well as send a scouting party to Wolverhampton to watch Wolves for the first time. 'The interest suggests just how seriously they are taking the event,' said a report on the paper's back page. 'They are not bothering to watch Arsenal – they saw them recently in Moscow, anyway – for the remainder of the team are going to White Hart Lane to see the Tottenham/Cardiff game.' The Russians would have different tales to tell when they reconvened at their Piccadilly hotel. While Spurs had lost an undistinguished, scrappy match 2-0 – both Cardiff goals coming from ex-Molineux man Ronnie Stockin – Wolves had turned on the style in putting five past Burnley, Swinbourne and Flowers each scoring twice to put them top of the table on their own. 'We go to make a plan to give you a hard time on Tuesday week,' Spartak president Vassily Kuzin had told James Baker after the game. '[They] may need that plan,' said Phil Morgan in the *Express & Star*. '[Wolves] showed them they have run into form at precisely the right time.'

But the Russians were feeling confident, too, as they settled into their routine. After a Turkish bath on the afternoon of their arrival – they had asked that two masseurs be available, the papers said – they had exercised on Green Park the next day. 'A pre-breakfast loosener,' reported the *Star*, before the players sat down to a meal of smoked salmon, fruit juice, boiled eggs, steak, and, 'for those extra carbohydrates to give energy', a large pot of fresh cream. The squad trained at Highbury that evening, and on Saturday night as well. 'Even Sunday will not be a day of rest for these football-minded Russians, who are leaving nothing to chance,' the article went on. 'They have asked Arsenal to provide training facilities for them at Highbury between one and three o'clock.' Their team to face the Gunners had already been announced: the same eleven that had humbled Anderlecht a few days before. 'I don't give Arsenal the slightest chance of beating Moscow Spartak,' the Belgians' Liverpool-born coach Bill Gormlie had said. 'Their physical condition is extraordinary. I think their defeat will be even heavier than in their recent match against the Dynamos in Moscow.'

But, contrary to most predictions, it was a much tighter game, one the Soviets were grateful, in the end, to win. 'Let me be the first to give Arsenal a whale of a cheer for the way in which they almost staggered most of the forecasters, including me,' said Clifford Webb in the *Daily Herald*. 'With magnificent determination, loads of courage, and, dare I say it, some surprisingly good long-ball play, they tore the robot mask off the Russians.

'Few could have expected such a gallant Arsenal retort to their licking in Moscow. They reduced Spartak to a scrambling level in the closing stages, and were themselves unlucky with some close first-class efforts.'

Arsenal had taken a first-half lead through Jimmy Logie's powerful drive, but goals either side of the break from Aleksei Paramonov and Nikita Simonyan had put the visitors 2-1 ahead with 35 minutes to play. Controversy, though, would follow, and from what must have seemed a scarcely believable source: Nicolay Latyshev, the same Russian referee that had overseen the 'farce in the fog' against Dynamo in 1945, who awarded the Gunners an indirect free kick for obstruction instead of a penalty when Arthur Milton was bundled over in the box. 'It was a penalty,' a fuming Logie said afterwards. 'If we'd got that we might have won.' The Arsenal captain didn't shake Latyshev's hand at the end of the game – not deliberately, the club later felt obliged to explain – but the crowd made its feelings known at the final whistle with a chorus of jeers and boos.

While Arsenal were happier with their performance – if not the final result – Spartak were keen to provide some mitigation for theirs. 'The lighting was not very good,' the *Herald* quoted the Soviet Sports Ministry's head of football Valentin Antipenok, who had accompanied the team on the tour, as saying, 'and it prevented our goalkeeper from seeing the ball when Arsenal scored their goal.' But radio commentator Viktor Kuprianov was more even-handed in his appraisal of why things hadn't quite gone according to plan. 'Probing for the sake of probing gets you nowhere,' he said on his Moscow-based *Sports Spotlight* show. '[It] is all well and good if it [reveals your] opponents' weaker points, but suppose it does not? Worse, suppose it shows up your own weak spots: what then?' Spartak would have to 'brush up their kicking' before they met Wolves, he added, the 'leading professional eleven [of] today'. They had shown the English champions their fitness and skill, but the chinks in their armour as well.

'Spartak have in abundance those most essential of soccer attributes,' said Phil Morgan, who was also in London for the game. 'Good individual ball control, almost constant movement and an enthusiasm that causes them to challenge for every ball. But, although they challenge so persistently, they are not good tacklers, and it was evident that they are not too happy when tackled hard.' They could expect plenty of that at Molineux, he added, tipping Wolves to have the edge overall. '[Spartak] are capable of giving the crowd a highly entertaining game,' he concluded, 'but I cannot see them [leaving] Wolverhampton unscathed.'

By then, the match at Molineux had already sold out: police horses had been deployed when the last batch of tickets went on sale to help control the expected queues. But there was an alternative option for those that had missed out – the BBC, which announced it would be providing television coverage of the second half of the game. Still rare for non-international matches apart from the FA Cup Final – and, given the logistical difficulties, virtually unheard of for any being played outside the capital – the Corporation paid £225 for the rights to the broadcast. Three extra lamps were added to each floodlight pylon to assist the cameras in the ground.

The fee, together with an increase in admission prices – of around three shillings for a stand ticket, one for the terraces – would help cover the heavy costs that hosting the tourists had incurred. 'The Football Association [has] intimated that the Spartak travel and hotel expenses [should] be equally shared by Arsenal and ourselves,' the board meeting of 14 October had heard, though the directors had decided that, with Highbury's capacity much larger than that of Molineux, efforts would be made to persuade the Londoners to take a more equitable share. But the hospitality, said the Russians, would be repaid in kind, as Wolves' much-trailed invitation to play in Moscow was finally confirmed. 'It is a Soviet custom,' Mr Antipenok told the *Express & Star*'s London correspondent, whose piece was splashed on the paper's front page.

As, too, was the news of Spartak's arrival in Wolverhampton, the Sunday before the game. They had allowed themselves a little sightseeing prior to their departure from London, taking trips to Windsor and Madame Tussaud's as well as Wembley, where they had watched England (including debutant Bill Slater) beat Wales 3-2. It was back to business in the Midlands, however, with a full training session under the lights at the Revo Electric ground – they had been offered the use of Molineux, but agreed with Stan Cullis's suggestion that, after recent heavy rain and a reserve match the previous day, it would be better to give the pitch some extra time to recover before their game – before some 'good English food' back at the town's Victoria Hotel. A reminder of their homeland was also on hand if required. 'Vodka,' said the *Sunday Mercury*, 'is always on sale in the cocktail bar.'

It was at Molineux that the stiff drinks might have been needed, though, as the weather threatened to throw a spanner in the works: thick fog had blanketed the country over the weekend, with worse forecast for the start of the week. A contingency plan had been agreed – should a postponement be necessary, the game would be played the next day – but, to general relief, the day of the match brought better news. 'The big red hammer and sickle flag of Russia was hoisted over Molineux at 9.50 this morning,' the *Express & Star* was able to report that afternoon. 'There is now no fog threat for [tonight's game].'

With Ron Flowers passed fit to play after missing the previous Saturday's trip to Deepdale – where Spartak's observers had again been present as Wolves and Preston drew 3-3 – Stan Cullis was able to name the same eleven that had scored nine against West Bromwich Albion and Burnley in the club's two most recent home league games. And some extra names, too: the use of substitutes had been agreed as a condition of the tour – for injured players only, it was decided, though Spartak had raised more than a few eyebrows at Highbury by replacing an apparently fit Viktor Voroshilov with ex-Dynamo striker Nikolay Dementyev for the last 20 minutes of the match – so Nigel Sims, Roy Pritchard, Eddie Clamp, Jimmy Mullen, Tommy McDonald and Doug Taylor were also included in the squad. The procedure for using them had since been clarified, but after the controversy at Arsenal – Tom Whittaker had been involved in a testy exchange with Mr Antipenok immediately after the game – the Wolves manager was determined to ensure the match at Molineux would be argument-free. 'Our players will be absolutely forbidden to make complaints or approach the referee,' Cullis told the *Daily Mirror*. 'They will accept every decision unquestioningly. If Spartak are awarded a penalty kick, it will be a penalty kick, with no recriminations, no excuses. Our players will be instructed to play this one hard, but also to play this one, above all, fair.' The message was crystal clear: the most eagerly awaited day in Wolverhampton's soccer history, as Phil Morgan put it, was going to be remembered for its football alone.

Spartak trainer Vasily Sokolov was also able to name his first-choice team, unchanged from the eleven that had won in London. Five had been in the USSR side that had held Hungary to a 1-1 draw in Moscow at the end of September, one of them the national captain, Igor Netto, who, with fellow half-back Nikolai Parshin, was marked as one to watch in the *Star*'s matchday preview piece. 'They work with a will and with a fitness which enables them to tear off in pursuit of their forwards before tearing back in support of their defence,' wrote Morgan, though the speed of Wolves' long-passing game, he added, might well catch them out. As, he went on, could the home side's quality in the individual battles that were likely to settle the game. 'Centre-half [Anatoli Bashashkin] is the stay-at-home type, tall, good in the air, but likely to find Wolves' Swinbourne about as much as he can handle,' he said, '[and] among the inside-forwards I cannot see [Nikita] Simonyan, as good as he is, getting much change out of Wright in top form.

'But this is not to say the Russians are incapable of giving a good account of themselves. Remember, they are playing for their country as much as Wolves are playing for theirs.'

And, after the national anthems and a pre-match lap of honour, both sides quickly set out their stall. The red-shirted visitors had the best of the early chances – only a goal-line clearance from Bill Shorthouse and a last-ditch tackle by Billy Wright prevented first Simonyan then Boris Tatushin from giving them the lead – but Wolves were soon creating opportunities as well, Spartak goalkeeper Mikhail Piraev twice keeping out headers from Bill Slater before a drive from Les Smith whistled inches wide. Back came the Russians, Aleksei Paramonov firing over from eight yards before Anatoli Ilyin forced Bert Williams into a save. It was anybody's game when half-time arrived with the score still tied at 0-0.

Despite the weather reports, it was to an increasingly foggy Molineux that the BBC's Kenneth Wolstenholme welcomed those tuning in to watch the second 45 minutes of the match: misty from the start – even without the clouds of cigarette smoke that were also billowing round – visibility inside the ground had steadily worsened as the first half had worn on. But the second saw Wolves' influence move in the opposite direction as Wright, Slater and Flowers tightened their grip on the game. 'By close marking and strong tackling they reduced the Russian attack to a thing of shreds and patches,' said Charles Buchan in the *News Chronicle*, and though Bashashkin, Netto and Mikhail Ogonkov did their best to keep the hosts in similar check, Dennis Wilshaw, Roy Swinbourne and Johnny Hancocks were a constant thorn in their side. In the 59th minute Piraev was beaten, but Hancocks's 20-yard shot smacked off the crossbar and back into play. Wolves were rampant, and it was surely only a matter of time before they found the game's opening goal.

And four minutes later they did, as the goalkeeper, challenged by Swinbourne, failed to punch a Bill Shorthouse free kick clear and Wilshaw, following up, hooked the ball in from six yards. Spartak responded with an immediate change – Ilyin sprinted across the field to deliver a message to Paramonov, who suddenly developed a limp – but Wolves' number 10 almost got another, Bashashkin coming in with the goal-saving tackle after Wilshaw had dribbled round Piraev's dive. By now the pace of the game was taking its toll on the visiting team. Ilyin came close again, but with Wolves keeping the tempo relentlessly high – a two-hour fitness session the morning after the Preston game (the first time in the 77-year history of the club that the players had trained on a Sunday) had kept them in the peak of condition – Spartak were struggling to cope. 'These Russians are … very fit,' Stan Cullis had told the *Daily Herald* after the match at Highbury. 'We are fit, too.'

Yet no one was expecting the visitors to implode in quite the way they did in the last six minutes of the game. Sixty seconds after Hancocks had deservedly doubled Wolves' advantage, squeezing between two defenders and past the onrushing Piraev before rifling the ball into the net, Swinbourne made it three, driving into the bottom corner from the edge of the box. Another effort from Hancocks was then ruled out for offside, but a minute later he scored again, knocking Wilshaw's deflected pass past Piraev from eight yards to complete what had become a crushing win. 'Never have I seen a more famous victory than the one the fighting-fit Wolves gained over Spartak under floodlights here tonight,' Buchan added in the *Chronicle*. 'They not only won handsomely but exploded the myth of Russian super-fitness … So tired, in fact, were the Russians that they lost control completely and on most occasions sent the ball straight to the feet of the opposition instead of maintaining their usual accuracy of movement.'

For Stan Cullis – initially so overcome with emotion he could do nothing except shake each of his players by the hand – it was the club's greatest achievement, 'greater than winning the FA Cup'. The manager had had a decision to make late in the second half when Eddie Stuart was left groggy after a collision with Netto seven minutes from time. Roy Pritchard prepared to come on as the South African was given treatment, but Cullis had sent him back to the bench. 'It is against British tradition to have substitutes,' he later told the press, 'and I was determined tonight, no matter what the result, to try to play the same eleven right throughout the game. I thought Stuart was only dazed and I was prepared to have him off for five minutes and play only ten men rather than bring on a substitute.' Cullis had said that nothing would be allowed to detract from his team's performance on the night, and he had been true to his word.

The television coverage, too, had been a resounding success. 'I was at home that evening, and I was told that I probably had a better view of that game than most of the spectators,' Bob Bannister told *Champions of the World*. 'The goals were scored on the South Bank: those in the North Bank couldn't see what was happening because it was an extremely foggy evening. Many people in the Waterloo Road Stand and the Molineux Street Stand couldn't see all that much [either], and it was in this period of time … that Wolves scored their four goals. So seeing it on television, it was misty but at least you could see it and have the satisfaction of seeing the ball go into the net.' Fortune, though, had played its part: while the newsreel cameras were set up on a platform built over the players' entrance in the Waterloo Road Stand, the BBC's main camera was mounted high on a floodlight pylon diagonally opposite, on the Molineux hill. 'Our cameras were at the wrong end when Wolves were attacking in the first half,' remembered Kenneth Wolstenholme, as quoted in the *Express & Star*. 'The score was 0-0 at half-time and then they scored four times at the right end of the pitch for us. It was pure luck on our part.'

But there was no such qualification in the headlines the next morning. 'Wolves bash the floodlights out of Spartak' announced the *Daily Herald*; for the *Birmingham Post*, the 'handsome defeat of Spartak's footballers' had restored the honour of the English game. 'At last we have had a badly needed victory for English football,' wrote Preston and England winger Tom Finney in his weekly newspaper column, which appeared in the *Express & Star*. 'I sat in the stand with the rest of the England party at Molineux, and you should have heard us cheering!

'This has been one of my busiest and most interesting weeks for a long time. On Saturday we had that hectic match with Wolves ... A party of Spartak officials had been watching our game and as I was leaving the dressing room afterwards the Preston chairman, Mr Nat Buck, introduced me to them. They realised then they would be up against it at Wolverhampton. I guessed they would be, because these Wolves are the best team in the country. We ourselves have been beaten by Manchester United, who are a fine enough side, but Stan Cullis's men have got the edge on all of us.'

Though a different sort of edge was on display in the Soviets' immediate reaction to their defeat – 'Moscow telephoned Wolverhampton 24053 for the result of last night's match,' reported the *News Chronicle*'s John Camkin. 'Mr Valentin Antipenok, chief of Soviet soccer, waited in the office at Molineux a few minutes after the end. I asked him through an interpreter: Will you attend the short press conference with Mr Stan Cullis? "Niet [sic]," came the reply. I persisted: What do you think of Wolves? "They are a good side," he admitted. Are they the best team Spartak have met? Came a most explosive "[Nyet] … Spartak played very, very badly"' – it had softened in time for the post-match banquet held later at the Victoria Hotel, where Mr Antipenok acknowledged that Wolves were well-deserving of their win having been much the better team. His comments were not repeated back at home: the result was initially ignored by *Pravda*, Russian radio and the official news agency, Tass. Only *Komsomolskaya Pravda*, a newspaper aimed at a younger audience, carried a report of the game.

But the news soon reached the House of Commons – Brighton MP Howard Kempton raised a cheer when he referred to Wolves' victory at the start of the evening's adjournment debate – and further afield as well. 'I was in the army, stationed in Singapore, when we took on Spartak,' supporter Harry Hunt, then aged 20, told me at his Compton home. 'My mother used to send me the *Wolverhampton Chronicle*, which was a very good paper for pictures in those days, so I could keep up with the results. I had my photograph taken with the match report and my friend Ernest Howells, who was from Albrighton. We sent it back to the paper, and they published it! It was quite exciting, really.' Phil Morgan's preview had concluded with his hope for a good game, 'something about which we can talk with pleasure for years to come'. For fans inside the ground and, like Harry, elsewhere, that wish was certainly granted.

The Soviets left Wolverhampton at 6.40am the next day, catching the train back to London three hours earlier than originally planned. But despite the haste of their exit, they had made a good impression on the town, and the wider country too, posing for photos and signing autographs to the very end of their stay. A single incident apart – there had been an attempt to throw pamphlets at the players as they boarded their coach outside the railway station when they had first arrived (the text urged the visitors 'to look around … and remember that Communism "takes away freedom",' said the *Express & Star*) – politics hadn't interfered. Football, said Mr Antipenok, brought nations together, and Spartak very much hoped to return. 'We have liked our visit here very much,' he told reporters before the tourists boarded their flight home on the Friday morning, 'and we send our greetings to all the sportsmen of Great Britain.'

Wolves made a profit of £3,554 4s 9d on the game – a payment of £2,400 had been sent to Arsenal as their contribution towards Spartak's expenses – but the prestige it had brought to both the club and the town was worth substantially more. 'Will you please convey to the lads the heartiest congratulations of the board and its appreciation for the way they played and fought to attain such a magnificent achievement,' said a letter from James Baker to Billy Wright, dated 19 November. 'It was not just a club victory, but one for England, and we are very grateful and proud of you.' Though Wolves were unable to show their thanks in other, more concrete ways – Football League regulations made it illegal to pay the players any more than the standard £2 bonus they received for winning an ordinary league game – the mayor was also keen to play his part in recognising the success of the team. But although the offer of a civic reception was courteously declined, both manager and players would have been pleased to read of one other piece of praise that was reported at the end of the week. Radio Moscow had expressed 'on behalf of football fans all over Russia, its hearty congratulations to Wolverhampton Wanderers', said the *Birmingham Gazette*. 'They had shown,' said the Soviet station, 'how football should be played.'

Wolves would fly the flag again less than four weeks later, in a match no less significant to national pride. The victory over Spartak, their 'greatest achievement', had delivered a shot in the arm to the English game: their next would bring them even greater, global renown.

One of the most important matches in the history of European football was about to be played.

Tuesday, 16 November 1954: Wolves 4 Moscow Spartak 0

Wolves: Williams; Stuart, Shorthouse; Slater, Wright, Flowers; Hancocks, Broadbent, Swinbourne, Wilshaw, Smith.

Spartak: Piraev; Ogonkov, Sedov; Parshin, Bashashkin, Netto; Tatushin, Paramonov (Isayev 65), Simonyan, Voroshilov, Ilyin.

Goalscorers: Wilshaw (63), Hancocks (pen 84, 88), Swinbourne (85).

Referee: B.M. Griffiths (Newport).

Attendance: 55,184.

8

Champions of the World: Wolves v. Honvéd, 13 December 1954

ON THE night of Wednesday, 13 October, as 40,000 fans were watching Wolves play First Vienna, other eager eyes were trained on a story that was developing elsewhere. Under the lights of Brussels' Heysel Stadium, Hungarian masters Honvéd had gone into the final third of their match against West Bromwich Albion two goals down. The history of more than just the Black Country rivals might have turned out differently had that scoreline stayed the same.

The team from the Kispest district of Budapest was, for many, the best club side in the world. Six of the eight internationals facing Albion had played in the World Cup Final in July. Gyula Grosics, Gyula Lóránt, József Bozsik and Zoltán Czibor had all appeared against England at Wembley as well, as had Ferenc Puskás and Sándor Kocsis, between them the scorers of 54 of the century of goals that won Honvéd their fourth league title in six seasons a little later in the year. In the nationalisation of sport that had followed the communist takeover of Hungary in 1947, the club founded as Kispest Atlétikai had become the army team, but despite the military ranks the players were given, football was still at its core. Honvéd were set up, effectively, as a training camp for the national side: the club was its backbone, and, compared with every other team in Europe, on a different plane.

Even though they had fallen short in Switzerland – their 3-2 loss to West Germany, the team they had beaten 8-3 in the group stage of the competition, became known to the winners as the 'Miracle of Bern' – Hungary's footballers had continued to show the rest of the world the way, not least England, who, in spite of everything, still clung to the hope that their 6-3 defeat the previous November had been a one-off after all. Determined to redeem themselves and show the worth still in the English style, they had travelled to Budapest for a rematch on 23 May, lining up in the same formation as they had six months before. An even bigger 7-1 hiding had exploded any lingering doubts, however, as to where football's balance of power now lay. 'The stark truth has been emphasised here even more than at Wembley,' Clifford Webb, one of many to say the same, wrote in the *Daily Herald*, 'that our fellows are slow and cumbersome and lacking in progress and ideas compared with the magnificently trained and tutored Hungarian side.' West Brom's meeting with Honvéd offered a chance to regain some of that lost pride[24]. A week after Arsenal's humbling at the Dynamo Stadium had dealt English football a further blow, the country was pinning its hopes on the FA Cup holders to strike one back for its troubled game.

---

24 The match was the second of a two-game Festival of Football organised by the Belgian newspaper *Le Soir*; Austria Vienna and Anderlecht had played earlier that evening on the same ground.

And, remarkably, it appeared as if they just might, Johnny Nicholls and Ronnie Allen putting Albion 2-1 in front after Puskás's first-minute goal. Then, on the hour, it got even better for the Baggies as Nicholls made it three, stabbing a shot past Grosics from Allen's deftly flicked through ball. But in a flash Honvéd were level, outside-left Czibor scoring twice in as many minutes, then ahead through Josef Szoviak, running in from the opposite wing. 'A fatal few minutes, those,' rued Pathé News commentator Bob Danvers-Walker before Kocsis sealed it with number five. Albion had looked as if they were going to pull off the 'footballing shock of the century', said the *Express & Star*'s 'Hill Top II', but had been unable to hold on to the end. 'For two-thirds of the game Albion outplayed Puskás and Co.,' he said. 'They matched them in every phase ... But whereas Honvéd were able to keep up the cracking pace for 90 minutes, Albion were a tired side at the end.'

It had been an epic struggle, but the questions for English football still remained: of approach as well as fitness, in which Honvéd had so clearly held the upper hand. 'I still firmly believe that the only way to beat these Hungarians is the methods that Germany used in the World Cup series: the long, sweeping direct methods,' wrote Newcastle and England striker Jackie Milburn in his column for the *Sunday Sun*. 'The Hungarians will tie any team up that plays the short-passing game.' The test of that theory would come at Molineux two months later when Honvéd faced the representatives of the other half of the Black Country: the team set up to play in exactly that style, and to whom the burden of national expectation had now been transferred.

There were, however, some hurdles to clear before Wolves' bid to bring them to the Midlands was resolved. West Brom were keen to organise a rematch, and, knowing that many of Honvéd's players would be in Glasgow for Hungary's friendly against Scotland on 8 December, they suggested a game at The Hawthorns a week later, to be played, given the ground's lack of floodlights, in the afternoon. But it was Wolves' existing offer that the Hungarians preferred: Albion withdrew their bid on 20 November, leaving the champions to dot and cross the details of the deal.

The on-off nature of the negotiations had kept Wolves on tenterhooks for a while. Though the club's directors had heard at their meeting on 4 November that Honvéd were willing to set a date – of Monday, 13 December, with the team also prepared, they were told, to stay on to the Tuesday if required – without the formal approval of the Hungarian Football Federation nothing could yet be guaranteed. The arrangements still hadn't been confirmed by the time of the Spartak game, though a half-time announcement had advised spectators to retain their half-tickets just in case. But finally, eight days later, everything was at last agreed. 'After Spartak come Honvéd!' said a jubilant *Express & Star*. 'Wolves, who have been delighted to get this most attractive fixture … are looking forward to meeting the side who, by general consent, are recognised – Wolverhampton, of course, excepted – as the best club eleven in the world.'

For Stan Cullis, it was a chance to test his methods against the country he viewed as their greatest exponent. While the newspapers had framed Hungary's Wembley win as the epitome of the continental style, Wolves' manager had watched their performance through very different eyes. What had struck both him and trainer Joe Gardiner – from their seats at the ground and in their subsequent studies of the cinefilm of the match he asked the Wolves board to buy – had not been the visitors' much talked about short-passing game, but the number of long passes they employed. As most observers' focus was on the former – 'a drive [that] gained pace after the World Cup of 1954', Cullis wrote in *All For The Wolves*. 'As many of the important games were televised from Switzerland to Britain, the spectators began to look for what they *thought* [his italics] was the basis of the continental game' – the long balls, he said, were ignored. 'The consensus of opinion decided overwhelmingly that we had lost decisively to a team which played football in tip-tap style on the carpet of Wembley,' he concluded. The reality, however, was not the same.

Hungary had made 94 long passes over the course of the match, said Cullis, more than 60 of which were in the air. Twenty-one of their 31 shots, he also noted, had followed moves of two passes or fewer, 12 of which – including three of their six goals – were from only one, a deliberate approach from the Hungarians owing to their assessment that the heavy nature of the Wembley turf meant that players could conserve energy by moving the ball forward quicker. 'The critics and the public,' he wrote, 'were misled, I think, by the particular brand of play employed by Hungary … at a time when they had the match well in hand. Then they used … an innumerable total of short passes for a specific purpose: [that of] denying [England] the ball.'

Cullis's figures had been provided by a man with whom his footballing philosophy had struck a chord: Charles

Reep, an accountant with the Royal Air Force stationed at nearby RAF Bridgnorth. A wing commander in rank and an avid follower of the game, Reep had devised a way of collecting in-match data to find the most effective styles of play. After offering his services to Cullis in the summer of 1951, he would provide the manager with analyses of his teams' performances for the next four years.

Reep had been inspired by a pair of talks on football tactics given by Charlie Jones, a key member of Herbert Chapman's two-time title-winning Arsenal side. He had been fascinated to hear of the emphasis Chapman had placed on the rapid transfer of the ball from defence to attack, and, equally frustrated by the general lack of such directness in the English game since the Second World War, he had set about the task of proving through statistics the optimal way for a team to score. Reep's system broke the match down into a series of shorthand symbols, designed to record the progress and outcome of each move. By the time Wolves met Spartak he had documented over 90,000 individual actions, gathered from more than 200 separate games.

His data had told him several things: that seven out of every nine goals came from moves of three passes or fewer; that those begun with a long ball from a team's own half were twice as effective as those built from sequences of short passes; and that possession regained in the attacking quarter of the field was most likely to end in a goal. 'The ultimate in goalscoring is now known,' Reep told the *News Chronicle* in an interview published on 18 November, two days after the Spartak game. 'Hungary's national side is 75 per cent along the road towards perfection: by using correct principles they have averaged four goals in every international.' Wolves, he said, were 60 per cent advanced, and improving all the time. '[Mr Reep] says without hesitation that the day could come quite soon when the Wolves could beat the Hungarian national eleven every time,' reported the *Express & Star*, also wanting to learn more about the man and his methods ahead of a then still potential Honvéd game. 'He has faith in his system and faith in Wolves as something approaching a wonder team if they apply it. And this is not something to be scoffed at, for it is one of those cases in which figures seldom lie.'

As could also be said of the score from Glasgow a fortnight later, as the current holders of the tag maintained their goals-per-game average with a 4-2 victory at Hampden Park. Hungary didn't have everything their own way in their first game on British soil since Wembley – Scotland pulled a goal back after going two behind, and, roared on by more than 113,000 fans, were inches away from an equaliser a few minutes before half-time – but they saw out the game comfortably enough despite the home side's best efforts to break them down. 'They tried, how they tried,' lamented the *Daily Mirror*'s Jimmy Stevenson after Kocsis's 89th-minute strike wrapped up the visitors' win, 'but those Scots footballers challenging the overpowering Hungarians failed.' Budapest radio was full of praise for the hosts – 'The victory is Hungary's, but the glory is Scotland's,' one announcer said, adding that the famous 'Hampden roar' had shaken wireless sets across the country – but, as West Brom had also found, failure, however glorious, was still failure in the end.

It hadn't been a vintage performance from Hungary, but there was still plenty for Wolves' observers in Glasgow to admire. 'I wanted to get a clear picture of their tactics, and I got it,' said Stan Cullis, who had flown up with Billy Wright for the game. '[We will] have to play good football. It is a fallacy to imagine they can be beaten merely by a tough team.' They were masters of technique, he continued, describing four sumptuous Puskás passes as being worth the price of admission on their own. But there was one further thing, said Phil Morgan, that the manager was 'at pains to make clear. Lest anybody thinks Mr Cullis is hoping for a sea of mud to cut down the Hungarians' speed and ball control,' he cautioned in the *Express & Star*, 'let me make it clear at once that mud is the last thing he wants.' It was an interesting comment to make in light of what would later transpire.

All of the Honvéd players who had appeared at Hampden would be playing at Molineux as well, Puskás told the press the day after the game: Bozsik, Lóránt and goalkeeper Lajos Faragó (who had replaced the unfit Grosics) along with Kocsis and himself, while Wembley wingers Czibor – who had sat out the match in Glasgow – and László Budai would also feature, he said. The latter, together with the rest of the Honvéd squad, flew in to London on Saturday morning, sharing the flight with the players and officials of Red Banner, who were playing Chelsea at Stamford Bridge on Wednesday afternoon. The reunited Honvéd party – which included Gusztáv Sebes, Hungary's deputy sports minister and the manager of the national team – took the train to Wolverhampton the next day: after being welcomed by James Baker and presented with bouquets in the national colours by the daughters of a family of émigrés now living in the town, they made the short trip from the station to Lichfield Street, where they checked in to Wolves' favourite Victoria Hotel.

Fifty minutes later the players were back on the coach to visit Molineux, where, in their red woollen tracksuits – Puskás apart, who stood watching the proceedings in his long leather coat – they worked off any stiffness from their travels on the ground's shale track. After a demonstration of Wolves' floodlights they then returned to the hotel, to share the now-traditional celebration banquet with their hosts, held before the game this time, as they planned to return to London straight after the match on the 11.45pm train. Warm words, as well as gifts, were exchanged. 'Billy Wright said he hoped [Wolves] would not have as much running about to do … as the England team at Wembley last year,' said the *Express & Star*, '[while the] thanks of the Hungarians for their welcome, and an invitation to visit their country, were extended by Mr Sebes. They had heard a lot about "the famous Wolves", he said.' Many eyes would be on the respective captains, said James Baker, as they faced each other as clubmen for the first time. Puskás was now an international celebrity, but so too, he added, was Wright: their duel would be a special feature of Wolves' meeting with 'the greatest team ever to come to the town'.

'Honvéd are the second sports party from a communist state to come to Wolverhampton within a month,' wrote Phil Morgan in the *Star*, 'but [they] and Spartak aren't quite the same. Spartak were small, silent and fidgety, like kittens on hot bricks: Honvéd are bigger, talkative and relaxed. Spartak ignored Russian exiles in Wolverhampton: Honvéd chatted and joked with countrymen who fled totalitarianism for democracy.' The heavy rain falling stubbornly on the town took some of those smiles away – 'in Hungary we do not play in such weather', manager László Marosi glumly told the press – but it could, at least, have been worse: nearly 70 counties were experiencing snow, ice, fog or flooding, said the *Birmingham Post*, as winter gripped the UK.

The tickets for the match had quickly sold out after going on sale the Sunday before. Strictly limited to those presenting counterfoils from the Spartak game at first, 48,000 were snapped up on the opening day. Demand, unsurprisingly, outstripped supply when the remainder went on sale on Monday morning, but confirmation that the BBC would be televising the second half of the game softened the blow for the unlucky ones again. The broadcaster had learned from the experience of Spartak, where the positioning of the camera had made close-ups of the North Bank goal impossible to achieve: that angle was now covered by an extra camera mounted on top of the Molineux Street Stand, with the others placed as before.

While Wolves were unchanged from the eleven that had beaten Spartak, there was a last-minute alteration elsewhere, as referee Mervyn Griffiths was forced to withdraw. Linesman Reg Leafe stepped up in his place, though it meant he missed out on the chance to try Wolves' latest piece of night-time kit: illuminated flags, the result of a suggestion by the manager after the poor visibility of the previous game. The battery-powered design incorporated five bulbs into each stave, for the official to switch on whenever a signal was about to be made. 'I congratulate whoever was responsible for producing [them],' World Cup referee Arthur Ellis said in the *Halifax Daily Courier & Guardian* after seeing them in action for the first time. 'I found them a great advantage over the ordinary flags under floodlight conditions.' They might also have a place, Stan Cullis suggested, on murky afternoons in the league.

Everything, then, was set, and Charles Buchan, for one, was expecting a high-scoring affair, one he felt the Hungarians would shade 4-3. 'Wolves have, I think, a more difficult task against Honvéd ... than they had against Moscow Spartak,' he wrote in the *News Chronicle*. 'It may prove a little beyond their powers. Honvéd include more than half of the Hungarian international side, among them four of the forwards who overwhelmed England 6-3 at Wembley. These forwards will, I fancy, be the match-winners.

'[But] one thing may help Wolves considerably: mud. Mr Cullis says it is really too heavy for both sides. I am sure, however, the Wolves will be more at home on a "glue-pot" than the Hungarians, who openly express their dislike of muddy conditions.' The Molineux ground staff had laid tarpaulins over the goalmouths in an attempt to keep them dry. After days of rain and frosty nights, however, a sticky surface was guaranteed.

But as evening arrived, nothing could dampen the enthusiasm of the fans soon packing every inch of the ground. The counting system on the turnstiles broke down half an hour before kick-off; while the official attendance was given as 54,998, it was clearly many more. 'We got there late because our train from Wednesbury was late,' said supporter Michael Taylor, ten years old at the time, 'and I'd never seen so many people in one place. We went up the South Bank, and I was lifted up and passed over everyone's heads down to the front, where there was a little wall. I always remember, because my grandad had given me pocket money and it all fell out on the way! They used to do that with all the children, to make sure they could see.' He was there in time to watch Wright and Puskás lead their teams out side by side and line up for the national anthems: the visitors, having shed their tracksuits to reveal their all-white kit with double red chest bands, then set off on their lap of honour, throwing carnations to the crowd.

The opening few minutes were something of a stalemate as the teams vied for possession of the ball: the centre of the pitch, said the *Daily Mail*, already resembled a cattleground after a four-day show in the rain. But any thought that Honvéd would be unduly hindered was soon dispelled by a quickfire brace of goals: the first in the 11th minute from a free kick awarded on the right-hand edge of the box after the ball struck Ron Flowers's hand, Puskás floating a cross into the middle for Kocsis to head home; then, after Faragó had smothered an attempt from Roy Swinbourne, a brilliantly executed counter-attack swept the ball upfield for Ferenc Machos to make it two. But Wolves still pushed forward despite the double blow, Johnny Hancocks, Dennis Wilshaw and Swinbourne forcing the Honvéd keeper into a series of desperate saves. The visitors held on until the interval, but the match was far from finished yet.

'We met Mr Cullis in the dressing room, and, to say the least, he gave us a spirited talk,' remembered Billy Wright in his book *Football Is My Passport*. 'We went back for the second half with the quiet confidence Stan can build up as a result of his tactical talks. We knew, for instance, that while we were two goals in arrears, the Hungarians had played extremely well to achieve this lead. At the same time, our football had been quite good, so there was no question of a "beaten team" going out to be slaughtered. We also appreciated that Wolves, by reason of their hard training, were in no way inferior to the Hungarians so far as physical fitness was concerned, and it was in this frame of mind that we set out to try and make amends for the two goals we had conceded.' With Honvéd's full-backs playing square to Wolves' wingers, Cullis told his team to get long balls out to Hancocks and Les Smith. 'You are too nervous,' the *News Chronicle* quoted him as saying. 'Get out there and play our normal game.'

And, almost immediately, came the reward. After Smith had shot a foot wide from 20 yards, Hancocks, dribbling into the box, was nudged off the ball by Ferenc Kovács. Unfairly, said Leafe, awarding a penalty in spite of the visitors' protests; Hancocks blasted it home, and Wolves were right back in the game.

Urged on by the crowd, the home side poured forward, looking for the equalising goal: the growing pressure Honvéd were under could now be measured in picked-off passes and the sight of Puskás, all but neutralised by a towering performance from Wright, drifting out to the left wing to try to find some space. On 76 minutes the Hungarians finally buckled as Swinbourne's downward header beat Faragó's despairing dive: then, a minute later, delight became delirium as the centre-forward ran on to Smith's diagonal ball to smash a third into the net.

Honvéd brought on fresh legs in the form of 18-year-old Lajos Tichy as they tried to get back on terms, but Wolves weren't going to yield now: their excitement at the final whistle was mirrored in scenes of wild celebration in the stands[25].

'The crowd went absolutely berserk,' supporter Derek Bodley remembered in *Golden Glow: Favourite Wolves Floodlit Matches 1953 to 2021*. 'My dad used to wear a trilby: he threw it up in the air and he never saw it again. Gloves, programmes: it was all thrown up in the air. I'll truly never forget it.' The players would be met with quite a sight when they arrived back at the ground the next day: 'I [had] never seen the terraces so littered in caps and shoes,' Bert Williams recalled in his 'book of fond memories', *The Cat in Wolf's Clothing*. 'There were so many fans in Molineux that the joy and exuberance of winning was reflected in the happy faces as they threw their caps and jumped for joy. Many a shoe or shoes were lost in the crowd, due to … people standing on each other's heels. One lady, who had lost both her shoes, actually came to the dressing room, and was given an old pair of football boots to go home in!' Another fan had an even more uncomfortable walk home. 'They even found a crutch!' chuckled Bill Guttridge in an interview included

---

25 The tension was drawn out just a little longer for those listening in at home. With less than a minute to go and Honvéd on the attack, the voice of BBC announcer Adrian Waller cut in to the radio commentary to introduce the evening's edition of the *Light Programme*. 'It is already half a minute past 9.15,' he had said before its opening number, *365 Kisses*, began. 'I will give the final result later.' Within half an hour, however, he was back with both the score and an apology after thousands of angry complaints. 'This is the kind of mistake we only make once,' a repentant Waller said, 'and, needless to say, I shall be wary of doing it again.'

in *Legends of Soccer: The One and Only Billy Wright.* 'A fella must have thrown his crutch up into the air and lost [it], and they found [it] on the terraces!'

More serious was the situation that quickly developed outside, as the wave of departing fans became a tsunami on Waterloo Road. 'I'd been lucky enough to obtain a ticket in the Waterloo Road Stand from a friend of the family who knew Roy Swinbourne,' said Graham Winwood, ten years old at the time, 'and I remember coming out on to Waterloo Road and trying to go towards the town centre where I had arranged to meet my father, who had been standing on the North Bank. I was carried some way down the road before I could get out of the crush and make my way back along.' There had also been similar scenes at the end of the Spartak game.

As the supporters made their way to the exits, an elated Stan Cullis was giving his assessment of the game. 'I am prouder than when we beat Spartak, if one can be,' he told the mass of assembled reporters. 'It was the most exciting game I have ever seen. In the first half, I was a little worried by the ease with which Billy Wright was drawn too far forward and left gaps down the middle, so I had a chat with him at half-time. After that, he and the rest of the team were inspired.' For Wright – for whom, as England captain, the victory was especially sweet – it was a 'wonderful achievement by a wonderful team', prompted by the manager's words. The part played by Charles Reep ('Wolves' back-room boffin', as he was inevitably described) was also acknowledged: the Wing Commander, who had taken the players through his information on Honvéd in the run-up to the match, would describe their performance as 'perfection' after going over his data on the game.[26]

An old Major Buckley trick had proved useful, too, if a little controversially, given Cullis's remark to Phil Morgan a few days before. On the morning of the match, the manager had sent three apprentices armed with hosepipes and a roller on to the already wet pitch with instructions to saturate it still more. One of them was future Manchester United manager Ron Atkinson, then 16 years old. 'We thought he was out of his mind,' Atkinson later recalled in *The European Cup 1955–1980*. 'It was December, and it had been raining incessantly for four days. [But] when I watched the match in the evening, I understood what he was up to. The Hungarians were two up in about 15 minutes, and playing superbly. It was the best football I have ever seen, brilliant first-time movement. But the pitch was getting heavier and heavier. In the second half, Honvéd were still leading 2-0 but they gradually got bogged down. Billy Wright and Ron Flowers kept slinging these huge long passes up to the Wolves forwards. The mud just wore the Hungarians out.' In the 30s, Major Buckley had often flooded the pitch to give his team an extra edge; his former

---

26 'I was on the South Bank with some mates from RAF Bridgnorth,' wrote W.T. Lloyd in a letter to Mike Crump in 2015. 'I know that Stan Cullis was the manager, but [the planning of] Wing Commander T.C. Reep [played] a great part in how the team performed at that time. I know this for a fact, as on a Saturday night as I served him dinner he would inform me of how many corners, free kicks and the like he had noted down in his own form of shorthand. He would have to have his full report done to hand in on Tuesday night for Mr Cullis's attention. He told me that the Honvéd game was perfection. His theory was that the shortest distance between two points was a straight line, so the fewer passes the better. Sadly, when he came to retire his commission in 1955 the club would not employ him, and, to put it mildly, he was not best pleased.'

captain had taken a leaf from his book (and, it appears, a few of his mind games, too), with a similarly effective result.

Conditions were, of course, the same for both sides, but Cullis knew his players' strength would see them through. 'We won because of our fitness, of our desire to win,' Billy Wright told Gerald Sinstadt. 'I know the pitch was a bit heavy – we always used to water the pitch anyway – but it was just superb fitness, and they didn't know how to cope with our attacking ability. They wanted to play like the Hungarians played: beautiful football, but at their own speed. At the back they always played it quietly, quietly, and when they broke, they broke fast.

'But we always played it quick from the start, and I think that's what upset the teams we played.' Honvéd – whose international contingent must have had flashbacks to the World Cup Final, where, on a similar surface, they had surrendered another two-goal lead – 'had the polish, the "overheads", magnetic ball control, jet take-offs', summarised the *Express & Star*, 'but Wolves had the fight, [the] English bulldog determination'.

The rest of the papers agreed. In newsrooms up and down the country, the mood was nothing short of triumphal. For Charles Buchan, Wolves had 'struck another decisive blow for British football with the greatest second-half rally I have seen in 40 years ... [it was] British football at its best'. That baton was picked up with gusto by the *Daily Express*, for which the result proved that the game in England remained 'the genuine, unbeatable article ... still the best of its kind in the world'. Dick Knight's column in the *Birmingham Gazette* was positively Churchillian in tone – 'British chests can burst with pride that grit and determination, the inheritance from our forebears, has put us right back on football's top floor' – while, for the *Daily Mirror*, 'Wolves the Great … had the Nelson spirit'. But it was another headline that made the biggest waves. 'Hail Wolves champions of the world now,' said the *Daily Mail*, apparently prompted by a remark from Cullis himself. Though he swiftly denied having made it – backed up by the *Express & Star*, which quoted Cullis as saying, 'No, I do not agree with that. You may say it for yourself if you wish, but please don't quote me as saying it,' in response to a question from a national journalist – it was a message that travelled far. As the English press united in praise of Wolves and their achievement, influential ears were pricking up elsewhere.

* * *

In Paris, Gabriel Hanot – the former French international, now *envoyé spéciale* of the prominent newspaper *L'Équipe* – had his own thoughts on the game to share. 'In this manufacturing capital of 130,000 inhabitants,' he wrote of Wolverhampton, 'football is a diversion, a rejoicing and almost an anthem of deliverance, especially when an atmosphere of rain and smoke falls on the town, as it did the day before yesterday … [Only the most] fanatical supporter of Honvéd [could have remained] indifferent to the sporting communion of the crowd.

'[But] before we declare that Wolverhampton are invincible, let them go to Moscow and Budapest. And there are other internationally renowned clubs: [AC] Milan and Real Madrid, to name but two. A club world championship, or at least a European one – larger, more meaningful and more prestigious than the Mitropa Cup[27] – should be launched.'

Later that same week, *L'Équipe* editor-in-chief Jacques de Ryswick fleshed out the details of the idea. Taking inspiration from the Campeonato Sudamericano de Campeones – the world's first continent-wide club football competition (the precursor to the Copa Libertadores), which, on a trip to South America, his colleague Jacques Ferran had witnessed at first hand – it was proposed that each country nominate one club side, to play the others home and away in a midweek European league. The principle was well received, though it soon became clear that most countries favoured a tighter, knockout format instead (concerns over fixture congestion were raised by West Germany, whose players were still part-time). But, significantly, the most enthusiastic response came from the Spanish Football Federation in Madrid. 'This project appeals to me enormously,' said its president Juan Touzón, as reported in *The European Cup 1955–1980*, 'and to my friend Santiago Bernabéu, the president of Real Madrid. We are ready to receive, in his stadium which has room for over 100,000 spectators, all the top teams in Europe and also those from behind the Iron Curtain.'

Suitably encouraged, *L'Équipe* drew up a list of 18 clubs to take part, selected by Hanot, Ferran and Jacques Goddet, the paper's managing director. Not all were league champions; the organisers wanted to know who would be

---

27 Officially entitled La Coupe de l'Europe Centrale, the Mitropa Cup was one of the first international club competitions in the world. Founded in 1927, participation was limited to the nation states of the former Austro-Hungarian Empire: it was discontinued after 1992.

involved before the current season ended, so there were inevitably some contentious calls. England's invitation, for example, went, not to Wolves, but Chelsea, though to John Motson and John Rowlinson in their book on the history of the competition, the London side was the 'logical choice … Not merely because they were in line to win the First Division championship [though Wolves had led the way for much of the season, Chelsea had replaced them at the top of the table in late March] but because, like Arsenal, they had established overseas connections.' The example of Swiss full-back Willi Steffen, who had played for the Blues in the 1946/47 season, and their attempt to sign Italian centre-half Carlo Parola from Juventus were offered as evidence of the club's apparently more outward-looking stance. For the panel to overlook the team whose win had kick-started the whole process was, however, eyebrow-raising to say the least: that Celtic and Aberdeen, Scotland's current and soon-to-be champions, were also overlooked – Hibernian, who finished nine then 15 points behind the respective title winners in 1954 and 1955, were invited to represent the country instead (that Hibernian's chairman was Harry Swan, who was also president of the Scottish Football Association and an enthusiastic supporter of *L'Équipe*'s proposal from the start, no doubt helped their cause) – puts a further question mark over some of the decisions it made.

But in the end, at least from England's perspective, it was immaterial. Though the competition was ratified by FIFA on 7 May – subject to UEFA agreeing to take on the responsibility for its organisation, which was confirmed at a joint meeting of the governing body and the *L'Équipe* committee in Paris on the 21st – Chelsea still needed the approval of the Football League to take up their place, and in that, Arthur Drewry, its outgoing president, had already made his opinion clear. Linking the success of the friendly matches Wolves and other clubs had played to a drop-off in league attendances in 1954/55, he used his address at the league's AGM on 4 June to caution against adding any further fixtures to an already crowded calendar of games. The league management committee – of which Blues chairman Joe Mears was a member – and its secretary, Alan Hardaker, followed the president's lead, not exactly refusing Chelsea permission, but suggesting that it would be inadvisable for them to take part. Mears and his board didn't have to agree, but dutifully fell in line: like the World Cup a quarter of a century earlier, the first edition of the European Champion Clubs' Cup, as it had now been christened, would proceed with England left behind. 'Our attitude to the European Cup was comparable to our later approach to the European Common Market,' said Roy Swinbourne in *The European Cup 1955–1980*. 'We would have been better off if we had gone in sooner. The fact that we waited meant that we had a lot of catching up to do.' There was no such malleability in Chelsea's successors: Manchester United would become the first English team to play in the tournament – now reserved for national champions only – after ignoring the same 'advice' the following year.

But for Honvéd, politics of a far more serious kind would rob them of the chance to show what they, too, might do. The collapse of the Hungarian Uprising in 1956 threw the country into turmoil, leaving the team a casualty in its wake: after refusing to return home from a European Cup fixture in Bilbao following the Soviet invasion of Budapest, its eventual breakup signalled the beginning of the end of the country's glory years as well. While most of Honvéd's players did go back to face the music before picking up their former careers, the national team would never recover from the permanent defection of three of its biggest stars: Puskás would enjoy a new wave of success at Real Madrid and play in another World Cup, with Spain; Kocsis would accompany Czibor to Barcelona, in whose famous stripes he would one day meet Wolves again.

Honvéd may well have dominated the early years of the European Cup had things turned out differently – that distinction would belong to Real Madrid instead – but their name will always be a part of its story nonetheless. That cold, wet night in December 1954, when Wolves overcame the seemingly invincible Hungarians and dragged the reputation of English football out of the mire was the catalyst for what has become the world's most prestigious club competition today. A tournament made in France, embraced throughout Europe, but born in the mud of the Black Country.

Monday, 13 December 1954: Wolves 3 Honvéd 2

Wolves: Williams; Stuart, Shorthouse; Slater, Wright, Flowers; Hancocks, Broadbent, Swinbourne, Wilshaw, Smith.

Honvéd: Faragó; Rákóczi, Kovács; Bozsik, Lóránt, Bányai; Budai, Kocsis, Machos (Tichy 84), Puskás, Czibor.

Goalscorers: Wolves – Hancocks (pen 49), Swinbourne (76, 77); Honvéd – Kocsis (11), Machos (14).

Referee: R.J. Leafe (Nottingham).

Attendance: 54,998.

9

Hammered and Sickled:
Wolves v. Moscow Dynamo,
9 November 1955

THOUGH THEIR league and cup challenge had faded
– seven losses in the final 12 games of the 1954/55 season,
including to Sunderland in the quarter-final of the FA Cup
and Chelsea, crucially, in the league, dashed their very
real hopes of a double – Wolves' wins over Spartak and
Honvéd had left them a club in demand. Within a week of
the victory against Honvéd, AC Milan were in touch over
the possibility of a game. Stan Cullis wanted his team to
prioritise the domestic campaign, however, so the proposal
from the Serie A leaders was shelved.

But the summer saw Wolves travel to Russia, to take
up the invitation extended to them during Spartak's stay.
Matches against the two Moscow teams offered the chance
of another statement win, but, in the wider political context,
the club's role in building relationships mattered more. On
that score the trip was successful, even if Wolves were less
so on the field.

Just as Cullis and his men arrived in the Russian capital
as England's principal football ambassadors, so the Soviet
Union was eager to show itself in the best possible light as

well. Like Arsenal a year earlier – when, apart from their time on the pitch, their hosts had gone out of their way to make them as comfortable as possible – the *Volki* received the warmest of welcomes, as did the 100 fans who travelled too (for an all-in fee of £180 per person, the Soviet tourist agency Intourist provided a lavish package, including first-class air travel, five-star hotel accommodation with four meals a day, match tickets, sightseeing trips with an interpreter, visits to the theatre, and journeys to and from the airport by car), among them Frank Mansell, the mayor of Wolverhampton, John Baird MP, and Sir Charles (known as Marcus) Mander, who would have the distinction of scoring a hat-trick in an unofficial supporters' game. A Pathé News cameraman was there to record the squad's visit to the Kremlin, capturing images of the players inspecting the famous Tsar Cannon and the snaking queues outside Lenin's tomb. 'British sportsmen and a British cameraman wandering freely around the Kremlin,' announcer Bob Danvers-Walker marvelled. 'Surely the Iron Curtain is melting away at last.'

There would be more history made at the Dynamo Stadium, where Dennis Wilshaw – with all due respect to Sir Marcus – became the first Englishman to score in the USSR. It was not before Wolves had conceded six, however – three without reply on 7 August, as Spartak exacted their revenge, then, five days later, three more in the first half against Dynamo, who, despite Wilshaw's second-half brace, held on to win by the odd goal in five. Wolves had shown far more attacking venom in what was a much tighter second game, but their lack of match practice was clear: coming in 'cold' to play Russia's two best teams in the middle of the

Top League season was always going to be a challenge, and Wolves' bid to become the first English side to win in the Soviet Union duly failed. They left with no complaints, but a couple of 'if only' moments to mull over on the plane: had Italian referee Vincenzo Orlandini upheld a late penalty appeal and Dynamo keeper Lev Yashin not denied Roy Swinbourne with an even later wonder save, the country might have been toasting something even more remarkable than all Wolves' achievements so far.

The first of the squad's two travelling parties arrived back in Wolverhampton on 14 August, six days before the new English season began: somewhat later than planned, after a delay in the customs hall at London Airport, caused by a long discussion over whether duty needed to be paid on the cameras the players had been given before their departure from Russia the day before, led to them missing their train. But in among the reports of the 'enjoyable, most successful and well worthwhile' visit given by James Marshall and the recently elected John Ireland at a meeting of the Wolves board three days later was an exciting piece of news: the promise of a new two-game tour of England by a leading Russian side, beginning with a match at Molineux in October. 'The chairman ... tendered congratulations on the party's safe return, the good job it had done and the arrangements made for a return game,' Jack Howley minuted. The Soviets had agreed to confirm the details, said Marshall, within the next ten days.

One lesson they had learned from their previous dealings across the Iron Curtain, however, was that nothing was ever as simple as it seemed. Ten days passed, then a month, but still no message came, leaving the directors to turn to FA secretary Sir Stanley Rous in their growing exasperation to see if he could get a reply. Sir Stanley had already tried to move things forward when he met his Soviet counterpart in Brussels on 19 September, offering games at Molineux, Roker Park and Old Trafford over nine days in November. With the silence from Moscow still deafening a week later, however, the Wolves officials began to turn their attention elsewhere.

Real Madrid were approached, so too Vasas of Budapest, who agreed to visit Molineux in mid-October. But more frustration was in store. 'In order to keep open for the promised visit of a Russian team to Molineux, Wolves had not, so far, arranged any floodlit games,' read a statement the board felt compelled to draft on 5 October. 'With no date yet arranged, Wolves arranged to play the Hungarian club, Vasas FC, at Molineux on Monday, 17 October, but this fixture has been cancelled, Wolves feeling that they could not play without a full first team which may not be available owing to the possibility of players being required for the Wales v. England and/or England "B" v. Yugoslavia matches to be played the same week.' It was decided, said a somewhat terser entry to the minutes of the same meeting, to ask the Football League if there was a rule which stated that the Football Association should consult them before drawing up its international schedule, and, if there was, whether that had taken place.

The directors also heard that a letter from Milan had been received, rekindling their earlier interest in setting up a floodlit game. A date of 16 November was subsequently proposed and accepted, but, with everything announced and ready to go, the arrangements again fell through.

Already depleted by injury, the Italians, too, had lost players to national call-ups, so pulled out the week before.

By then, however, the news for which Wolves had long been waiting had, at last, arrived. Moscow Dynamo would be visiting Molineux on 9 November, the Soviet authorities confirmed, before playing a second, yet to be chosen side five days later. For that, Arsenal and Chelsea threw their hats into the ring, both with memories of 1945, but Sunderland – then flying high in the First Division, a point behind leaders Manchester United but with two games in hand – were awarded the game instead. 'From the English point of view it must be evident that the Russians have chosen two tough matches, for neither Wolves nor Sunderland can be easily beaten on their own ground,' said the *Express & Star* on 2 November as the shared arrangements for the visit were agreed: the clubs each undertook to provide Dynamo with £300 in spending money – later upped to £540 – and Stanley Rous, in due course, with their receipts. Perhaps mindful of Wolves' efforts to negotiate with Arsenal over the costs of the Spartak tour – discussions that, even then, hadn't been satisfactorily resolved – Rous would decide how the final bill was split between the two hosting teams. Wolves' efforts to persuade Arsenal to take a fairer share rumbled on into the next year but, despite not being satisfied by the Gunners' response, by August 1956 they had decided to let the matter drop.

It didn't leave a lot of time to pull everything together, but Wolves had already taken steps in advance. Colour-coded tokens had been issued to the 43,000 fans who attended the league match against Chelsea on 24 September, guaranteeing each of them a ticket for the game – the colours corresponded to different times of sale, to cut down on the length of the queues – while referee Arthur Ellis, who had overseen the 2-2 draw between the USSR and France in Moscow at the end of October, was lined up to take charge. The BBC, which had offered Wolves £350 for permission to televise the second half of the now abandoned match with Milan, came back with a bid of £750 for the rights to the Dynamo game instead, offering an extra £250 if commercial television was excluded from showing any footage of it, too. Just two months after the launch of ITV, which had already screened live football in the form of the second half of the floodlit friendly between Spurs and Vasas on 12 October, its influence had netted the club its first four-figure broadcast deal.

Described by Phil Morgan, a little euphemistically, as 'the team of the Soviet civil service' – they were affiliated to the Ministry of Internal Affairs (MVD) and the recently restructured KGB – Dynamo had gone one better than Wolves in retaining their league title the previous season, pushing Spartak into second place once again. Seven of the eleven who would play at Molineux were either current or future Soviet internationals, including Yuri Kuznetsov, who had scored two of Dynamo's three goals against Wolves in August, and Genrikh Fedosov, who got the other. With skipper Konstantin Krizhevsky and left-back Boris – brother of Yuri – Kuznetsov, Moscow-born inside-right Fedosov would be part of the Soviet squad that reached the quarter-finals of the World Cup in Sweden in 1958. Standing supreme, however, was Lev Yashin: '"The Lion",' said Phil Morgan, 'or, as I described him after seeing him thwart Wolves on his own ground, "The Leaping Leopard".' The 'Black Spider', as he became more commonly known, was a player ahead of his time, known for his commanding presence in the box as well as his spectacular reflex saves. The only goalkeeper to be named European Footballer of the Year – the forerunner to the Ballon d'Or – Yashin would help the Soviet Union win gold at the 1956 Olympic Games and the inaugural European Nations' Cup in France four years later. Boris Kuznetsov and Vladimir Ryzhkin would also be part of the USSR's gold medal-winning squad, along with eight of the Spartak team that had played at Molineux: Mikhail Ogonkov, Anatoli Bashashkin, Boris Tatushin, Aleksei Paramonov, Anatoli Isayev, Nikita Simonyan, Anatoli Ilyin and Igor Netto. The latter would also captain the Soviet side that won the European Championship in 1960.

Dynamo arrived at London Airport at lunchtime on Saturday, 5 November, where they were met by Sir Stanley Rous and, rushing into the hall after climbing up a downward escalator just as the players were coming in, a slightly out of breath James Marshall. 'I only heard late last night that the party was arriving here today,' the Wolves director said to the *Express & Star*, having completed the journey from Wolverhampton by taxi after catching an early morning train, 'and I particularly wanted to be here to greet our Russian friends.' The welcomes over, it was then the visitors' turn to dash away: some to watch the Second Division game between Fulham and Bristol Rovers, the others to Kenilworth Road, where Wolves were playing Luton Town. They would have been heartened by Luton's 5-1 victory, Wanderers' heaviest loss of the whole campaign – 'The Wolves defenders will have to tighten up if they are to hold Moscow Dynamo,' said the *Birmingham Gazette*, 'whose representatives must have watched the gaps appear with considerable glee' – but also aware that Wolves hadn't lost a match at Molineux in almost a year. The 20 goals they had scored in the six home games of the present season provided another good reason for Dynamo to avoid any chicken-counting as of yet.

After a night in a hotel near the Soviet Embassy in Kensington, the tourists travelled to the Midlands on Sunday afternoon, going straight from the railway station to Molineux, coach full of luggage and all. A two-hour session of jogs, sprints and ball work followed, ending with an eight-a-side practice game, played first in daylight then under the floodlights, switched on as darkness began to fall. 'The ground was greasy, and I looked for a sign whether this affected Dynamo,' said the watching Phil Morgan. 'It made no difference at all. They took it in their stride, and the ball, too, [which they took] at a furious speed, any slackening of which brought a sharp "faster" from [coach Mikhail] Yakushin.' Satisfied with their night's work, the players had dinner at the Victoria Hotel then unwound at a local cinema, where they saw the Jane Russell and Jeanne Crain musical *Gentlemen Marry Brunettes*, the follow-up to *Gentlemen Prefer Blondes*. 'Although they did not understand more than a word or two, there were the curves and the music, which are the same in any language,' wrote Morgan. Like the movie, Dynamo were also hoping to provide a worthy sequel to a hit that had gone before[28].

---

28 The team saw another film on the Tuesday evening, too: of themselves playing Wolves in Moscow the previous August, taken by John Ireland. 'It happens that Mr Ireland is also vice-president of the Wolverhampton Rotary Club,' the *Birmingham Gazette* reported the following day, 'which was holding its usual weekly meeting in the hotel where the Russians are staying. So the Rotarians welcomed the Russians in to the show.'

Ivan Sharpe's column in the match programme explained how they would try to do it. 'The style of play of the Dynamo men seems to be drilled, but is effective and attractive,' he wrote. 'Their formation is not unusual so far as continental formations go, but the emphasis is on slick movement, positional play and distribution of the ball. Like the Hungarians, they have the knack of mixing the short- and long-passing game. The through ball between centre-half and full-back is ever in mind, and attackers are ready to race through the gap.

'The general impression is this, then: crisp, nippy, mobile players, all pulling together all the time, and calling for the best from practically all opponents.'

After reversing the now familiar ritual by presenting the Dynamo players with bouquets of flowers before the game, it was Wolves, however, who first showed those characteristics as Arthur Ellis got the match under way. Johnny Hancocks and Jimmy Mullen immediately found their rhythm, the former showing how much the team had missed him in Moscow – he had chosen, as usual, not to fly – while Billy Wright and Bill Slater were similarly imposing as the visitors struggled to get into the game. With Roy Swinbourne injured, 19-year-old debutant Jimmy Murray was leading the line, showing already the striker's instinct that had secured his selection in the role ahead of Dennis Wilshaw, playing alongside him at inside-left. After five minutes he had the chance to make the perfect start, but his shot from Mullen's pass was straight at the keeper. The warning signs were there, though, and it wasn't long before Wolves' efforts were rewarded with a goal.

It came just before the quarter-hour: from a Hancocks corner, Mullen's sliced shot spun into the path of Slater, who, after hitting Murray with his first attempt, beat Yashin with his second from eight yards. Four minutes later the left-winger tried again, his powerful volley from Hancocks's cross bringing the save of the match out of the Russian. He was not to be denied for a third time, however, as, four minutes into the second half, he added a suitably glorious finish to a brilliant Wolves move. Slater flicked Bert Williams's clearance on to Murray, who fired a great ball across the field for Mullen to collect and dribble towards goal. Shrugging off two challenges from Anatoli Rodionov, he cracked a right-footed drive past Yashin to double his side's lead.

It had been, so far, a one-sided affair, Wolves enjoying the bulk of the possession as they shut their opponents almost completely out of the game. 'Tackle hard and quickly, and don't give the Russians a chance to work on the ball,' Stan Cullis had said before kick-off, and it had, up to now, paid off, but a slight easing in Wolves' tempo was all Dynamo needed to finally exert some pressure themselves. Using the extra yard or two they had so far been denied, the visitors started to find the accuracy their passing had lacked, putting together a series of moves that asked questions of the hosts for the first time. After 58 minutes Yuri Kuznetsov's shot beat Williams but came back off the post, while a drive from the right-hand corner of the box from Vladimir Ilyin – the scorer of two of Dynamo's five against Arsenal in 1954 – was gathered by the keeper and gratefully cleared. But on 62 minutes the inside-left finally broke through as Bill Shorthouse failed to clear Vladimir

Ryzhkin's probing ball, allowing Ilyin to turn and beat Williams from the edge of the box. Another cross from Ryzhkin was headed in by Fedosov shortly after, but the would-be equaliser was disallowed for offside.

It wasn't all Dynamo by any means, as Murray crashed a header off Yashin's bar; there was always danger when Wolves moved forward, especially as the Soviets pushed for a second goal. 'It was near the end that we saw the real team spirit of Wolves in action,' said Alan Williams in the *Birmingham Gazette* the next day. 'The Dynamos whipped the ball around brilliantly and yet they could not force a way through.' Wolves, the 'pride and joy of English football, [had] rocketed British sporting prestige to Everest heights', said the paper. The wider reaction was on a similar plane, as Wolves, already the only British side to have beaten a Soviet team, added Dynamo to their list of victims, too.

The players toasted the victory with lemonade, while, along the corridor, the Russians consoled themselves with tea. 'I think the 1945 team were more accurate,' said Yakushin, Dynamo's coach on that original tour. Vice-president Alexei Kuprianov identified the offside decision as the crucial moment in the game, but he also paid tribute to the 'outstanding class' of English football, particularly that of Wolves. That they had secured the win without two of their main stars – Ron Flowers, out with a knee injury, had been replaced by Eddie Clamp – made the feat all the more impressive. 'He played well,' said Cullis of Jimmy Murray's start to what would be a 299-game Wolves career, 'considering what the match was.'

But the harsher side of football in the 50s was about to become reality for Wolves' first-choice number nine.

With 17 goals in 11 games, Roy Swinbourne had made an exceptional start to the season, hat-tricks against Cardiff City and Huddersfield Town and a four-goal showing against Manchester City putting him in contention for a first call-up to the full England side. The injury that had kept him out of the Dynamo match – in trying to avoid a collision with a group of boys who had been allowed to sit at the edge of the pitch at Luton, he had pulled a muscle in his thigh – had seemed, in itself, to offer little cause for alarm. But after four weeks on the sidelines, he made his return at Deepdale on 3 December, and, in a challenge with Tommy Docherty in the final minute of the game, suffered a badly twisted knee. 'He told me the mishap was purely accidental,' said the *Lancashire Evening Post*'s Walter Pilkington, 'and that, far from being kicked, he was not even touched. He fell awkwardly and could not get up, hence the stretcher.' Perhaps brought back too soon – Swinbourne later said that the lack of strength in his leg had contributed to the severity of the injury – the extent of the damage would become more apparent as the weeks and months wore on. He would undergo three operations, but none would succeed: at the age of just 26, the hero of Honvéd had played his final game. 'As [Stan Cullis] said when Swinbourne announced, with obvious regret, the result of his chat with the specialist, this is one of the biggest single blows the club has suffered in recent years,' wrote Phil Morgan when the news was finally confirmed. 'I would go further and describe his premature retirement as a blow to football as a whole. There were few who played [the game] better, more diligently or more fairly.'

Dynamo's match against Sunderland was, for the Russians, a happier occasion, Ilyin's goal four minutes from time inflicting a first home defeat on the team now leading the First Division on goal average, still with their two games in hand. With a win and a loss, the Soviets left with an identical record to that of Spartak, and with a similar souvenir as well: a suit-length of the finest English fabric, presented at the midnight banquet that had followed the Molineux game. 'We thought it would be a sensible gift which the Russians would appreciate,' said James Baker, quoted by the *Halifax Daily Courier & Guardian*, 'knowing that cloth from the West Riding is better than anything in Russia.'

But the tone of this second visit had been different from the first: 'much more free and easy' in the words of Clifford Webb, 'no secrets about the team, no conferences behind closed doors. Plenty of laughs.' A shopping trip around Wolverhampton – 'There is so much in the windows,' Krizhevsky had said, 'that choice is difficult' – and, in the company of the Wolves squad, to a show at the Dudley Hippodrome, had shown the public something different from the polite but earnest persona Spartak had projected: one in keeping with what Wolves had experienced in Moscow, when their hosts had grasped every opportunity to show the world that things after Stalin had changed.

Politics, however, was only ever a surface-scratch away. When Spartak had played Arsenal the year before, Russian radio had broadcast commentary of the game while the authorities jammed the BBC's Russian language coverage at the same time; now, the Foreign Office had refused to allow the Soviets to broadcast from Molineux after receiving no assurance that it wouldn't happen again. 'The Russian authorities are perfectly aware of our attitude,' said a statement in response to the Soviet Embassy's protest. 'They know that if they do not jam our broadcasts, they will be given all the necessary facilities here.'

Back in August, Pathé News had forecast the melting of the Iron Curtain, but it would be more than 30 years before such incidents were consigned to the past. Images such as those of Wolves in Moscow had raised hopes of building a new and lasting understanding; by the following year, however, those of Soviet tanks on the streets of Budapest ensured the Cold War froze once more. But while the optimism that surrounded Wolves' game against Dynamo wouldn't last, it was fitting that the two should meet just as the world was filled with it again. On 9 November, three months after the centenary of Molineux was marked by a recreation of their floodlit friendly in August 1989 – and 34 years to the day after the original game was played – the Berlin Wall, symbol of all that had divided East from West since the end of the Second World War, began to be taken down.

Wednesday, 9 November 1955: Wolves 2 Moscow Dynamo 1

Wolves: Williams; Stuart, Shorthouse; Slater, Wright, Clamp; Hancocks, Broadbent, Murray, Wilshaw, Mullen.

Dynamo: Yashin; Rodionov, B. Kuznetsov; Baykov, Krizhevsky, Sokolov; Shabrov, Fedosov, Y. Kuznetsov, Ilyin, Ryzhkin.

Goalscorers: Wolves – Slater (14), Mullen (49); Dynamo – Ilyin (62).

Referee: A.E. Ellis (Halifax).

Attendance: 55,480.

10

The Match That Never Was: Wolves v. Athletic Club de Bilbao, 14 March 1956

THOUGH A large part of the latest instalment of Wolves' floodlit story had been of cancelled plans, the club had more high-profile games in the pipeline for the first months of the new year. A rematch with Honvéd was proposed – the Hungarians were very open to a return – while a visit from Athletic Club de Bilbao, vying for the Spanish title, was fixed for the middle of March. But first came a second team from Argentina: San Lorenzo, who arrived in Wolverhampton looking to improve on Racing Club's performance of two years before. Wolves' elimination from the FA Cup had made it possible to host the Primera División side on 28 January as part of their European tour. Like the trip they had made to Pittodrie in similar circumstances in 1954, Stan Cullis wanted to make the most of his players' free afternoon.

Kicking off at 3pm, the match wasn't a floodlit friendly, though the lights were switched on in the second half as the daylight began to fail. By then Wolves were 4-1 up, Hancocks (from the penalty spot), Wilshaw and Broadbent (twice) with the goals in a game that would have a moment of controversy as well. After Broadbent completed his hat-trick with Wolves' fifth, Mervyn Griffiths's decision to award the hosts another spot kick prompted a furious response from the visiting team, 19-year-old forward José Sanfilippo leading the rush of players who pushed and jostled the Welsh referee as they protested their innocence after Norman Deeley was brought down. Somehow the ringleader stayed on the field – even after grabbing the ball and booting it into the crowd – and Hancocks's penalty was saved. 'Instead of it being a dull afternoon with "nothing doing" on our ground, we at least had … plenty to talk about,' said Phil Morgan in his programme note for the Central League match at Molineux the next weekend. So, too, had the fans of Coventry City after the Argentines' visit to Highfield Road, as another mêlée over a disputed penalty call culminated in Sanfilippo kicking referee Arthur Ellis in the shin. With police officers on the pitch as the player was dragged away, Ellis declared the match abandoned. The teenager didn't feature in San Lorenzo's final game against Southampton, no doubt to the relief of Arthur Smith, the next official taking charge.

Athletic Club had been engaged in a different sort of battle, with Barcelona at the top of La Liga, a fight the two would take right down to the wire. The Basque team's acceptance of Wolves' invitation to visit Molineux on 14 March had been confirmed on 17 January, the club agreeing to cover its own expenses, hotels excluded, in exchange for Wolves doing the same in a return. The match with Honvéd, too, was agreed, its date set for nine days earlier, making an attractive package for the BBC and ITV to try to secure. The latter offered £1,500 for permission to televise one or other of the games, the BBC £500 less but with add-ons including radio and overseas coverage that gave the possibility of more. On 1 February the commercial broadcaster was awarded the rights to the Athletic Club match: Arthur Ellis was approached to officiate, and the tickets were put on sale. But while the final arrangements for the game were concluded – down to the ordering of cut-glass gifts to present to the club and squad – a request from Budapest to postpone the Honvéd fixture until the end of the month gave a hint of the troubles to come. '[The] official reason is they were delayed on tour in Turkey,' wrote Jack Harkness in the *Sunday Post*, '[but] my own feeling [is that] the Honvéd postponement is tied up with a threatened strike action by players in England. The old snag has cropped up: English players are not allowed extra pay for these floodlight games. And a "no extra pay, no floodlight play" campaign is in full swing. My forecast? We'll see no Honvéd until the financial air is a bit clearer.'

While the growth in floodlit friendlies had provided clubs with a lucrative new income stream, the fact that players were unable to share in it had been a source of tension for some time. Though the Football League had made some concessions towards the playing of competitive floodlit football at their AGM in 1955 – after a meeting of the FA in February had announced that cup matches up to and including the second round could be replayed under lights if required, the league had agreed that postponed fixtures could be similarly rescheduled if both teams involved consented – a motion giving clubs the power to pay their players for any additional matches was voted down. A maximum weekly wage of £15 was in force, with all other payments strictly controlled. When Peter Broadbent qualified for a benefit in February 1956, for example, Wolves had to apply to the league for permission to give him the £150 he was due. 'Why no extra pay for floodlit games?' Tom Finney had asked in his newspaper column back in 1954. 'I know [floodlit football] is fine for spectators and club treasurers, but the question is whether with 42 league games in a season – 46 in the Third Division – and cup matches as well, professional footballers should be expected to undertake these additional commitments.

'There remains a very strong feeling, with which I agree wholeheartedly, that the player should receive extra payment, beyond the £2 [bonus] for victory [now permitted to be paid].'

Some clubs had already tested the waters. Hull City's attempt to invite 'prominent players to take part in a floodlight match on 9 March 1953 ... offering a substantial match fee' had been given short shrift by the Football League – 'The secretary was instructed to write to Hull City and ask ... what terms they had suggested to the players,' reads an entry to the minutes of the management committee meeting on 1 February. 'The secretary was also instructed to issue a circular to clubs pointing out that the rules did not permit of [sic] any payment to players taking part in friendly matches under floodlight, other than the normal bonus' – while Wolves' proposal to pay players £5 per game, up to a maximum of £25 a season, fell on similarly stony ground. But with television coverage now adding even more money to the ever-growing pot, something had to give. Wolves' match with Athletic Club was in the firing line as the situation came to a head.

On 4 March the Players' Union – now the Professional Footballers' Association – announced a ban on its members appearing in floodlit matches, to remain in place until the Football League agreed to institute negotiations on the issue of overtime pay. Due to come into force on 13 March, the Third Division South game between Brentford and Swindon Town was going to be the first affected. However, after the match was brought forward by a day to beat the boycott, the floodlit friendly at Molineux was now under the spotlight instead.

On 7 March, a week before the game, union chairman Jimmy Guthrie met the Wolves playing staff at the Molineux Hotel. 'We've got to do something,' Roy Swinbourne remembered him saying. 'Fifty-five thousand [crowds], and you're only getting £2.' The reality was even worse as the payment was also liable for tax, the players eventually only taking home 25 shillings (£1.25). As their union rep, it fell to Swinbourne to coordinate the players' response. 'I called a meeting of all the lads in the visitors' dressing room,' he said in *Talking With Wolves: An Oral History of Wolverhampton Wanderers*. 'There were 25 of us, all union members, in that room. We took a vote on a slip of paper. I counted them and it was very close, but it was against playing.

'I had to go up and tell Stan. I walked up the old passageway from the visitors' dressing room, past the home dressing room, the physio's room, the boardroom, the secretary's room: all the way up to the top to Stan's office in the corner. I knocked and went in and said, "Stan, we've had a meeting and the vote is that we don't play." Whoosh! He went at me. He said, "It's a sell-out, we've sold all the tickets. I'm sending for the chairman. You go back and get Bill Shorthouse and Billy Wright and the three of you come back here and sit in this office." I said it had all been done democratically. It was a secret ballot and it had gone against the club. It was very close. He still said to go and fetch Bill and Billy.

'So I went back down and said, "He wants to see us." So we went up and we sat in the office and we waited for [James] Baker to come. It seemed to take hours. Anyway. I think he was sympathetic, old Baker was. He said, "If the Football League said we could pay you £100 for playing this game, we'd pay you. But we can't, we have to abide by the Football League. The rules say we can't pay you for these extra games. You just get a bonus and that's it. But if the Football League would change the rules and say it's £100 a game for floodlit games, we'd pay you." And we knew that, because we always got what we were entitled to: always first-class hotels and everything.'

The decision, though, had been made. Guthrie met with the players again before he left for London – 'The Wolves players are not against their club,' he reiterated to the press. 'They have supported the union. They are against the Football League, who are against overtime payment' – and, despite the manager's insistence that he would 'pick 11 reserves if I have to', the match was called off the same day. 'The timing of the ban made Wolves the "guinea pigs",' said the *Daily Mirror*'s Ross Hall, 'and the union's position had undoubtedly been strengthened by this demonstration of support from the staff of so famous and powerful a club.' The league and union met four days later, the former agreeing to the latter's terms; a further meeting on the 16th then confirmed that payment for matches 'extra to [the] normal club programme' would be allowed, according to the management committee's minutes, as well as for televised games. The decision was ratified at the league's next AGM on 2 June. Win or lose, a minimum sum of £2 – a maximum of £3 – would be paid to each player for every additional game. 'I am happy to report that meetings have taken place in a cordial and friendly atmosphere,' announced Arthur Oakley, now the Football League president, as reported in the *Leicester Evening Mail.*

The withdrawal of the strike action came too late for Wolves and Athletic Club, however. Though their intention was to reschedule the match when time allowed, the Basques' plans to visit Molineux never came to pass. *Los Leones* wrapped up their sixth La Liga title on 22 April, earning a place in the European Cup, where they would defeat Wolves' other prospective opponents, Honvéd, who, for very different reasons, would also be unable to rearrange their Molineux game.

The story of the last few months of 1955, then, became that of the season as a whole, as the matches against Athletic Club and Honvéd were added to the list of games organised but never played. Molineux would host its first floodlit league match on 18 April – a rearranged meeting with Tottenham Hotspur, originally scheduled for 3 March – but Wolves' floodlit friendly against Moscow Dynamo turned out to be the only one of the campaign: a famous but solitary night in what was otherwise a frustrating year.

11

English Lessons: Wolves v. CCA Bucharest, 29 October 1956

AS THE fight for extra pay had illustrated, the number of teams playing floodlit football was continuing to rise. Ten of the 22 First Division clubs had floodlighting in 1955; by the end of 1957, that number had grown to 19, a total that now included West Bromwich Albion, Chelsea and Manchester United, who, as Old Trafford's system was developed, had been playing their European Cup matches at Maine Road. But while many were investing in their first set of lights, Wolves were now looking at upgrading theirs. A major overhaul of their training ground at Castlecroft was also under way, including the fitting of floodlights for the first time.

Though the lighting of the facility had been talked about back in 1951 – the newspapers, as we have seen, suggested that that was where Wolves' initial ambition lay – it wasn't until 1955 that bids for the work were sought: a quote (of a very precise £1,394 3s 2d) from France's Electric being accepted along with one of £3,170 from another company involved in the installation of the Molineux lights, A.M. Griffiths and Son, for the building of a gymnasium and stand. William France was subsequently asked for his thoughts on improving the Molineux floodlights as well; the designer of Wolves' first lighting system would begin to draw up plans for their second over the course of the following year.

Fixture-wise, the 1956/57 season began with a sense of déjà vu. A floodlit friendly against West German champions Borussia Dortmund was arranged for mid-October then cancelled – Dortmund now had a match at Maine Road after being drawn against Manchester United in the first round of the European Cup – while an invitation to play Red Banner on Thursday, 29 November was reluctantly declined, falling a day after England played Yugoslavia at Wembley and one before Wolves travelled to Newcastle for their league fixture at St James' Park the next day. New dates for both matches would, however, be agreed, as would two more floodlit friendlies: against Valencia – who Wolves would meet (as they had planned with Athletic Club) in a two-legged, European Cup-style tie – and Romanian side CCA. The country's 'golden team' would visit Molineux on 29 October, kicking off a much busier year.

But before that came another floodlit first. In addition to the changes approved in relation to players' pay, the Football League's AGM on 2 June had supported a further proposal from the management committee, lifting all restrictions on the agreed use of floodlights for competitive league games. Wolves' match against Luton Town on 29 August was the first to be played under the new ruling, beginning in natural light at 7pm and concluding under artificial as the clock approached nine. It turned out to be an evening very much in keeping with the sense of occasion. '46,000 fans get soccer-drunk' read the headline in the *Daily Mirror* the next morning; 'Wolves and Luton go goal-crazy'.

Watched by a new signing – goalkeeper Malcolm Finlayson, who had joined from Millwall for £3,000 earlier in the day – and featuring debutant Gerry Harris at left-back, five first-half goals saw Wolves come from two down to beat the Hatters 5-4. 'Memories of Spartak, Honvéd and Dynamo were starkly recalled as Wolves overthrew an almost equally brilliant Luton Town,' said the *Birmingham Gazette*'s report, not the only one to evoke Wolves' earlier exploits in its description of the game. Five more part-floodlit league matches were also planned for Molineux's winter programme, with two more agreed with Newcastle and Leeds United for the team to play away.

Wolves' first floodlit friendly in almost a year promised to be a similarly memorable night. Founded less than a decade earlier, the Romanian army team – Casa Centrală a Armatei translating as 'Central House of the Army' – had already become the country's leading side, winning five national cups and a hat-trick of league titles between 1951 and 1953. On 22 April, Romania had beaten Yugoslavia – a feat England had not yet managed – with a team made up exclusively of players from CCA; a 2-1 victory for the 'soccer soldiers' over Spartak in Moscow, too, showed they were very capable of giving Wolves a testing game.

While Billy Wright's 78 international caps hadn't yet included a match against Romania, his manager had good reason to recall England's first meeting with the nation's footballers on the eve of the Second World War. On 24 May 1939, Stan Cullis had become his country's youngest professional captain, leading the team to a 2-0 victory in Bucharest in front of 40,000 fans. 'The deft touches and clever movements of the Englishmen repeatedly had the home defenders running the wrong way, and this, combined with the robust style of the Englishmen, tended to upset the Roumanian [sic] players who became somewhat temperamental in the second half,' reported the *Birmingham Post*: 'Cullis ... played very well and had a steadying influence on his team when the [Romanians] in desperation attempted to force their way through.' Romanian football had come a long way since then, but CCA wouldn't find his approach any less uncompromising as a manager than it had been as a player on the field.

The visitors had made an excellent impression in the first three matches of the tour. After drawing 1-1 with Arsenal on 16 October and 3-3 with Sheffield Wednesday on the 22nd – fighting back from 3-1 down – they had overturned a three-goal deficit at Kenilworth Road to beat Luton 4-3. Two goals from inside-right Gheorghe Constantin had kept up his record of scoring in every game, while striker Ion Alecsandrescu – known as *Sfinxul* ('The Sphinx') – had got the other two. 'The [Romanians], having tasted blood ... never looked back,' said the *Daily Herald*, praising them for the attacking flair that had brought them a deserved win. 'Once more the task of upholding English soccer prestige has been dropped in Wolves' lap,' said the *Express & Star*. 'Wolves, who would perhaps have preferred the first crack at the continentals, get the last, and it is with the responsibility that somebody, at least, can beat the [Romanian] soldiers' team.'

Though CCA's only other experience of floodlit football had been in their win at the Dynamo Stadium, they had already shown their capacity to adapt, embracing a more direct approach from Hillsborough onwards after being criticised for their shot-shyness before. Some tactical shortcomings, however, had also been identified as ripe for Wolves to exploit. '[Their] wing-halves lie deep, and at times leave a big midfield gap in which Wolves' inside-forwards may be able to work with advantage,' said 'The Scout', giving his appraisal of the team's performance at Highbury for the next day's *Express & Star.* 'For all their skill and all-round ability, they are no Honvéd, and if Wolves tackle hard and go straight for goal, the Central House of the Army may have to be put in order after [the game].'

While the Romanians named an all-international eleven for the match at Molineux, Wolves had some new faces in their ranks. Malcolm Finlayson had been called into senior action a little earlier than anticipated after Bert Williams sustained a finger injury in mid-September, and the Scot had retained his place despite the England keeper being fit again. Gerry Harris, too, had made the most of his opportunity after replacing Bill Shorthouse at the start of the month, playing every game as Wolves climbed from ninth to sixth in the league. Also included was winger Harry Hooper, signed for £25,000 from West Ham in March. His arrival – the club record fee more than funded by the sale of Les Smith and Nigel Sims to Aston Villa and Peter Russell to Notts County – had sent the loudest signal yet of a changing of the guard, with the man he replaced, the now 37-year-old Johnny Hancocks, relegated to the reserves.

Hooper had been on target as Wolves prepared for CCA's visit with a 3-1 win over Cardiff City, his penalty in the 40th minute adding to goals from Jimmy Mullen and Colin Booth, who was also getting a run in the side. With Peter Broadbent dropped, Jimmy Murray continued at inside-left and Dennis Wilshaw at number 9. Broadbent would make an appearance from the bench, however, the first Wolves player to do so in their Molineux floodlit games.

CCA – who, after watching the Cardiff match, had trained under the lights for an hour – lined up in a system of three backs and two half-backs, with skipper Alexandru Apolzan, wearing 3, in the central role. But Wolves didn't take long to break the formation down, Murray opening the scoring after only two minutes from Billy Wright's pinpoint through ball. A quarter of an hour later it was two, Apolzan's clumsy block on Hooper giving away a penalty which the winger dispatched with aplomb. Although Wilshaw had to leave the field after a collision with goalkeeper Costică Toma ten minutes later – Murray moved into the centre-forward position with Broadbent slotting in at inside-left – the hosts still had most of the ball, slinging their customary long passes from the centre to the wings. There was no addition to the score, however, as Reg Leafe blew his whistle for half-time.

The visitors made two changes, replacing Victor Moldovan and Ion Alecsandrescu with Iosif Bükkösy and Gheorghe Cacoveanu – the former because of injury, sustained in a first-half clash with Harris, the latter tactical, after Wright had barely given the striker a kick of the ball – and, in the early part of the second half, CCA had their best spell of the match. Threatening another comeback, the Romanians would have narrowed the gap but for an excellent save from Finlayson after Ştefan Onisie burst through. But unlike Wednesday and Luton, the scare only got Wolves going again. Straight from the goalkeeper's clearance, Murray collected the ball and found Broadbent in space; his shot gave Toma no chance, and effectively killed off the game.

Wolves weren't done yet, however, as two goals in three minutes turned the win into a rout, Murray again the provider as Booth scored the fourth before he rounded off a man-of-the-match performance by turning home Broadbent's parried shot for number five. It hadn't been a classic Wolves performance – it hadn't needed to be – but there was no arguing with the final score. 'Rah, rah, rah!' said David Williams in the *Daily Herald*. 'Rampaging Wolves have done it again. Spartak, Honvéd, Dynamo: and now the all-international [Romanian] soccer soldiers. Wolves have well and truly thrashed them all.'

CCA had been, as 'The Scout' had predicted, no Honvéd, but they had shown more than a glimpse of what they could do; in Gheorghe Constantin, the papers agreed, they had a special player, 'a master-footballer' said the *Birmingham Gazette*'s John Davies, 'if ever I saw one'. But they had been outclassed by Wolves, and, in an echo of the national side's experience against Cullis's England in 1939, outmuscled, too. 'We appreciate playing at Wolverhampton and we love to play football, but we have never met such hard fighting and barbaric tackling for the ball,' grumbled coach Ilie Savu after the game. 'Wolves' technique is very good, and we congratulate them on being the better side, [but] we have met this hard tackling against the other British teams, and we just cannot take any more.' The tourists were keen to expose themselves to it further, however, as they looked to improve. 'They were so impressed by what Wolves had to show them ... that they immediately asked the Molineux club to go to Bucharest, there to show the natives the sort of stuff that had stopped CCA in their tracks,' wrote Phil Morgan in the *Express & Star*. 'They wanted a date next May, but Wolves, feeling they have done what was asked of them for the time being, will think it over.'

Though they still had much to learn about the realities of playing abroad, CCA continued to dominate at home. The season would end with their fourth national title and qualification for the 1957/58 European Cup, where they lost 3-1 to Borussia Dortmund in a first-round play-off in Bologna after the aggregate score from the two legs was tied at 5-5. They would get no further in their next five appearances in the tournament, but history would be made in their seventh, when, as Steaua Bucharest in 1986, they became the first team from the Eastern Bloc to win the competition, defeating Terry Venables' Barcelona in a penalty shoot-out after the final's first goalless draw.

Ion Alecsandrescu was there for Steaua's greatest day. CCA's centre-forward in their game at Molineux was now president of the club and the architect of the side that had shocked the Spanish champions in Seville. *Sfinxul*'s 18 league goals 30 years earlier had taken them on their first European adventure; now he watched on, a legend of Bucharest, and the link from one 'golden team' to another.

Monday, 29 October 1956: Wolves 5 CCA Bucharest 0

Wolves: Finlayson; Stuart, Harris; Slater, Wright, Flowers; Hooper, Booth, Wilshaw (Broadbent 28), Murray, Mullen.

CCA: Toma; V. Zavoda, Apolzan; Ivănescu, Onisie, Bone; Moldovan (Bükkösy HT), Constantin, Alecsandrescu (Cacoveanu HT), F. Zavoda, Tătaru.

Goalscorers: Murray (2, 74), Hooper (pen 18), Broadbent (61), Booth (71).

Referee: R.J. Leafe (Nottingham).

Attendance: 47,284.

12

Relief: Wolves v. MTK Budapest, 11 December 1956

WHILE THE match with CCA had made a gross profit of £6,440, Wolves were hoping that their next floodlit friendly would bring in much more. The game against Red Banner – who had now made known their wish to go by their original name of MTK (Magyar Testgyakorlók Köre, translating as 'Circle of Hungarian Fitness Activists') – would be played in aid of the Hungarian Relief Fund: the club was anxious to support the humanitarian efforts now in full swing after the collapse of the revolution in Budapest.

Emboldened by Soviet premier Nikita Khrushchev's call for the 'de-Stalinisation' of the USSR in a speech in February 1956, Hungary's student-led protests against the country's communist government had looked, for a while, like succeeding. 'The rebels' determination to achieve freedom has [shone] like a bright star over a battlefield,' said an *Express & Star* editorial on 29 October. 'It has shown that once the blood of a nation is up in a cause of snow-white purity, even tanks and artillery have a hard task in the face of unquenchable resolve.' The reality, however, had been different: on 4 November, 12 days after the uprising had begun, it was over, crushed by the 17 divisions of Red Army troops ordered in to the country to put it down. Thousands had been killed or wounded and nearly a quarter of a million people displaced. The Western allies were united in their condemnation of Khrushchev and his government but, their eyes also fixed on the developing crisis in the Suez Canal, stopped short of sending military aid.

MTK – their former moniker coming from the club's affiliation to the ÁVH, Hungary's loathed and now disbanded secret police – had arranged their tour of England before the rebellion had begun: the invitation to Wolves, turned down for the aforementioned reasons on 3 October, was extended as they drew up their itinerary for a planned four-match stay. But now, visits to Molineux, Brighton and Hibernian were added to the games already scheduled against Sunderland, Portsmouth, Tottenham and Manchester City. 'When it became known that they were open to arrange fixtures additional to those planned for their original tour, we were only too happy to suggest a game as a means of helping the relief fund, and Red Banner [sic] were equally willing to accept,' said a note in Wolves' match programme. 'Thus, in a surprise fashion, we have been able to add just one more to the list of outstanding foreign teams who have appeared under the Molineux lights.'

MTK had, like Honvéd, left Budapest on 1 November with the blessing of Imre Nagy, the leader of the new Hungarian government Khrushchev's forces would shortly overthrow, travelling to Vienna in an ad hoc fleet of Chevrolet cars (Honvéd, journeying by bus, went on to Brussels, where they would eventually play the second leg of their tie with Athletic Club de Bilbao). But as the situation in Hungary changed, so, too, did their plans: the extra games they arranged were also necessary to support the players financially as they waited to see if it was safe to return. After six matches on the continent – the penultimate one in Munich, where, according to a report in the *Daily Record*, they beat 'Munich' (whether Bayern, 1860 or another club is unclear) 4-1 on 17 November – they arrived in England seven days later. 'The team … was sent out of Hungary just before the heaviest fighting by prime minister Nagy, who thought that they would be better able to serve the cause of the country by playing sporting football outside it than by remaining,' said the *Nottingham Guardian*. 'When the players left Budapest they took with them one case, with handkerchiefs the only additional personal belongings to the clothes they wore. They reached London with new overcoats and hats, [all] gifts from the German, Belgian, Austrian and Luxembourg people, who, said the manager [Miklós Gáspár], "have been so generous to us".'

They arrived with a piece of news, as well, that alleviated some of the anxiety they had experienced. 'I managed to speak to my wife, who is in Budapest, by telephone two days ago, and she contacted the wives of the players,' said Mr Gáspár. 'The players' families, we were very relieved to find, are all safe, but some of their homes have been destroyed by gunfire and Russian tanks and they are destitute.' The players had donated £5,000 of the money they had earned so far to the relief fund; the proceeds from their matches at Brighton and Hibernian were also now earmarked for the appeal.

Quite apart from the cause for which they were playing, the prospects for a large crowd were good.

Unlike Honvéd, the 'super team' effectively created by the state, MTK had been a major force in Hungarian football long before the communists came to power. They, with Ferencváros, had dominated the domestic league, winning 32 of the 45 official Nemzeti Bajnokság ('National Championship') titles between them before the nationalisation of Hungary's clubs in 1949. But while MTK were then aligned with the ÁVH, their long-time rivals were considered unsuitable to carry the name of the army because of the nationalistic traditions of the club. While Ferencváros became the team of the state food workers' union, the ÉDOSZ, Kispest Atlétikai, then with just a single Hungarian Cup to their name, were the beneficiaries instead. As Honvéd, they would win the league in five of the next seven years.

It was at MTK, though, that the foundations of Hungary's international success had been laid, as coach Márton Bukovi shifted the role of the centre-forward from target man to 'false 9'. Wing-half Péter Palotás was the first to play in the position for the club and, in due course, the national side, but it was Nándor Hidegkuti who made it his own, complementing the partnership of Puskás and Kocsis with his skill and tactical guile. 'He was a great player and a wonderful reader of the game,' said Puskás, as quoted in Jonathan Wilson's *Inverting the Pyramid: A History of Football Tactics*. 'He was perfect for the role, sitting in front of midfield, making telling passes, dragging the opposition defence out of shape and making fantastic runs to score himself.' Now 34, the destroyer of England at Wembley in 1953 had lost none of his mystique: 'Hidegkuti shows why he's World No. 1' announced the headline in the

Daily Herald after he had scored one and made the other as MTK drew 2-2 with Sunderland in their opening game on 26 November. 'It was magic. It was Hidegkuti. The world master centre-forward took charge of this game and saved it for the Hungarians when Sunderland seemed to be strolling home.'

Though the morning of the 28th brought some alarming news – Viennese radio was reporting that the Hungarian Football Federation had told MTK to be home by 10 December, threatening the match with Wolves – the tourists were determined to continue as planned. 'We have not received any communication from Budapest,' said Mr Gáspár, quoted by the *Birmingham Post*, adding that both the MTK management and national body were fully aware of their whereabouts. 'Have no fear!' Béla Miklós, the Hungarian-born travel agent who had organised their itinerary, told the *Daily Herald*. 'We will see the tour through as arranged.' It carried on, with first an upset then a shock, as a 2-1 loss at Fratton Park was followed by a 7-1 mauling at White Hart Lane. 'Britain is best – Spurs prove it!' crowed the *Herald*, not about to let an opportunity for some triumphalism, whatever the circumstances, pass by. 'A crowd of 31,000 staggered fans saw the homeless Hungarians shattered by a home side which included five reserves!'

They were better on 6 December, beating Manchester City 3-2, but then fell to an even more stunning defeat two days later, to Brighton, then of the Third Division, who won 5-3. By then the Hungarians had decided to abandon the Scottish leg of their tour – with a week between the games in Wolverhampton and Edinburgh, they felt that its costs would be more than the likely reward[29] – but they were ready for the match that had, since its confirmation, been the focal point of their plans. 'We are reserving something special for the side that beat Honvéd, Spartak and Moscow Dynamo,' said Mr Miklós. Molineux, he promised, would see the best football of their trip.

It was, of course, hardly surprising that MTK hadn't yet shown their greatest form. The cloud that had overshadowed the visit hung heavy over the pre-match banquet as well. 'I don't think we could have met under worse circumstances,' said James Baker as he welcomed them to the town. 'We would like you to know that everybody in England would like to do their utmost to put things right.' The civic motto, Out Of Darkness Cometh Light, was appropriate, he added, 'Win or lose, we are grateful to you for coming and we hope the day is not far distant when you can invite us to Budapest.' The visitors were given knitted pullovers as their gift from the club: another practically minded present, for which they had each been fitted in the town that afternoon.

Both managers delayed naming their respective elevens until just before the kick-off at 7.15pm. Hidegkuti, 'as anxious to play as are the Wolverhampton crowd to see him', had received treatment on a damaged thigh muscle

---

29 There had originally been a fourth 'extra' match announced – against Shamrock Rovers, to be played in Dublin on 15 December – but, after being mentioned in several different newspapers over several days, reference to it suddenly stopped. The proposal had definitely been abandoned by the time of the cancellation of the Hibernian game; the reason given by Béla Miklós refers to an empty week between the Wolves and Hibs matches, which the Rovers game would have filled. An enquiry to the Irish club has yielded no further information. MTK had expressed their disappointment at the gates of their earlier games, however, so perhaps, like Hibernian, the match was called off over fears that the takings wouldn't justify the expense of playing.

earlier in the day, while injuries to Dennis Wilshaw and Colin Booth had brought Johnny Hancocks and Pat Neil into the reckoning, the former for the first time since a goalless draw at Villa Park eight months before. The senior man would have to be content with a place on the bench, but 19-year-old Neil, signed from Portsmouth in August, was given his first-team debut on the left wing. Right-back George Showell would play his first floodlit match, too, in the absence of Eddie Stuart, who was recovering from an ankle injury. But Wolves fans were perhaps most delighted to see that Hidegkuti was fit enough to start: his 58 appearances for Hungary took the number of international caps represented in the visitors' line-up to a remarkable 241.

And, despite a treacherous pitch – solely down to rain this time, unaided by any apprentice with a hose – MTK made good on their pledge to the town, turning on the style from the off. Bert Williams had already made two big saves by the time they scored a deserved opening goal: István Szimczák shot and Williams dived, pushing the ball acrobatically off the line, but Péter Palotás was there to knock in the rebound as the goalkeeper desperately tried to get to his feet. But the lead lasted just four minutes as back came Wolves, a corner from the right finding its way to Neil, free on the left, whose first-time shot flew through a ruck of players and into the corner of the net. As the crowd caught its breath, Harry Hooper twice went close, his first effort being tipped over the bar and second deflected on to the post. MTK keeper János Veres had to make three more good stops before the whistle went for half-time.

It was Williams who was first in action as the second period began, however, as he closed down a clean-through

János Molnár then touched Szimczák's drive over the bar. Both teams were creating their chances through the wings, and even with Hidegkuti on the field – he had been withdrawn at the interval – there had been little to choose between two fine half-back lines that were dominating the middle of the pitch. The full-backs were performing admirably too, particularly those of MTK – 'The two Kovács [Ferenc and József] were almost irritatingly cool,' said Phil Morgan's report the next day – but there was still plenty of goalmouth action to enjoy. That there was no addition to the score was entirely due to the continued brilliance of Williams and Veres, who both gave near-faultless displays. The visitors were aggrieved in the dying minutes when Arthur Ellis waved a very good penalty shout away – a challenge by George Showell was, said the *Herald*'s David Williams, 'as clear a foul as I ever saw' – but 1-1 it stayed; the closest Wolves had come to surrendering their unbeaten record, said the papers, after MTK had finally shown their teeth. 'This touring Hungarian side has been kidding us,' said Williams. 'Those defeats by Portsmouth, Spurs – and especially Brighton – must have been so much Magyar tomfoolery. They played in the real Hungarian style: fast and incisive in attack and more resolute in defence than any other continental side I have seen.

'I was hoping to write rah, rah, rah, rah – and for the fifth time, rah – for Wolves. It was not to be.'

But this was a game in which football was always second to bigger things. 'One could not escape the impression that Wolves did not unleash their full floodlit fury on the worried Hungarians,' wrote Phil Morgan in the *Express & Star*. 'This mood was reflected in the crowd, who, it seemed to me, just could not bring themselves to making the visitors' task any harder by harassing them with the Molineux roar. Instead, it became the Molineux murmur, and quite often a murmur of appreciation for the artistry of the visitors.'

The supporters had, though, raised the roof for Johnny Hancocks, who replaced Jimmy Murray with eight minutes to go. But it wouldn't be a fairy-tale ending for the man remembered as one of Wolves' greatest-ever players, who had only three touches of the ball: one a lobbed shot from an indirect free kick, one last effort on goal in what would be his final appearance in the senior team[30]. After turning down offers from several clubs – including one from former Wolves coach George Poyser, now in charge at Notts County – he accepted the post of player-manager at Cheshire League side Wellington Town in June. When he left, his record of 167 Wanderers goals was bettered only by that of 'Artillery Billy' Hartill, who scored 170 for Major Buckley's team between 1928 and 1935.

Pat Neil, meanwhile, had done more than enough to retain his place for the weekend's trip to Maine Road: not that every Wolves supporter was familiar with him as of yet, despite his performance against MTK. 'In those days the team used to travel on a corridor train to the matches, and a mate and I ended up on the same train to Manchester, where Wolves were playing Man City,' Keith Perry recalled. 'We plucked up a bit of courage and went into the players'

---

30 At the board meeting held at Molineux the following day, it was noted that Hancocks had 'refused to play in the position selected for him' against MTK and that 'a warning and severe caution should follow'. On 27 December, it was recorded that a notice to that effect had been posted in the dressing rooms.

carriage, and the likes of Bill Slater, Billy Wright and Ron Flowers were sitting there playing cards. I went up and asked if I could have their autographs, and I got the whole team: Mullen, Mason, Showell, Williams, I got them all.

'Well, all except one, and I've always regretted it. Because I didn't recognise Pat Neil, I didn't ask him. He must have thought I was a right prat! But I got all the others. I got Billy Wright twice, in fact, because I got him at the start and then again on my way out as well!' Keith would surely have put it right had their paths crossed on the way home: Neil had grabbed the decisive goal as Wolves beat City 3-2[31].

MTK flew from London Airport to Munich the same day, having taken some time to weigh up their next move. 'Whether all the players will return to their homes I cannot say,' Béla Miklós had said in the *Huddersfield Daily Examiner*. 'Some Hungarians participating in the Olympic Games in Melbourne decided otherwise [34 athletes, coaches, writers and administrators defected to the West] and that may prove to be the case here, too.' But while Honvéd would continue their tour with an unauthorised trip to South America in the new year – after which the defections of Puskás, Kocsis and Czibor were confirmed – MTK, now back in Vienna, resolved to return to Budapest.

---

31 Pat Neil's time at Molineux would be short-lived, despite his scoring start. After making just three more appearances he left in the summer, later returning for a second spell at Fratton Park before giving up the game to focus on an academic career. 'I was called in to play against the touring Hungarian team Red Banner [sic] and scored the equalising goal that saved Wolves' unbeaten record against continental teams,' he recalled in an interview in 2009, 'but when national service and a posting to Cyprus took over, it was difficult to continue to play for Wolves.'

'We are anxious to get back to Hungary to give presents to our families for Christmas,' said Miklós Gáspár. Defender József Zachariás – who, while away, had heard that his house had been destroyed in the fighting – quoted a proverb to the waiting reporters: 'Everywhere is good, but best is home.'

They departed having raised £10,000 for the Hungarian Relief Fund, a total that included a donation of £2,213 3s 4d from Wolves, who had, as promised, given their share of the receipts to the appeal (it would have been £4,160 had Wolves' application to Customs and Excise for exemption from paying Entertainment Tax in the circumstances – charged at 18 per cent of the total takings – not been refused). But while Hungary's clubs, Ferencváros included, reclaimed their old identities as football in the country uneasily resumed – joined, in due course, by the Honvéd players who also decided to return – the impact of the defections was compounded by a heavier blow.

Hungary's under-21 squad had been in Switzerland when the revolution began. None would ever go home, adding the loss of the country's next generation of talent to that of its current stars. The Mighty Magyars had dominated the global stage, winning 58 and drawing ten of the 69 internationals they had played since 1950: now, six years on, in the turbulent aftermath of the revolution, the golden age of Hungarian football was at an end.

Tuesday, 11 December 1956: Wolves 1 MTK Budapest 1

Wolves: Williams; Showell, Harris; Slater, Wright, Flowers; Hooper, Mason, Murray (Hancocks 82), Broadbent, Neil.

MTK: Veres; F. Kovács, J. Kovács; I. Kovács, Börzsei, Sipos; Sándor, Palotás, Hidegkuti (Kárász HT), Molnár, Szimczák.

Goalscorers: Wolves – Neil (10); MTK – Palotás (6).

Referee: A.E. Ellis (Halifax).

Attendance: 43,540.

13

Blitzkrieg: Wolves v. Borussia Dortmund, 27 March 1957

THOUGH MTK hadn't followed Honvéd in openly defying the Hungarian authorities while on tour, several of their players had still been keen to stay in the West if they could. Ferenc Kovács and Ferenc Sipos had expressed their interest in signing for an English team; so, too, had Károly Sándor, who had met representatives of Birmingham City during the squad's final days in the UK. 'Even if they are willing to come and the FA and Hungarian [Football Federation was] agreeable, there are still plenty of snags to overcome,' West Bromwich Albion manager Vic Buckingham, who approached Kovács and Sipos by letter after getting the go-ahead from Major Wilson Keys, cautioned in the *Birmingham Post*. It was Stan Cullis, however, who struck while the iron was hottest, moving to sign the 19-year-old István Kovács, MTK's youth international right-half.

On 18 December – a week after watching Kovács at Molineux – Cullis travelled to Switzerland to speak directly to the player himself. After MTK had left England, he had chosen to join up with the under-21 squad rather than stay with the team. '[Cullis] was busy in the early hours of the morning telephoning the continent,' reported the *Daily Mirror*, 'then, with a hasty goodbye to his wife[32], he disappeared from Wolverhampton and flew to Geneva. Neither his wife nor any Wolves official knew where he was going.' When the under-21s had decided that they wouldn't be returning to Hungary, Kovács had sent a message to the Wolves manager asking for his help. 'I would like to join Wolves and live in England,' he said again when they met in a city cafe. An agreement was struck that evening, and he accompanied Cullis back to Wolverhampton the following day.

It would be, said the *Mirror*, the first test case to discover whether a Hungarian player could play for an English team. The formal permission of the FA, Football League and Hungarian Football Federation was required before he could do so, and then, only as an amateur while the FA's two-year qualifying period for an overseas player was served. 'There may be a difference if a player is a refugee and he intends to remain here permanently,' a spokesman for the league suggested, but the position of the Hungarian authorities on the matter was less than clear: the mixed messages coming out of Budapest were summarised in a *Daily Record* opinion piece, published on Christmas Day.

---

32 Stan Cullis's all-consuming focus on his job made such incidents far from unusual. When Wolves visited the USSR in 1955, for example, his family was the last to know. 'My mum didn't know that he was going to go,' Andrew Cullis told *Champions of the World*. 'We were at home, my sister, myself and my mum, saying, "Where is dad? The supper is ready!" It was only when we watched [the news on] television [that we realised what was happening]: there were the Wolves, getting on a plane to go to Russia. That's how we knew dad was not going to be home that night, or for about a week! He'd forgotten to tell my mum. And that was not unknown, that sort of, "Where is he? Oh there he is!" My mum was very patient!'

'I do not intend to extend merry Christmas greetings to Hungary's football officials,' wrote sports editor James Cameron. 'For they have in the past few days been messing around with the future careers of players who have, in the jerseys of Red Banner [sic] and Honvéd, adorned the international football scene ... First we had minister of sport Sebes telling the Hungarians in Brussels that the Honvéd and [MTK] boys needn't return to Hungary unless they wanted to, [and] that they might play for any foreign club: then, on Sunday [the 23rd], Budapest Radio announced that permission would not be given to any Honvéd or [MTK] footballers to play for any club outside the country. Now, from Vienna, comes a report that the Hungarian [Football Federation has] decided that no Hungarian refugee footballer will be given permission to play abroad.' Five names were 'particularly mentioned' in the ban, he continued: Puskás, Kocsis, Grosics, Sándor and B international forward István Szolnok, who had played in MTK's 5-3 defeat to Brighton earlier in the month. 'And all this in the season of goodwill and peace toward all men,' Cameron concluded. 'Let's keep politics out of sport.'

As he waited for a definitive judgement from the federation, Kovács could only train, working in a drawing office in Wolverhampton to support himself in the absence of a paid contract from Wolves. He was, however, allowed to play in a charity match at the Revo Electric ground, appearing for a Bert Williams All Star XI against Wolverhampton Boys' Club on 28 March. 'Kovács played a fine, foraging game for the All Stars, distributing well,' reported the *Express & Star*. 'He laid on a pass for [Arnold] Rodgers [of Shrewsbury Town] to open the scoring after

12 minutes and did precisely the same thing a minute later, when Rodgers obtained his second goal.' The Hungarian added a couple himself as, in front of 2,700 fans, the All Stars ran out 8-2 winners in the end. '[He] played quite well,' said Cullis in the *Sports Argus*, 'but he's dreadfully short of match practice. We're keeping in touch with the FA, but there's no news yet.'

For Kovács's prospective team-mates, by way of contrast, it had been a particularly busy month, taking in a midweek trip to Spain to play the first leg of their double-header with Valencia as well as five First Division games. And, the day before the charity event at the Revo, another floodlit friendly: the rescheduled match against Borussia Dortmund, the new power in the German game.

Dominant in the Oberliga West (with the Oberliga Süd, the strongest of the five regional top-flight leagues established in the country after the war) and soon to retain their national crown, the still-amateur eleven had pushed Manchester United all the way in their European Cup meeting five months before. In the first leg at Maine Road on 17 October – watched by a crowd of 75,568, the biggest yet for any English floodlit game – goals from international forwards Helmut Kapitulski and Alfred Preissler had seen them narrow the gap from three down to give themselves a more than fighting chance of going through. 'After a masterful first half ... the "Busby Babes" were made to look very young and very fallible,' said George Follows in the *Daily Herald* the next day. 'They had to cling by their bootlaces to a one-goal lead.' It had, as it turned out, been enough – the second leg in Dortmund finished 0-0 – but the Germans had shown themselves to be a side 'well worthy of our interest', said Phil Morgan in the match programme, 'and well capable of making one of the strongest [challenges] yet to our unbeaten record in special floodlit games against foreign opponents'.

Though their earlier plans to visit Wolverhampton had fallen through, Dortmund had been to the Midlands before. On Wednesday, 31 October, in between their European ties, they had played Birmingham City in the first floodlit game at St Andrew's, mounting another impressive comeback from 3-1 down to draw 3-3. Wolfgang Peters and Kapitulski – together with the unfortunate Johnny Newman, whose own goal had given them an early lead – were on the scoresheet, but the whole team had impressed. 'Courtly in manner and remarkable in football skill,' said the *Birmingham Post*, '[they] proved great favourites with the crowd.'

Their style of play was 'good English First Division standard', wrote Ivan Sharpe in the match programme. 'I was present at the World Cup Final ... when the West German international team sprang that surprise win on Hungary, and the similarity to English methods was noticeable on that great day. The higher class and more ornamental style of their opponents did not worry them: they kept at it and wore them down. They were less a team studded with stars than a compact, cohesive eleven who got on with it in a workmanlike way. And that is the kind of test awaiting the Wolves.' Though none of Dortmund's three capped players had appeared in Bern, goalkeeper Heinz Kwiatkowski had made his international debut in the group game against Hungary in Basel – something of a baptism of fire against Kocsis, Puskás and Co.: Germany's

8-3 loss remains their heaviest in a World Cup to date – but he had shown his quality on plenty of occasions since then, including at St Andrew's and Maine Road.

While the visitors named, with one exception, the same side that had played in Birmingham – first-choice striker Alfred Kelbassa, previously injured, had by now returned – Wolves again delayed announcing their eleven until just before the match was due to begin. Bill Slater and Harry Hooper had missed the weekend's trip to Arsenal – Slater had been absent since the beginning of February after being carried off during Wolves' defeat to Bournemouth in the FA Cup fourth round – but both were passed fit to play. The other change saw 18-year-old left-back Colin Tether given his second first-team start in place of Gerry Harris, now rested after playing 25 consecutive league games.

Originally planned as an all-ticket match, a lack of sales meant there was also entry at the gate, but despite extra advertisements in the newspapers on the day of the game, only the floodlit friendly against Maccabi was attended by fewer fans. But those who were there were treated to an exceptional encounter, one in which the tables were very nearly turned on habitual fast-finishers Wolves as Dortmund mounted another spectacular late charge.

It had been all Wolves at the beginning, a wave of home attacks forcing the Germans on to the back foot, and, very quickly, behind, as Peter Broadbent slipped between two defenders and slotted the opener home. A couple of minutes later it was nearly two, centre-half Max Michallek heading off the line to keep Jimmy Mullen's effort out, while, soon after, Kwiatkowski's terrific point-blank save prevented a second Broadbent goal. But the next to score were

Dortmund, from just their second attack of the game. Billy Wright headed away a centre towards Eddie Stuart, but before the defender could react Alfred Niepieklo nipped in, flashing the ball past Williams to peg Wolves back to 1-1.

For the Germans, the equaliser had come not a moment too soon, and they at last began to find their feet, sweeping forward with growing confidence and speed. But Kwiatkowski was still the busier of the two keepers, denying Flowers, Wilshaw then Hooper with brilliant saves: on 38 minutes, however, he could do nothing to keep out Jimmy Murray's delicate lob, and when Murray turned provider two minutes later, his pass setting Wilshaw off on the mazy run he capped with the goal of the game, Wolves looked to be home and dry.

Murray had had a hand in the first goal as well, but, still suffering the after-effects of a bout of flu, he didn't appear for the second half: his replacement, Bobby Mason, lasted only ten minutes before he, too, had to depart, making way for Mickey Lill having tried but failed to continue after taking a stud to the leg. Dortmund, meanwhile, had a substitution saga of their own: Aki Schmidt had come on for Preissler at the start of the second half, but when Kelbassa had gone down with an injury almost immediately afterwards, the Dortmund captain had then had to return. By that time his side's prospects were looking even bleaker; Hooper's stabbed finish, on 55 minutes, had given Wolves a 4-1 lead.

But the return of Preissler seemed to have a galvanising effect as the visitors began to gather some momentum again. In the 62nd minute Schmidt, now at centre-forward, got away from Stuart to score their second, while eight minutes later Niepieklo bagged another after Wright and Stuart between them failed to clear. As Dortmund threw everything forward, Peters crashed a shot off the inside of the far post, the ball rebounding fortuitously into the arms of Williams in one of the last acts of the game. 'Few teams from the continent have mounted their Molineux attacks with such speed,' Phil Morgan enthused in the *Express & Star*, 'few have played with such a mercurial forward line, and even fewer have shown such effective first-time passing or better anticipation in the use of the spaces ... [The crowd] gave complimentary applause to these part-timers who played their football on blitzkrieg lines.' It was a Wanderers win, but no canter: for the second floodlit friendly in succession, they only just held on.

Wolves – who had worn an all-white kit to allow Dortmund to play in yellow, pairing their change shirts with shorts borrowed from Birmingham City for the game – had been thankful for the presence of Wright, Flowers, Wilshaw and Broadbent, while Tether, too, had acquitted himself well. The teenager wouldn't have a chance to build on his solitary league appearance, however: after three more years of reserve team football, he moved on to the newly rechristened Oxford United, having failed to make a permanent break into the senior side.

The two teams parted in a shower of mutual compliments, both in appreciation of each other's football and the spirit in which it had been played. It had been, said Morgan, a match well worth its place in Wolves' floodlit annals, even if the size of the crowd meant it wasn't a particularly lucrative one. Once the necessary tax and Dortmund's fee had been deducted from the gross profits –

the Germans had received their guarantee of £2,000, being greater than half the net gate – Wolves were left with just over £195.

But their next floodlit friendly was only a fortnight away. And, after a controversial defeat in Valencia, Wolves were not only out to maintain their unbeaten Molineux record, but gain some revenge.

Wednesday, 27 March 1957: Wolves 4 Borussia Dortmund 3

Wolves: Williams; Stuart, Tether; Slater, Wright, Flowers; Hooper, Murray (Mason HT, Lill 55), Wilshaw, Broadbent, Mullen.

Dortmund: Kwiatkowski; Burgsmüller, Sandmann; Schlebrowski, Michallek, Bracht; Peters, Preissler, Kelbassa (Schmidt HT), Niepieklo, Kapitulski.

Goalscorers: Wolves – Broadbent (2), Murray (38), Wilshaw (40), Hooper (55); Dortmund – Niepieklo (13, 70), Schmidt (62).

Referee: B.M. Griffiths (Newport).

Attendance: 26,900.

14

Culture Clash: Wolves v. Valencia, 10 April 1957

CULLIS'S MEN had had an afternoon to forget on the Iberian Peninsula – beaten 3-1 by the Primera División side – but a memorable trip overall. Arranged to coincide with Valencia's Las Fallas festival, the squad had arrived in time to sample some of its main events: one of them a bullfight at the Plaza de Toros, where matador Miguel Báez Espuny, the celebrated *El Litri*, was on the bill. 'It was a wonderful initial experience for most of us,' reported Phil Morgan, who had travelled out with the team, 'and if our sympathy was rather with the bull, there was all-round admiration for the skill of the men in the ring.' They all found the sight of the picador's (thankfully well-padded) horse being butted considerably less appealing, however, while the crush to get into the stadium was breath-taking in a very literal way. 'The possession of a ticket meant nothing to the crowds milling around,' the correspondent remarked. 'The bullfight business retains so much of its tradition that turnstiles would probably be regarded as modern and out of place.' The attendance figure for their game at the Estadio de Mestalla 24 hours later would be similarly, if not quite so chaotically, vague.

Differences in footballing culture would be a feature of the match on 19 March; Valencia, well-drilled and at ease in the conditions – the temperature was in the 80s – also benefitted from what Morgan described as the referee's 'peculiar' reading of the rules, of which Wolves frequently fell foul. 'I can only describe it as a travesty of the English conception of the game,' he telephoned back to the *Express & Star* after watching local official Tamarit Falaguera penalise Wolves' tackling again and again. 'Stanley Cullis was more blunt. He just said it was ridiculous.' The bone-dry pitch didn't help the visitors' efforts to find some rhythm either, but, mitigations or not, their performance was still disappointingly under par. 'There was not the zest and certainly nowhere near the necessary drive to beat this team,' rued Morgan, 'who became more and more confident as the game went on.' Injury was later added to insult as, watching the festival's closing firework display with the players from the balcony of the City Hall, the reporter was hit on the head by a spent rocket falling from the sky. '[It left] me with the only battle scar of a notable tour,' he said, '[but] I was more fortunate than one of the vice-presidents of the Valencia Football Federation, who had entertained us so royally.' Quite what mishap had befallen the poor man, however, never made his final dispatch from Spain.

Exactly three weeks later, Valencia arrived in Wolverhampton for the return. They had flown in to London Airport on 8 April, spending a night in the capital before travelling up to the Midlands to prepare for the 'vengeance game', as the *Star* was billing it, the next day. 'One cannot forget the handicap the Wolves suffered: the Spanish referee's interpretation of the rules as they apply to bodily contact and foot-raising,' said Morgan. 'Tomorrow, however, things will be a little different, for there will be in control none other than Mr Arthur Ellis, a man well used to the idiosyncrasies of the continentals.' Valencia would have to play their football the English way, and it would now be Wolves with the advantage in the game.

Not that it would necessarily be an overwhelming one. While Valencia played in a typically European style, full of slick passing and intelligent running off the ball, they were not afraid of a tackle, as Quincoces, for one, had shown in Spain, coming out well on top in his battle with Harry Hooper, who had struggled to make any sort of impact at all. The centre-half was one of the six full internationals in Valencia's starting side: Pasieguito, Antonio Fuertes, Daniel Mañó and Ignacio Eizaguirre were also included, as was striker Vicente Iborra, who had been left out in favour of on-loan Dutch international Faas Wilkes at home. The Spaniards would be lining up in a 3-2-5 formation, said the *Express & Star*, listing the English-style shirt numbers that they had agreed to wear. It was a powerful-looking eleven, the paper reported, with plenty of incentive to do well. '[Wolves'] record has been well publicised abroad,' wrote Ivan Sharpe in the match programme, 'and the visitors are out to destroy it.'

Wolves welcomed back two of the four first-choice players who had missed their trip to Deepdale the previous weekend: Billy Wright, who had been on international duty against Scotland at Wembley, and Dennis Wilshaw, now recovered from the flu. George Showell, who had stood in for Wright at centre-half, was named at right-back – Eddie Stuart, injured on Saturday, would play only two more games that season, both for the reserves – while Norman Deeley was again preferred to Jimmy Mullen, who had been dropped. Bill Slater was also injured, but Wolves' other Preston absentee, Jimmy Murray, was in contention for a return. In the end, however, 20-year-old Bobby Thomson was given the number 8 shirt instead, and his senior debut.

The Dundee-born forward had waited a while for his chance – he had signed professional forms in 1954 – and it took him just nine minutes to make the most of it as he flicked Eddie Clamp's attempted shot from Hooper's corner past Eizaguirre and into the Valencia net. The Spanish keeper – on loan from Osasuna and one of the stars of the first tie – had already saved well from Wilshaw, and though the visitors launched some counter-attacks (with winger Mañó, another who had impressed in March, at their heart), it was their defence that continued to be stretched. Peter Broadbent was unlucky to see a goal disallowed for a foul then a header cleared off the line, but in the 43rd minute Thomson was there again to nod in Deeley's free kick and put the hosts firmly in control.

Half an hour into the second half, from another set piece, Clamp made the game safe, planting Broadbent's rolled-back pass from the edge of the penalty area just inside the far post. There had been plenty of other chances, too: Hooper had a couple of shots well-saved and Deeley and Wilshaw both went near, while after the match Broadbent was still convinced that his first-half effort kicked off the line by Esteban Areta had, in fact, been a goal. But Wolves were more than comfortable in a match in which they seldom hit top gear. 'Without reaching great heights, the play was attractive,' said the *Birmingham Post*, but it had lacked the thrill of earlier games.

Valencia had been disappointing, offering little beyond the early exchanges. Inside-right Fuertes had linked up well with Mañó, but with Showell effective and Wright imperious, their other forwards had found it all but impossible to break through. 'There was never much doubt about Wolves' ability to avenge their Mestalla Stadium defeat,' said Phil Morgan. 'With a three-goal margin, they may feel justice was served, even if many of the 25,310 spectators would have been happier if the advantage had been pressed home to produce the runaway victory their superiority warranted. The score, however, was sufficient to give them the win on aggregate of the two games with the Spaniards.'

Though Wolves had been efficient rather than spectacular in claiming their tenth floodlit friendly win, the evening had been a personal triumph for Bobby Thomson, one rewarded with a league debut against Newcastle that weekend, which he marked with another goal. But with the fit-again Jimmy Murray ahead of him in the manager's plans, it would be his only other appearance in the senior side. Like Colin Tether, he would have to move to find regular first-team football, in his case to Aston Villa, for whom he signed in 1959.

After their third-placed finish in 1955/56, Wolves ended the league season in sixth, 16 points behind Manchester United, who claimed the First Division title for a second successive year. Dominant at home – their record of 17 wins was better than their championship-winning season of 1953/54 – their away form had badly let them down: 12 losses on the road coupled with only three wins had kept a handbrake on their challenge from the start. The team would have a new look going forward after Harry Hooper moved on: an incident on the club's close-season tour of South Africa in May had brought him into conflict with the manager, who never selected him in the league again. At the end of November, he was sold to Birmingham City for a fee of just under £20,000; Norman Deeley took over at outside-right, and was a virtual ever-present the next year.

Wolves also had to admit defeat in the long-running saga of István Kovács, just as the situation had looked to be resolved. In early April, his clearance from the FA had finally come through, allowing him to sign amateur forms: on the 19th he had played, and scored, in his first game in gold and black, a 2-1 win over Wulfrun College Old Boys in the Wolverhampton Amateur League. But on 14 August, ten days before the start of the new season, came a hammer blow as the club learned that Kovács's name was on a list of players suspended at the request of the Hungarian authorities until 21 April 1958. 'Kovács became a Wolves player after the Football Association had failed to receive a reply to letters sent to the Hungarian [Football Federation] regarding his future,' reported the *Western Mail*'s Derrick Collier. 'But now, in view of the statement from the international body [FIFA, under pressure, had endorsed the Hungarians' ban], this permission has been withdrawn.' Reluctantly, his name was removed from Wolves' books. 'There is nothing we can do about it,' a frustrated Stan Cullis said in the *Sports Argus*, 'but I do think FIFA could have taken a firmer stand.'

Unfortunately Kovács's story did not end there, as, on 12 November 1958, the *Birmingham Post* reported his conviction for theft. 'István Kovács (21), a Hungarian footballer who was formerly on the books of Wolverhampton Wanderers FC, pleaded guilty at Wolverhampton yesterday to two charges of shoplifting,' the paper said. 'He asked for four similar offences to be taken into account. Kovács, of Allan Road, Wolverhampton, was conditionally discharged for stealing nail varnish and put on probation for stealing women's clothing. He was hoping to emigrate to British Nyasaland, it was stated. Kovács received a secondary school education in Budapest before coming to England. He never played for Wanderers because of the suspension of Hungarian footballers in this country. After a year in a Wolverhampton factory, he went to Germany for six months to play for Borussia Dortmund. He returned to Britain and had been unemployed since.' His lesson, unfortunately, was not learned: in December 1958 he breached his probation order with a theft from a Birmingham branch of Woolworth's, and was jailed for 12 months. 'Whether István remained in this country is not known, but it is more likely he returned to Hungary,' wrote Steve Gordos. 'Perhaps if he had been allowed to play for Wolves as soon as he arrived in England, things might have turned out very differently.'

There had been other partings, too. In March, Bert Williams had announced that the current season would be his last; after 420 Wolves appearances and 24 national caps, football's original 'Cat' – a nickname bestowed upon him by the Italian press after his performance in England's 2-0 victory over the *Azzurri* at White Hart Lane in 1949

– had more than repaid the £3,500 the club had paid Walsall for his services in September 1945. 'Here is a man who has made goalkeeping an art,' wrote Phil Morgan in tribute. 'Blessed with unusually fine athletic physique … he adapted his supremely fit body to the peculiar needs of his calling, and brought to the English scene something of the continental style of agility.' In *All For The Wolves*, Cullis gave a vivid example from a match at St James' Park. 'Jackie Milburn … drove the ball for the top corner of the net, and Williams began to jump for it,' he recalled, '[but] on its way, the ball was deflected by an outstretched boot to the other side of goal. Somehow, Bert changed direction and managed to push the shot away. Milburn – and 50,000 spectators – could not believe their eyes.' Wolves fans had seen plenty more wonder saves over the course of his illustrious Molineux career.

Williams joined Bill Shorthouse and Roy Swinbourne, whose retirements had also been confirmed – 'three good Wolves men and true' as they were described at a dinner organised in their honour by the *Express & Star*. Donations had been collected for presentations to the players and tickets for the evening – priced at £3 3s – sold. Held on 25 April at the Victoria Hotel, it capped the very fondest of farewells.

There was also one other, final goodbye to say as the 1956/57 season drew to a close: to the floodlights that had served Wolves so well for the past four years. The club's upgraded system would be installed over the summer, for use in the new campaign: one that would see more Wanderers history written, and perhaps their greatest floodlit win of all.

Wednesday, 10 April 1957: Wolves 3 Valencia 0

Wolves: Williams; Showell, Harris; Clamp, Wright, Flowers; Hooper, Thomson, Wilshaw, Broadbent, Deeley.

Valencia*: Eizaguirre (1); Piquer (2), Quincoces (5), Mestre (3); Pasieguito (4), Sendra (6); Mañó (7), Fuertes (8), Iborra (9: Pla 65), Areta (10), Vila (11).

*With English shirt numbers, as listed in the *Express & Star*.

Goalscorers: Thomson (9, 43), Clamp (77).

Referee: A.E. Ellis (Halifax).

Attendance: 25,310.

15

A New Everest: Wolves v. Real Madrid, 17 October 1957

WILLIAM FRANCE'S proposal for Wolves' new floodlights had been received on 30 January, after a none-too-subtle nudge from the board. 'As nothing [has] been heard from [Mr France] regarding a scheme to improve Molineux's lighting,' read a slightly tetchy note from a meeting held the previous November, 'was he interested?' He was, giving first his apologies then two alternatives for the directors to consider: one a like-for-like replacement of the existing system, with new galvanised steel pylons and extra lamps at a cost of £10,838; the second a scheme for slightly taller but significantly cheaper towers made of tubular steel – as Birmingham City had installed at St Andrew's the year before – for £8,184.

Wolves were, however, thinking of something bigger, and so a third plan from France's Electric was prepared, this one gaining the directors' approval at their meeting on 1 April. At 146ft, Molineux's new galvanised steel pylons would stand 50ft taller than before, each platform carrying 48 lamps but with capacity for 60 if required. Projectors from Holophane, Revo and the General Electric Company had been tested, Revo winning out thanks in part to a cast-iron guarantee: should the lights prove unsatisfactory, the company said, they were prepared to leave them in place until the club found a replacement then give a full refund on their return. 'Wolverhampton Wanderers, pioneers of floodlit football in Britain, will have a new set of lights before the start of next season,' the *Birmingham Post* excitedly announced a few days later. 'The new [system] will double the lighting power.' At £23,112, the cost of the new structure was more than twice that of the original, too. Wolves paid France's Electric an extra £312 for push-button remote control and £292 for taking down the existing equipment and towers.

But though the board had hoped that that work would begin at the end of the 1956/57 season, Wolverhampton's Town and Country Planning Department was less enthusiastic when the proposal reached its door. James Baker and John Ireland met with the committee on 25 April to explain the scheme, answer questions and request permission to proceed: its judgement, however – when it eventually arrived – was hardly a ringing endorsement of Wolves' plans. 'The committee are of the opinion that the erection of the pylons would be, or is likely to be, detrimental to the amenities of the town, and indeed they gather that your company did not dissent from this view,' read the town clerk's letter to the board a month later, 'but having regard to the case made by your company's representatives the committee decided, with some hesitation, to grant permission for a temporary period of five years … In granting this permission, the committee ask your company to give consideration to any technical developments in floodlighting which may take place during [this time] to see whether it would be practicable and reasonable to avoid the use of pylons altogether, or, alternatively, to make the upper portion of the pylons, or the staging carrying the lights, retractable when not in use.' Obstruction lighting may also be required, he added, should the nearby aerodrome at Halfpenny Green expand. Assurances on both counts were given, and the dismantling of the old towers finally began.

Various other clubs had already expressed an interest in buying them, including Barnsley, Bolton Wanderers and Walsall, who had enquired about whether the system would be available for sale as early as the middle of March. The price was set at £6,500: too much for Walsall and Bolton, sadly, while Barnsley wanted more time to decide. It was to Blackpool, however, that the lights were sold, once a little quibbling over the bill had been sorted out. 'Information [has] been received … that [Blackpool are] prepared to purchase the installation, but understood from Mr Oakley that the price was £6,000,' Jack Howley minuted on 11 April. The confusion was cleared up, Blackpool received the planning permission that allowed them to go ahead with the purchase, and, on 29 August, they settled the account for the full £6,500.[33]

---

33 Blackpool had hoped to have the Molineux system installed at Bloomfield Road for the start of the new season and the beginning of a mooted floodlit football league – they had purchased the lights on the advice of a group of London consultants, who were working on a plan to floodlight Bloomfield Road – but it was subsequently decided that it didn't meet their needs after all. 'It soon became apparent that the scheme as originally proposed to us could be improved upon, and then we were relieved of the urgency by the decision not to operate a floodlit league for 1957/58,' said chairman Albert Hindley. Blackpool postponed their installation to the summer of 1958, and sold Wolves' system on to Grimsby Town. It remained in place at Blundell Park until the summer of 2019.

By then Molineux's new towers had been assembled, and an additional service cable laid; Wolves had given the Midland Electricity Board a contribution of £750 towards the cost of the work. But time was now of the essence. Behind schedule because of the initial delay, William France was asked to confirm, in writing, that as many men as possible would be assigned to the installation as the start of the new season approached. It wasn't, unfortunately, finished in time – planned floodlit games against Bolton and Chesterfield reserves had to be played in daylight hours instead – but, on Wednesday, 2 October, the lights were at last ready to be unveiled. It was a happy occasion all round: Wolves celebrated their completion with a 4-0 thumping of Tottenham Hotspur that sent them to the top of the league, and William France was told that, like the mayor and local MPs, he could have a complimentary match ticket whenever he wished from now on.

There was only one team the directors had wanted for the floodlights' official opening a fortnight later, however, a side they had tried to get to Wolverhampton twice before. Real Madrid had underlined their status as Europe's leading side with a 2-0 win over Fiorentina in the European Cup Final in May, retaining the trophy they had dominated since its introduction the season before. First proposed in July, their visit to Molineux had been confirmed at the beginning of September after Stan Cullis had flown out to Madrid to finalise the details himself. 'All who have seen Real Madrid pronounce them a team in a thousand,' said Phil Morgan in the match programme. 'As one well-known football writer has put it, they have to be seen to be believed. Now we get the chance to see for ourselves, and we look forward with the keenest anticipation to watching a team who by reputation put the accent on attack.'

Manchester United knew all of that at first hand. In April, having followed up their first-round win over Borussia Dortmund with victory over Athletic Club de Bilbao, the English champions had met Real in the semi-final, going down 5-3 on aggregate after a 3-1 loss in Madrid and a 2-2 draw at home. Goals from Tommy Taylor and Bobby Charlton added some respectability to the final scoreline after a brilliant first-half display at Maine Road had sent the holders four goals clear, but United had never looked like repeating their earlier feat against Athletic Club, when they had come back from two goals down. 'The old comparison of a crude battle-axe against a fine Toledo blade was never more apt,' said Archie Ledbrooke in the *Daily Mirror*, reflecting on a night in which the Busby Babes were comfortably outplayed.

Their tormentor-in-chief had been Alfredo Di Stéfano, the brightest of Real's galaxy of stars. The Argentine-born centre-forward had scored seven goals in the competition, including one in the first match against United and another in the final, repeating his feat of the year before. 'To be honest, I was terribly pleased I wasn't playing,' said Bobby Charlton of the Madrid leg of the semi-final, as reported in *The European Cup 1955–1980*. 'I saw Di Stéfano and these others, and I thought, "These people just aren't human. It's not the sort of game I've been taught."'

The Spaniards arrived in Wolverhampton on the afternoon of 16 October, heading out to Molineux for a training session after checking in to the Victoria Hotel. 'The Scout' was on hand to describe their routine, meticulously managed by coach Luis Carniglia. 'This was more than an ordinary ... hour of training,' he wrote in the *Express & Star*. 'Everything was done with methodical exactitude, from the eerie whistle of exhaling breath – a weird sound in the vast deserted stadium – to short bursts of sprinting, conducted in the precision timing of Carniglia's whistle.' Most eyes, though, were on Di Stéfano as he went about his work: 'quietly, without ostentation', said the reporter, 'and there was nothing immediately obvious to mark him as reputedly the world's highest-paid player. But just one piece of trickery was enough. He trapped a fast-moving ball, chipped it forward two or three yards and it rolled right back to his feet! The amazed looks of the few who noticed it bore testimony to the sheer wizardry of the action.'

But there were, as Charlton had witnessed, plenty more magicians for Wolves to worry about as well. Di Stéfano's provider-in-chief, winger Francisco 'Paco' Gento, had earned the nickname *La Galerna del Cantábrico* (the 'Gale of the Cantabrian Sea') because of his exceptional pace and thunderous shot, while French international Raymond Kopa was universally recognised as one of the finest inside-forwards in the world. Montevideo-born centre-back José Santamaría was another lynchpin of the team, a key member of the Uruguay side that finished fourth in the 1954 World Cup. Fellow defender Marquitos, meanwhile, had a reputation as 'the best of stoppers,' according to the match programme, 'seldom beaten in the air'. There was a familiar name, too, that of goalkeeper Rogelio Domínguez, Racing Club de Avellaneda's man of the match at Molineux in 1954: 'then a gangling youth, now matured to muscular manhood,' said 'The Scout'. Quality was everywhere, however, and, even though they were missing three outfield players from their first-choice eleven – José Becerril, Enrique Mateos and their captain, Miguel Muñoz – Real were still supremely confident for the game. 'We have 22 players all capable of playing well in first-team places,' an official was quoted by the *Express & Star* as saying. 'We are in the same position as a side like your Manchester United: plenty of splendid reserve strength.' Wolves would be needing theirs, too: Billy Wright was away on international duty, leaving George Showell the unenviable task of marking Di Stéfano and Eddie Stuart the honour of captaining the side.

But impressive though their opponents were, the hosts weren't about to be cowed. Still top of the First Division with nine wins out of 13 – the latest a 5-1 thrashing of Birmingham City, which stretched their lead over second-placed West Brom to two points – Wolves had every reason to be confident, regardless of their opponents' pedigree. 'I, for one, am not taking it for granted that the champions of Europe must necessarily become the champions of Wolverhampton,' Phil Morgan wrote in his preview in the *Express & Star*. 'Wolves can treat [Real] with respect, but that is a much more different thing from viewing them with something akin to awe and starting somewhere near a goal down in consequence. Let it be rather the other way round in the light of current form and past achievements.'

He needn't have worried. The match – which kicked off at 7.35pm, timed to allow a neat 8.30pm start for second-half coverage on ITV – began with Wolves on the attack and very nearly taking the lead: less than four minutes in, Jimmy Mullen found himself one-on-one with Domínguez, only to tangle the ball in his feet. But it was the visitors who struck the first blow, Ramón Marsal's towering header from Joseíto's corner putting them in front on the quarter-hour. Soon after, Di Stéfano could have doubled their advantage, but mishit his shot wide. Wolves went close again – Santamaría only just cleared an effort from Ron Flowers off the line – but they were glad of referee Maurice Guigue's intervention in another Real attack not long before half-time, the French official blowing his whistle just as Gento drove a shot into the net for an incident off the ball. Di Stéfano was the player penalised, apparently for shouting something at Eddie Clamp. Exactly what was unrecorded, but it 'obviously could not be construed as Spanish good wishes', the *Birmingham Post*'s Cyril Chapman remarked.

Luis Carniglia brought on fresh legs at the interval, Marquitos for Ángel Atienza at the back and Héctor Rial for Gento on the wing, but, seven minutes into the second half, it was Wolves who finally had a spring in their step as Finlayson sent a clearance towards the Madrid penalty area, Santamaría misjudged the bounce as Murray flicked it on and Peter Broadbent, challenged by Marquitos, lobbed home. Wolves were now rampant, visibly panicking the Real defence in their assaults up the field, and it was no surprise when, eight minutes later, they went into the lead. Mullen forced a corner, Deeley swept it over and Jimmy Murray headed in, a virtual carbon-copy of the Spaniards' opener in the same minute of the first half. The visitors sent on Antonio Ruiz as they tried to stem the tide, but it was the hosts now in charge, and Real chasing the game.

But just as Wolves were looking dominant, the visitors found an equalising goal when a defensive slip let Marsal through, who feigned to shoot with his right foot then knocked the ball past Finlayson with his left. Wolves, though, were not to be denied and with ten minutes remaining, Dennis Wilshaw hooked Mullen's near-post cross into the net for a sensational winning goal. Wolves 3 Real Madrid 2; to the utter delight of another 55,000-plus crowd,[34] a new footballing Everest had been scaled.

Showell, Wilshaw and Gerry Harris (who, remarkably, had played for England's under-23s against Romania the night before) had been outstanding: so too Murray, who had given the famous Santamaría a torrid time. But every one of the eleven, the papers agreed, had more than played their part. 'Wonderful Wolves!' said the *Daily Herald*'s Peter Lorenzo. '[They] did what champions Manchester United … couldn't do, beat the European champions, the Latin champions and the Spanish cup holders all rolled into the marvel team that Madrid undoubtedly are: or, rather, were, until they arrived at Molineux.'

Just as the victory over Honvéd had inspired several reporters to find their inner Churchill, so the spirit of Sir Francis Drake was evoked in some of the other coverage the next day. For the *Lancashire Evening Post* it had been a re-enactment of the Armada, another triumph for England against overwhelming force, and one in which, through television, the whole country had been able to share. 'Stop me for [being] a hopelessly nationalistic reactionary,' said the unnamed author of the paper's 'Tele-Viewpoint' column, 'but I think it matters a very great deal when we beat these foreign

---

34 It wasn't quite a record attendance – the floodlit friendlies against Moscow Dynamo and Spartak had been seen by a handful more – but it brought in a record sum of £12,397 0s 6d, which left a net profit of £6,931 11s after Real's fees and expenses were paid.

champions, and this, apart from its sporting implications, was very good television. All England must have been with that delirious Wolves crowd when the golden shirts crashed home that winning goal against the proud Dons.

'The opposition – a BBC play, *To Love and to Cherish*, concerning the problems of a parson, two of whose daughters get mixed up with the innocent parties of divorce cases – was very weak and watery stuff by comparison.'

Wolves' win over Honvéd was the most historically significant of the floodlit friendlies – both in the context of English football's immediate past and the near future of the European game – but their defeat of Real Madrid was perhaps the greatest footballing achievement of the 16-match series. Already European champions twice over, Real would extend their run of consecutive European Cups to five, culminating in the 7-3 victory over Eintracht Frankfurt in 1960 that is still regarded as a seminal moment in the history of the sport. The shockwaves from their loss at Molineux led to a rematch being hastily arranged, but that Wolves not only held their own in the Spanish capital but should probably have won again said it all. So mortified were the Madrid fans, recalled Bobby Mason, a scorer in the 2-2 draw, that they 'lit candles in mourning for their team as they had never been beaten or drawn at home to foreign opposition'. Stan Cullis's delight with his players, in turn, was equally clear. 'I would like to strike a medal for every one of them,' he told the press after the game.

The match at the Bernabéu, played after two more away games at Hibernian and Anderlecht, was Wolves' last floodlit friendly in a season that would end with their second league title win. Confirmed with a two-goal victory over second-placed Preston on 19 April, Wolves had topped the table ever since the defeat of Spurs, eventually finishing five points ahead of Cliff Britton's team and 13 clear of Tottenham in third. It was far from the club's only honour in what was an exceptional year: Wolves also won the Central League, the Birmingham League, the Worcestershire Combination, the Worcestershire Combination Cup and the FA Youth Cup; every trophy but the FA Cup, which, even in the circumstances, the manager wasn't prepared to disregard. 'I am very proud and have never seen players work so hard, but I've got to graft some steadiness on to my team,' Cullis, always looking for more, said. 'It was also that shortcoming that lost us the quarter-final at Bolton.'

But now, of course, Wolves' attention could turn towards another cup at last. 'It is surely not difficult for people outside Wolverhampton to understand the excitement with which we look forward to the Wolves taking part in next year's European Cup competition,' said Clem Homer, the mayor, at the civic banquet given in honour of the club on 22 May. 'This [is] only as it should be,' commented the *Birmingham Post*, 'for the Wolves [have] pioneered international football at club level in this country. They [know] that the Wolves [will] add fresh lustre to their already great record on the international football field.'

But the 1957/58 season will always be remembered for the tragedy that touched it as well. Six days after the banquet, Real Madrid claimed their third European crown; for many, however, it was a victory overshadowed by thoughts of what might have been.

* * *

'Matt Busby, to us, was "Uncle Matt",' Andrew Cullis remembered in *Champions of the World*. 'My father knew him well, and when Munich happened I remember coming home and meeting my sister at the gate of our house, and she said to me, "Uncle Matt has been hurt. We must pray for him."'

On 6 February 1958, British European Airways flight 609 crashed as it attempted to take off from Munich-Riem Airport in Munich, West Germany. On board was the Manchester United team, travelling home from a European Cup quarter-final tie with Red Star in Belgrade. 'Uncle Matt' would have the prayers of many more families with him in the days and weeks ahead.

The Munich air disaster claimed the lives of 23 passengers, including eight of Busby's players: Geoff Bent, Roger Byrne, Eddie Colman, Mark Jones, David Pegg, Tommy Taylor, Billy Whelan and, 15 days after the accident, Dudley-born Duncan Edwards, who passed away in hospital at the age of 21. 'No words can express our great sorrow at the terrible tragedy that has overtaken your club,' read a telegram sent from Molineux to Old Trafford on the day of the crash. 'Please convey our deepest sympathy to all relatives. Signed, directors, officials and players of Wolverhampton Wanderers.'

Wolves had been due to play United two days later, and were in Blackpool, famous for its iconic tower, when the news from Germany came through. 'We often stayed at the Norbreck Hotel, even when we were playing somewhere like Old Trafford,' Eddie Stuart recalled in *Wolves: The Glory Years*. 'About eight of us were in a restaurant near the tower on the Thursday when a reporter raced in and told us, "You won't be playing against Manchester United at the weekend. There's been an air disaster."

'About an hour later, we were going back to the hotel on the tram and passengers openly wept. Although there wasn't much TV in those days, word was getting round by wireless about what had happened. We were very upset. We had good pals on that plane.'

The sense of shock is preserved in the minutes of the directors' meeting being held in Wolverhampton at the same time, during which a phone call from the Football League was taken, confirming the postponement of the game. 'Manchester United is a wonderful club with whom we have always had the happiest association, which makes it specially a great blow,' an entry reads. 'The catastrophe causes a loss which will be felt by those interested in association football the world over.' A collection in aid of the dependents was organised for the match against Birmingham City on 22 February: £473 was raised, the equivalent of around £8,800 today.

Among those who also lost their lives in the tragedy were Frank Swift – Bert Williams's predecessor as England goalkeeper, now working for the *News of the World* – and Archie Ledbrooke of the *Daily Mirror*. The *Daily Herald*'s George Follows, born in Walsall – who, as a young reporter, had worked for the *Express & Star* – was another of the eight journalists who never made it home. And, for Wolves, there was another poignant name: that of Béla Miklós, MTK's travel agent for their tour of Europe in 1956, who had organised United's trip to Belgrade. His wife Eleanor was badly injured, but mercifully survived.

One of the first telegrams Wolves received on 19 April was from Matt Busby, congratulating them on their title win. Stan Cullis would treasure the message from his friend, and deeply appreciate the gesture made by United's players when they met Wolves two days later, the outgoing champions paying tribute to the new with a guard of honour before they played their rearranged game. Wolves won the match 4-0, adding to the 3-1 victory they had secured over them at Molineux in September; had they beaten rather than lost to relegated Sheffield Wednesday in their final match of the season the Saturday after, Wanderers would have equalled the top-flight record of 66 points, set by Arsenal in 1931.

Had Munich not happened, some have wondered, would the championship have gone the other way? 'By February [United] were fourth [sic] in the table, but they'd lost just once in 13 games,' reports *The Munich Air Disaster*, a YouTube film made by the *Manchester Evening News* to mark the 60th anniversary of the tragedy in 2018. 'Busby's Babes were being tipped for yet another league title.' The reality, however, suggests that it wouldn't. United – who were lying third at the time of the crash, six points behind Cullis's men – would have needed to win 27 of the 28 available points from their last 14 games to overhaul Wolves' lead (assuming that Wolves would still have dropped the six points they did with a resurgent United on their tail). 'No team had ever won 14 successive games in First Division history,' wrote Steve Gordos in his biography of Cullis, *Club and Country*. 'In no way should the tragedy that befell United be allowed to undermine Wolves' triumph.'

But United's time would come again. They reclaimed the title in 1965 and 1967 and, in the final of the 1968 European Cup, won the trophy they might well have collected a decade earlier had the accident not occurred. 'Surely the spirits of the men of Munich must have hovered over Wembley last night,' said the Manchester paper after their 4-1 victory over Benfica, completed with survivors Bobby Charlton and Bill Foulkes in the side. 'Certainly they could not have been far from the thoughts of Matt Busby, who survived to tread the long road back from that disaster of ten years ago.' Few begrudged the soon-to-be Sir Matt and his team the emotional success they had earned.

Thursday, 17 October 1957: Wolves 3 Real Madrid 2

Wolves: Finlayson; Stuart, Harris; Clamp, Showell, Flowers; Deeley, Broadbent, Murray, Wilshaw, Mullen.

Real Madrid: Domínguez; Atienza (Marquitos HT), Lesmes; Santisteban, Santamaría, Zárraga (Ruiz 64); Joseíto, Kopa, Di Stéfano, Marsal, Gento (Rial HT).

Goalscorers: Wolves – Broadbent* (52), Murray (60), Wilshaw (80); Real Madrid – Marsal (15, 72).

*Listed in some reports as a Marquitos own goal.

Referee: M. Guigue (France).

Attendance: 55,169.

16

Mixed Returns: Wolves v. South Africa, 29 September 1958

WITH THEIR first European campaign about to begin, Wolves arranged just a single floodlit friendly for the following year. Their return to South Africa the previous summer had been another popular success – Wolves' request to the FA to be included on the itinerary for the latest visit of the South African national side to the UK was a thank-you from the Molineux board.

The club's second African tour had taken place while their new floodlights were being installed, a visit that saw them score 49 goals in eight matches while conceding only nine in reply. Jimmy Murray had set the tone in Wanderers' opening game on 4 May, bagging all five in their 5-2 win over Southern Transvaal, while Jimmy Mullen scored two then four as the tourists twice reached double figures – 10 and 11 respectively, against South Rhodesia and North Rhodesia – to bring the trip to a close. It was one of Wolves' opponents, however, who most caught Stan Cullis's eye: 17-year-old Cliff Durandt, who the manager moved to sign after seeing him score twice for the Southern Transvaal President's XI in Johannesburg on 21 May. The South Africans lost 7-3, but, as Cullis told reporters, he knew within ten minutes that Durandt had a football brain. Accompanied by director James Marshall, the inside-forward boarded the boat from Cape Town to Southampton on the 31st, and on 17 August, he lined up for the Whites in the traditional pre-season game against the Colours and scored his first Molineux goal.

Wolves would play their full South African contingent against the Springboks on 29 September: Durandt, Eddie Stuart – who again captained the side – and 18-year-old Des Horne, who had signed for the club as a youth player from Durban Railways two years before. The outside-left had, like Durandt in 1957, made an impression in 1958's pre-season game, scoring in the Colours' 6-5 win to earn a starting spot in the league. The champions' strength in depth had been noted, too, with several big names included in the Whites – nominally the Central League – side. 'When Stan Cullis can put out a couple of teams like these for his public trial, it's sure confirmation that the Wolves are probably stepping out for one of their best-ever seasons,' said the *Birmingham Mail*. 'Just imagine it: Mullen, Slater, Showell, Booth and [Jackie] Henderson[35], all in the "[reserves]"!' After sitting out the games against Nottingham Forest and West Ham, Jimmy Mullen, now 35, regained his first-team place from the youngster for Wolves' trip to Stamford Bridge on 30 August, but he would make way for Horne on eight further occasions over the course

---

35 Scotland international Jackie Henderson had been signed from Portsmouth in March 1958 after making more than 200 appearances, mostly at centre-forward or outside-left, in nine years at Fratton Park. His time at Molineux, however, was short: after scoring three goals in eight league starts for Wolves in 1958/59, he moved to Arsenal the following October for £20,000. He would play 103 times for the Gunners, scoring 29 goals, before joining Fulham in January 1962.

of the year: one of them the Charity Shield match against FA Cup winners Bolton Wanderers on the evening of 6 October, in which Durandt would score again.

The South African squad arrived in Wolverhampton on 28 September, fresh from a 5-3 victory over British Universities in Reading the day before. After a 2-2 draw with Headington United in their first match 11 days earlier, they had also beaten Bedford Town and Norfolk County FA: the latter, like British Universities, a representative team their predecessors had also met in 1953. There were echoes of the previous visit in the town's welcome to their guests, too, as a civic reception in the mayor's parlour began their four-night stay. 'Wolverhampton may not be quite as beautiful as some places you may see on your tour,' said Councillor Homer, as quoted by the *Express & Star*, 'but we make up for that in other directions.'

South Africa had already named their strongest eleven for the match manager Pat Murray had described as the plum game of their tour, two of whom – Les Salton and one-time Wolves target Wally Warren – had played at Molineux in 1953. Captained by 29-year-old centre-half Gillie Petersen, the team also featured Charlie Hurly (who had attracted similar interest from Wolves after they saw him in 1951), former Northern Ireland amateur international Jackie Scott and Henry Hauser, brother of Blackpool's Peter, a tall and creative wing-half. '[The South Africans] are a team to be taken seriously in their own right as footballers,' wrote Phil Morgan in the *Star*. 'And it is another significant fact that much of the improvement they are showing today may be traced to things they learned from the Wolves on two highly successful tours to the Union. At their best they are capable of giving the full Wolves team a good run for their money, and they are entitled to a special welcome in Wolverhampton, if only to acknowledge the fine reception Wolves got when they were in South Africa a little over 12 months ago.'

A crowd of only 13,511 turned out to watch the South Africans' return, however, perhaps influenced by the absence of Billy Wright and Peter Broadbent from the Wolves line-up – both in Belfast, preparing for England's match against Northern Ireland at the weekend – and several other changes to the regular first team. While Cliff Durandt and 'stalwart standby' George Showell replaced the international absentees – for Durandt, it was his first call-up to the senior side – Stan Cullis made three further alterations to the eleven that had just played Tottenham Hotspur in the league, bringing in Gwyn Jones and Mickey Lill for Gerry Harris and Jackie Henderson, who himself had been standing in for the injured Norman Deeley, as well as Horne for Mullen. Bobby Mason, meanwhile, continued at inside-left, a role he had shared with Colin Booth since Dennis Wilshaw's departure for Stoke City the December before. With Jimmy Murray now established as Wolves' first-choice centre-forward, Wilshaw had made only a dozen appearances in the first months of the new season, mainly at number 10. After scoring 113 goals in 219 games in gold and black – adding to his 10 in 12 for the national side – he would play 95 matches for the Potters over the next four years, and score another 41 league and cup goals.

As they had against Dortmund, Wolves offered to wear their all-white kit to allow their guests to play in their regular green and gold; another example of the spirit of friendship and reunion, as the *Birmingham Post* put it, that surrounded the build-up to the game. But the match itself was a turgid affair, Wolves vastly outclassing their opponents in every department but unable to make it count. They scored in the 15th minute, Horne volleying in a high corner from Lill, but despite long periods of sustained pressure they couldn't find another goal. With minutes remaining Warren (twice) and Salton nearly embarrassed them, too, but delayed their shots long enough to allow Finlayson to smother them at their feet, the third time at the cost of a kick to the head: 'a risk,' said Phil Morgan, 'that he should never have been called on to take in a game as one-sided as this.' It was a 'chance-frittering' evening, he wrote, of which the crowd quickly grew tired, many supporters leaving early while those that remained gave vent to their feelings by cheering the South Africans into the late rally that so nearly brought them a goal. 'And that,' said Morgan, 'at Molineux, on a floodlit occasion particularly, was a sorry state of affairs indeed.'

After two more days in Wolverhampton, the tourists travelled on to Bangor, where, on 4 October, they beat Wales' Amateur XI 3-1: they later defeated the Republic of Ireland B, Northern Ireland FA and Combined Amateur League XIs and, in Wigan on the 18th, a Lancashire Combination team 6-2, their biggest win of the tour. The Springboks' fortunes in their other matches against league opposition were more mixed, however: they drew 3-3 with Heart of Midlothian in Edinburgh and 2-2 with Southampton, then of the Third Division, under the floodlights at The Dell, but lost 7-4 to Everton then 9-1 to Preston North End, for whom Tommy Thompson scored five times. A little pride was restored when Chelsea, like Wolves, were kept to a single goal – 'The Springboks' defence was solid as rock,' said the *News Chronicle*, after only Jimmy Greaves broke through – but they shipped another seven in their farewell match against Peterborough United on 8 November. After three more games on the continent, they sailed home with a record of seven wins and four draws from their 20 matches played.

By then, however, Wolves' attention was firmly focused on their own European plans. The draw for the first round of the European Cup had been made on 8 October, pitting them against Schalke 04, who had broken Borussia Dortmund's two-year run of West German titles with a 3-0 victory over Hamburg in the final of the Deutsche Fußballmeisterschaft – the end-of-season tournament for the regional Oberliga champions and runners-up – on 18 May. Schalke had struggled through the European Cup's preliminary round, needing a play-off to get past Danish side Boldklub after losing the away leg 3-0, eventually going through with a 3-1 win in Enschede after a 5-2 victory at home. 'Schalke can add themselves to such outstanding foreign visitors to Molineux as Honvéd, Moscow Spartak, Moscow Dynamo and Real Madrid,' said Phil Morgan in the match programme for the first leg on 12 November, 'and they may note that the last-named, current European Cup holders did not leave the English Midlands unscathed.' It was Wolves who were left licking their wounds, though, after a thoroughly professional Schalke display.

The damage was done at Molineux, where, despite having only seven shots on goal to Wolves' 29, the Germans claimed a 2-2 draw. Sticking resolutely to their tactical plan – the defence, reinforced by an extra man, doggedly refused to be drawn out of shape, while a skeleton attack of three forwards waited to hit Wolves on the break – the visitors were prepared to let the hosts dictate the pace while they patiently bided their time. Numerous attacks were fended off – goalkeeper Karl Loweg and left-back Otto Laszig deserved an 'Iron Cross of football' for their part in keeping Wolves' forwards at bay, said the *News Chronicle* – before Schalke made theirs count with the opening goal. Peter Broadbent's second-half brace put Wolves level then ahead, but Willi Koslowski's 88th-minute equaliser stunned the crowd into silence and left the Germans favourites for the return. Six days later Wolves threw everything at their opponents again – 'Seldom has a British team battled so bravely on foreign soil as the eleven gold-hearted, gold-shirted Wolves warriors did in a blood-tingling second half,' wrote Peter Lorenzo in the *Daily Herald* – but after conceding two more counter-punch goals, the game slipped away. 'Just one sharp-shooting forward, just one man like Nat Lofthouse or Derek Kevan,' John Camkin lamented in the *News Chronicle*, 'and Wolves would now be in the last eight.'

They would, however, have another chance to get there soon enough. Wolves ended the season as league champions again, making virtually certain of their second successive title on 18 April with a 5-0 hammering of Luton Town[36]. The celebrating crowd leapt the barriers at the final whistle

---

36 All but certain of the title because of their superior goal average over Manchester United, Wolves put it beyond doubt four days later with a 3-0 home win over Leicester City.

and gathered in front of the directors' box, calling for Stan Cullis to appear. He remained inside, however, already focused on what was ahead. 'This time we should put up a better show in the European Cup,' he told the press. 'We've got a more settled team.'

* * *

And, a year later, they did, though they needed another big night at Molineux to defeat East German champions ASK Vorwärts in the preliminary round. After going down 2-1 in the away leg on 30 September, second-half strikes from Broadbent and Mason gave Wolves a 3-2 aggregate win, despite Karl-Heinz Spickenagel's heroics in the visiting goal. 'The "Heinz" must stand for 57 varieties of fantastic goalkeeping,' Ian Wooldridge had remarked in the *Chronicle*, but Wolves had done enough to earn a second trip behind the Iron Curtain, this time to face Red Star Belgrade – another unknown quantity, Malcolm Finlayson recalled, but one they took in their stride. 'Stan hadn't been able to send anyone out to watch them play,' the goalkeeper remembered in *Wolves: Match of My Life*. 'So when we arrived … Stan asked a British diplomat from the embassy to come in and tell us about the team. This guy came in and told us how the goalkeeper was a cat and saved everything, the full-backs were brick outhouses and the forwards could score goals at will. Stan listened and then said ironically, "I don't know why we've bothered to come then! Now I'll tell you what we are going to do."' At the aptly named Stadion Partizan, his players faced not only the Red Star team and an extremely hostile crowd, but a German official who penalised them 43 times. 'Who paid this referee?' joked one of the local journalists as decision after decision went the home side's way, but a 1-1 draw put Wolves in the driving seat for the second leg, which they duly won 3-0.

Their reward was a quarter-final with Barcelona, a tie that would again set Cullis's tactical methods against those of a top continental team. Wolves' direct, muscular game had brought them a decade of success: an FA Cup and three league titles as well as those iconic floodlit wins. But now they were taken apart by a side on which they could barely lay a glove, losing 4-0 at the Camp Nou on 10 February then, most painfully of all, surrendering their unbeaten record against foreign opposition at Molineux with a 5-2 defeat on 2 March. 'And, make no mistake, Wolves didn't play badly,' wrote Peter Lorenzo in the *Daily Herald*. 'But in terms of soccer skill, method and execution, it was almost a different game.'

There had been plenty of input from some familiar names beforehand. Real Madrid coach Emil Östreicher, once of Honvéd, warned Barça that they would need a lead of at least three goals to give themselves a chance – 'no foreign side will ever win at Molineux', he told the *Herald* – while advice on how to beat the Spaniards from ex-Barcelona assistant trainer Emilio Aldecoa (who, after arriving in England in 1937 as a refugee from the Spanish Civil War, had played for Wolves for two seasons during the Second World War) saw him variously branded as a traitor to his country and a spy by the furious Barça fans ('I don't care,' he shrugged: 'I just wanted to help my old club'). But ultimately it was another returnee who put the seal on Wolves' fate: Sándor Kocsis, the scorer of Honvéd's opening goal at Molineux six years before. Now back in the

Midlands in the colours of his new team – easing back into action as he recovered from a broken leg, he had missed the Camp Nou game – he struck four times, snuffing out any distant hopes Wolves may have had of salvaging the tie.

Lluís Coll, Luis Suárez and Ramón Villaverde were outstanding, as was Barça centre-forward Eulogio Martínez, whose skill was particularly appreciated by the crowd. 'Kocsis scored four goals,' said supporter Michael Taylor, 'but I have never seen a player before or since who stood out in a game as much as Martínez did. He was absolutely brilliant. Although I was disappointed that we lost, it was just unbelievable the way this Barcelona team played. I came away from the ground telling everybody that that was one of the most exciting teams I'd ever seen, and it still is to this day.' The striker can be seen executing what we should rightly call the 'Martínez turn' in the Pathé News footage of the match. Later labelled the 'Cruyff turn' after Johan Cruyff demonstrated the move at the 1974 World Cup, the Paraguayan maestro was baffling defenders with it at least a decade and a half before.

Although, for Stan Cullis, European success always came second to winning honours at home – 'My ambition as manager was to win the First Division championship, not the European Cup,' he later said, as reported in *The European Cup 1955–1980*. 'To win the European Cup required a different style: it required players to go against their natural game, and this I was not prepared to do' – the defeat to Barcelona showed just how far advanced the best continental teams now were: cosmopolitan in their make-up, and, as Manchester United had found in their semi-final loss to Real three years earlier, ruthlessly astute. Bravery and effort were no longer enough in this new, global game. Wolves' dazzling results against Spartak, Honvéd, Dynamo and Real suddenly seemed to belong to a very different time.

'I used to think it was right for a team to go out and play the game naturally: to work things out as the game developed,' Billy Wright wrote in *One Hundred Caps and All That*. 'That was until I met the crack continental sides. They showed football played to a highly organised plan. And I saw it again in Barcelona.

'Here was the well-thought-out, Hungarian type of attacking game. It was the big difference between Wolves and the Spanish champions. It is the big difference between English football and the best of the game abroad.

'We haven't a chance of equalling these people until we start thinking a lot more about the game: about method and tactics. I know from experience that Wolves do think a lot about style and method: manager Stan Cullis is constantly working on it. But the ability and thought to make it work has got to come from the players. And I maintain that the Wolves players have got to think much more.'

Yet despite the exhibition they had put on in the quarter-final, Barcelona did not go on to win the 1960 European Cup, beaten 3-1 at home then again away in the semi-final by Real Madrid, who met, and defeated, Eintracht Frankfurt in the final at Hampden Park. The Catalans would have to wait until the tournament's 37th year to finally win it for the first time, just before it was rebranded as the UEFA Champions League. For Wolves, their quarter-final appearance remains – at time of writing – their last in the competition their original floodlit victories had helped inspire.

Monday, 29 September 1958: Wolves 1 South Africa 0

Wolves: Finlayson; Stuart, Jones; Slater, Showell, Clamp; Lill, Durandt, Murray, Mason, Horne.

South Africa: Smith (Brakpan United); Williams (Queen's Park [Martin, Western Province]), Denysschen (Queen's Park); Hauser (Johannesburg Rangers), Petersen (Boksburg), Rufus (Stella); Hurly (Marist Brothers), Scott (Salisbury Police), Salton (Berea Park), Warren (Marist Brothers), Barratt (Queen's Park).

Goalscorer: Horne (15).

Referee: W. Clements (West Bromwich).

Attendance: 13,511.

17

A Final Flourish: Wolves v. Dinamo Tbilisi, 10 November 1960

THOUGH STAN Cullis had pointed to his settled side on the day Wolves' third league title had been won, the 1959/60 season had begun with a seismic change. The retirements of Billy Wright and Jimmy Mullen took away the last playing link to Wanderers' pre-war age: both one-club men, Mullen with 486 senior appearances and Wright 541, their departures represented the end of an era for team and fans.

'My hero was Billy Wright,' supporter Harry Hunt told me. 'The only time I put a poster on my wall, it was him. I remember trying to get his autograph as a kid. I deliberately went to this dog show where he was presenting the prizes, just to get his autograph. I won a poetry competition, a road safety poetry competition, when I was 14 or 15, and he was presenting the prizes, a week before the FA Cup Final in 1949. My prize was a pound's worth of savings stamps. And I couldn't talk to him at all: I couldn't wish him good luck for next week or anything, I was just speechless.

'Of course I was prejudiced – I saw no wrong in him, ever – but he never seemed to give a foul away. I can remember different things he did, like taking a free kick against Huddersfield, I think it was, and scoring direct from it. Jimmy Mullen was another favourite of mine. He was a smashing fella. He'd speak to anybody.'

Amid the avalanche of tributes paid to the Wolves and England captain was a homage from the Soviet Union – 'Of all the players to visit this country from abroad, Billy Wright can be proud that he won the hearts of the Moscow crowds,' a state radio correspondent, recalling Wolves' visit to the Russian capital in 1955, was quoted as saying by the *Birmingham Post*. 'The news [of his retirement] was met here with dismay' – while the contribution of Mullen, who had asked to be released from his contract so he could concentrate on the sports shop he was now running in the town, was summed up succinctly by a paragraph in the *Birmingham Weekly Post*. 'One thing we admired [was that] he was never afraid to admit that he was strictly a one-footed player and a purely orthodox winger,' wrote columnist 'G.J.B.'. 'But what a magical left foot that was. Molineux will miss those stinging acute-angled shots and those slide-rule centres.' The league championship – all but clinched seven days after Wright won his landmark 100th international cap – provided a fitting conclusion to two legendary Molineux careers.

It was so nearly three in a row at the end of the following season – Wolves finished just a point behind Burnley, despite scoring more than 100 league goals for the third year in a row[37] – but they had won England's other major

---

37 After scoring 103 and 110 league goals in their back-to-back championship seasons and 106 in 1959/60, Wolves would break the century barrier for the fourth successive time in 1960/61, scoring another 103.

prize, a brace from Norman Deeley and a Mick McGrath own goal giving them a 3-0 victory over Blackburn Rovers in the FA Cup Final on 7 May. It also gave Wolves entry to a new European competition, beginning in August, the Cup Winners' Cup – not yet under the jurisdiction of UEFA – which, with only ten teams involved in its initial pilot run, they entered at the quarter-final stage. Drawn against Austria Wien (who had also received a bye through the cup's preliminary round) they played their first leg at the Praterstadion on 12 October. Their third successive season of continental competition would see them, at least on paper, go further than they had gone before.

A combination of the post and, after Red Star, another controversy-courting German referee frustrated Wolves in Vienna: the former hit several times, the decisions of the latter, Albert Dusch, prompting Stan Cullis to march into his room at half-time to protest about his handling of the game. 'I have never seen Cullis so angry as he was at the end of the match,' said the *Daily Mirror*'s Bill Holden after goals from Hans Riegler and Werner Huschek had rubbed salt into Wolves' wounds. His players had the final word at Molineux, however, as two goals each for Peter Broadbent and Johnny Kirkham – a late replacement for the ill Ron Flowers – and a lob from Bobby Mason put Wolves through with a 5-0 win, 5-2 overall.

It set up a semi-final against Rangers, a team Wolves' directors had considered as a potential floodlit friendly opponent three years earlier, naming the then-Scottish champions as their third-choice option to inaugurate Molineux's new lights should their approach to Real Madrid fail. The Glasgow side had gone one better than the Midlanders in the European Cup the previous season in reaching the final four, and, after wins over Ferencváros (who had been Hungary's league runners-up the previous season; initially it had been down to each country's national football federation to decide its entrants, despite the competition's name) and Borussia Mönchengladbach, the Scots were confident of doing so again. Both teams were hit by injury before the first leg at Ibrox on 29 March, but Wolves showed it more: badly missing the influence of Peter Broadbent, they fell to a 2-0 defeat which, even with the forward's return and a noisy Molineux crowd, they couldn't overturn. Rangers progressed to the final where they met Fiorentina – coincidentally, Wolves' second-choice option for their friendly in 1957 – and lost 4-1 over the two legs in May.

'I think [the game at Ibrox was] the only match in my whole career where I didn't do much at all,' Ted Farmer recalled. 'We were completely outplayed. Peter Broadbent was injured, so there was no supply. I ran my heart out but couldn't get anywhere. They then dropped me for the return.

'[Eleven days earlier, I had played] against Birmingham City. I scored four and went in at full-time and the chairman of the club, Jim Marshall, came up to me and said, "Son, you've done great today. Go to my tailors …" – I thought, I'm to get myself a suit or something – "… and get yourself a tie!" That was my reward for scoring four goals!'

Wolves hadn't arranged a home floodlit friendly for the 1959/60 season – with their European Cup fixtures, there had been no need – but the offer of another glamour game had piqued their interest in the summer. A match against Bahia, winners of the Brazilian Série A in 1959, had been provisionally arranged for October, but that was quickly trumped by a second proposal that arrived from the FA – for another game against Moscow Dynamo, who were planning a new three-match tour. Wolves accepted the governing body's invitation to host the Russians on 10 November, and the Bahia plans were scrapped.

The arrangements for the visit had been made – down to the acceptance of an offer from Lt. Col. R.L. Hargroves for the band of the First Battalion, the Staffordshire Regiment, to provide the musical entertainment at half-time – when news of a change came through. Dynamo would not now be coming to England, the board heard on 2 November, eight days before the game was due to be played; another Soviet Top League side, Dinamo Tbilisi, would be fulfilling the fixture instead.

The team from the east of Georgia was a 'surprise package' in more ways than one, wrote Phil Morgan – 'We know they were losing cup finalists to the Moscow Torpedo club, who also won the league championship [on 31 October, Dinamo had been beaten 4-3 by Torpedo after extra time], but apart from that we know little,' his note in the programme admitted – but, whether Wolves' expected opponents or not, they still promised to give them a good game. West Bromwich Albion had rated Tbilisi as the best of the sides they had faced when they had visited the Soviet Union in 1957 (having also drawn 1-1 with Zenit Leningrad and beaten Red Army team CSKA 4-2), and though their first match in England hadn't gone exactly to plan – a 5-0 drubbing by Sheffield Wednesday at Hillsborough on 7 November had prompted some brutal reviews from the press – Tbilisi were still bullish about their chances at Molineux. 'We shall do better tonight,' an unnamed official from the Soviet team told the *Daily Mirror*'s Bill Holden, who had sought him out at the Victoria Hotel. 'We are now acclimatised.'

They were. The players so roundly derided two days earlier were completely transformed, treating the 34,000 supporters at Molineux to some sparkling attacking play. 'The Russians [sic] no longer had snow on their boots,' said Cyril Chapman of the *Birmingham Post* after another special night at the ground.

Dinamo had rung the changes after their humbling in Sheffield, dropping left-back Givi Khocholava and right-half Jemal Zeinklishvili while reshuffling the rest of the team. Givi Chokheli was moved from left-half to left-back and Shota Iamanidze from inside-left to left-half. Valery Voronin (guesting from Torpedo Moscow) took over from Eduard Toradze at right-half, while the veteran Avtandil 'Basa' Gogoberidze replaced Iamanidze at inside-left. Capped three times between 1952 and 1954, the 38-year-old Gogoberidze's international days were now over, but Dinamo did have another star in their ranks: outside-left Mikheil Meskhi, a member of the Soviet eleven that had won the European Nations' Cup in Paris in July. Centre-forward Zaur Kaloyev had also been part of the successful squad: with 20 goals, he had finished as the Top League's leading scorer at the conclusion of the domestic season a few weeks before.

Wolves, in contrast, were unchanged from the side that had just beaten Nottingham Forest 5-3, a match that had seen Peter Broadbent notch up their 4,000th Football

League goal. But another Wolves scorer was by now grabbing the headlines: the 20-year-old Farmer, whose brace against the Reds had taken his season's tally to seven in as many games. The hero of the club's remarkable victory over Chelsea in the final of the FA Youth Cup in 1958, when Wolves had overturned a 5-1 first-leg deficit with a 6-1 win inspired by four Farmer goals, he had made his senior debut at Old Trafford on 24 September, scoring twice in a 3-1 success. Even though he would miss the last five matches of the season through injury, he would still finish it as Wolves' top scorer, with 28 goals in 27 league games[38].

Farmer would add two more to his total against Tbilisi, but not until after the Soviets had shown their own attacking prowess. Twice in the first minute they caught Wolves offside then swept upfield to take the lead in the second, a fast, low centre from outside-right Tengiz Melashvili evading everyone but Meskhi, who rifled the ball in from the opposite side. A gift from Chokheli gave the hosts an equaliser almost immediately, Farmer pouncing on the defender's errant back-pass to score, but Gogoberidze was there ten minutes later to head Meskhi's centre past Malcolm Finlayson and put Dinamo 2-1 ahead. The same combination produced a third a minute before the interval: a cross from Meskhi, a shot in off the bar from Gogoberidze, and Tbilisi were two goals clear.

It was nothing less than they deserved. Far from the team that had stumbled its way through the match against Sheffield Wednesday, the Georgians had looked to be the

---

38 Famously, Farmer's 21st senior appearance for the club came on his 21st birthday on 21 January 1961, during which, against Everton, he scored his 21st goal.

side in form, the forwards switching and interchanging their positions with polish and confident speed. Meskhi, the 'Georgian Garrincha', had lived up to his nickname, giving Eddie Stuart a particularly uncomfortable time. The interval arrived with Wolves still up against it, and needing something special to avoid a heavy defeat.

Stan Cullis made a change, bringing on Cliff Durandt in place of Norman Deeley, and, on the hour, the gap was narrowed to 3-2 when Eddie Clamp pushed a free kick to Bobby Mason at the edge of the Dinamo area, and the right-winger cracked a shot home. But it was the visitors who seemed to take most inspiration from it as their forwards swung into action once more. On 68 minutes Gogoberidze set up Meskhi for a fourth then, two minutes later, Melashvili fed Vladimir Barkaia, who made it 5-2. The echoes of Barcelona were deafening, and, with the contest seemingly over, some fans started to leave.

But Wolves weren't about to let lightning strike twice. On 78 minutes, from a ball launched forward by Finlayson – not long back on his feet after a nasty tangle with Meskhi – Durandt raced through the middle to score, then Farmer's powerful cross-shot three minutes later made it 5-4. With the Dinamo defence now in panic and the 'Molineux roar' deafening again, Jimmy Murray completed the revival in the 88th minute, climbing above a crowd of defenders to nod an Eddie Clamp cross home. Three goals in ten minutes, and there was very nearly a fourth, as the irrepressible Farmer took the ball away from Sergej Kotrikadze but, wide and off balance, he was unable to get a clean shot away. It added a final twist to an extraordinary match that left the newspapers grasping for superlatives again. 'I would sooner face a herd of rampaging elephants ... than the Wolves in full cry,' wrote Tom Duckworth in the *Sports Argus*. 'Few other clubs could have turned a 5-2 deficit into a 5-5 draw.'

The game would be the highlight of the tour for Dinamo Tbilisi – who maintained a consistent, if unwanted, record by conceding five again in their final match against Tottenham Hotspur, Barkaia scoring twice in reply – and prove to be the last of the great Molineux floodlit friendlies as well.

The footballing world had changed since Wolves' lights were first switched on back in 1953. With the advent of regular European football and the growth of the domestic floodlit calendar, the novelty of watching night-time matches against foreign opposition had passed. It would be two more years before Wolves' 16th floodlit friendly reprised the most famous of the series of games, and by then, the club's position as one of the dominant forces in English football was also, sadly, on the wane.

Thursday, 10 November 1960: Wolves 5 Dinamo Tbilisi 5

Wolves: Finlayson; Stuart, Showell; Clamp, Slater, Flowers; Mason, Murray, Farmer, Broadbent, Deeley (Durandt HT).

Dinamo: Kotrikadze; Sichinava, Toradze, Chokheli; Voronin, Iamanidze; Melashvili, Barkaia, Kaloyev, Gogoberidze, Meskhi.

Goalscorers: Wolves – Farmer (2, 81), Mason (60), Durandt (78), Murray (88); Dinamo – Meskhi (1, 68), Gogoberidze (12, 44), Barkaia (70).

Referee: R.H. Davidson (Airdrie).

Attendance: 34,006.

18

Curtain: Wolves v. Honvéd, 3 December 1962

NATIONAL PRESTIGE was still at stake, the *Express & Star* insisted, when Honvéd returned to the Midlands in December 1962. Lying second in Nemzeti Bajnokság I, a place above MTK, they 'still [ranked] as distinguished', said the paper, 'in their home soccer sphere'. But where the Hungarians' first visit to Molineux had sparked a clamour for tickets and a jam-packed, capacity crowd, their rematch with Wolves was watched by just 13,914 fans – an indication of just how different things were compared with eight years before.

It had been a long road back for Honvéd from the turmoil of 1956. After completing their tour of South America at the start of 1957 – they had played five games against Flamengo in Rio, São Paulo and Caracas, winning two, losing two and drawing one – what remained of their squad had headed back to Budapest, ready to face the sanctions the Hungarian Football Federation's new president Márton Nagy had threatened in a final bid to force them home. Already without Kocsis, Puskás and Czibor – Nagy's strong-arm tactics had, unsurprisingly, only hardened their resolve to stay away – they soon lost Gyula Grosics, too, sent to play for the rural team Tatabánya Bányász by the authority on his return. All but assured of a sixth league title when the revolution had begun, Honvéd were now so weakened that they would have been relegated at the end of the season had the federation not decided to expand the top division from 12 teams to 14. 'There have been changes,'[39] Phil Morgan said, with some understatement, in the match programme, 'since that first meeting back in December 1954.' Honvéd had finished second in the league in 1958 then third in 1959, but two more decades would pass before they won the championship again.

But there were still some familiar faces in the party that arrived at Molineux. Though Lajos Faragó was the team's only surviving player from 1954 – striker Lajos Tichy, a second-half substitute in the earlier game, was out injured – Wolves were pleased to welcome Gyula Lóránt and József Bozsik back as well, the former now coach, the latter president of the club at which he had spent the whole of his playing career. They met the three in the Wolves eleven that had also played in 1954: Bill Slater, Peter Broadbent and Ron Flowers, now captain of the side. 'They perhaps more than any others on the ground tonight will be anxious to see our local team repeat the thrilling success of eight years ago,' added Morgan. 'It is they who will remember the roar as the game turned our way.'

Others recalled it, too. As a boy, Alan Hinton had been in the crowd for several floodlit friendlies, including

---

39 Unlike MTK and Ferencváros, those changes hadn't extended to a restoration of Honvéd's pre-communist name. In 1991, however, the club revived the 'Kispest' prefix from their previous title, becoming Kispest Honvéd FC.

the Honvéd game, dreaming of playing for Wolves, he later said, on the famous Molineux turf. 'As a youngster, to watch such a high level of play in those games was thrilling,' he wrote in his autobiography, *Triumph and Tragedy*. '[My friend] Roy Morley and I actually sneaked in to the Victoria Hotel in Wolverhampton to get autographs from the likes of Ferenc Puskás and Nándor Hidegkuti. We were spoiled for great football, and then for me to be thrown in among it all just a few years later was nothing less than incredible.'

The 20-year-old winger was one of the clutch of young players Stan Cullis had now brought in to the side. After finishing third behind champions Tottenham Hotspur in 1960/61, Wolves had flirted with disaster in 1961/62, ending the season in 18th, their worst league finish since 1933. Two more products of the club's youth system – 20-year-old outside-right Terry Wharton and, two days shy of his 19th birthday, left-back Bobby Thomson (not to be confused with the club's former striker of the same name) – also lined up against Honvéd, as did two 23-year-olds, inside-forward Chris Crowe and goalkeeper Fred Davies, who had taken all but permanent ownership of the number 1 shirt from Malcolm Finlayson after breaking in to the first team at the start of the year. A cold sidelined another member of the group the press had christened the 'Cullis Cubs', centre-forward Barry Stobart, a member of Wolves' FA Cup-winning team in 1960 but who was only now, in the absence of Ted Farmer, getting an extended run in the side. After scoring eight goals in the ten games he had played at the start of the season (four of them coming in the 8-1 demolition of Manchester City on opening day), Farmer had suffered the latest in the series of injuries – recounted in heart-rending detail in his autobiography, *The Heartbreak Game* – that would end in his retirement from football four years later at the age of just 26.

Cullis's focus on youth had led to more departures as well. Norman Deeley had been sold to Leyton Orient, Eddie Clamp to Arsenal, the manager believing that, in Johnny Kirkham, he had a ready-made replacement already on his books. Bobby Mason was now with Chelmsford City, Eddie Stuart with Stoke, where, in September, he had been reunited with Clamp, whose year-long stay at Highbury had been ended by another former team-mate, now the Gunners' manager, Billy Wright, who didn't see a role for the hard-tackling half-back in his future plans. Stuart, who had taken over as Wolves captain when Wright had retired, would skipper the Potters to the Second Division title at the end of the season: a doubly momentous occasion in the club's centenary year.

There was plenty more nostalgia in the air as Honvéd walked out at Molineux again, despite the modest crowd – the bitterly cold weather hadn't helped the club's efforts to attract a larger number of fans. 'My tip to Wolves: don't arrange floodlit matches for this time of the year,' advised Alan Lake in the *Sports Argus*. 'The weather will nearly always wreck them.' But there was perhaps some intuition, too, in the decision of many to stay away. 'Wolves, as we already knew, were not the same,' Phil Morgan, now writing under his own name in the *Express & Star* – 'Commentator' no more – would say, 'and Honvéd, as we were soon to discover, have not yet recovered from the migration of their former star turns.'

The exception was Faragó: a stand-out for the visitors in 1954, now the player of the game. The Honvéd keeper was quite brilliant, compounding some early Wolves wastefulness – Crowe the most glaring culprit, volleying wide from close range having seemingly done the hard work in bringing an awkwardly high ball under control – with save after magnificent save. Jimmy Murray (recalled in place of Stobart after three games in the reserves) was repeatedly denied – so too Hinton, once with the aid of a post – while a full-length dive kept out a dipping shot from Wharton destined for the bottom corner. Flowers, too, saw a goal-bound free kick punched firmly over the bar. '[Faragó] went through the entire syllabus on "how to be a successful goalkeeper" as he leapt, dived, twisted, punched and kicked the almost continual succession of shots from all the Wolves forwards and [wing-halves],' wrote Morgan in the *Star*. The supporters showed their appreciation of his skill, but also made plain their exasperation at the number of chances slipping by.

But Wolves had, at least, been creating them. Honvéd, by way of contrast, had hardly troubled the home defence at all. But the longer the match went on, the more the visitors fancied their chances of stealing a goal, and, after István Vági had gone close and Bobby Thomson had cleared another Honvéd effort off the line, the fans' fears became reality as, with just five minutes left, the Hungarians snatched the lead when Imre Komora's chip found György Nagi, who gleefully drove home. The fat was in the fire, said Morgan; the hosts suddenly had a fight on their hands.

But at long last, Wolves made their superiority pay. Sweeping forward once more, they besieged Faragó's goal, and, with three minutes to go, a scramble in the box ended with Hinton slamming the ball emphatically into the net. But there was no moment of Swinbourne-like magic to round off the comeback this time; Wolves pushed hard for a winner, but couldn't find a way past the keeper again. 'Apart from those last hectic five minutes any resemblance between last night's game and the epic of eight years ago was confined entirely to the names of the clubs,' sighed Phil Morgan, the headline to his report also not mincing its words. 'Such a really poor showing,' it said. 'Wolves save their bacon but do not enhance [their] reputation.'

The friendship between the clubs certainly had been, though: at the banquet held the previous evening and then again at the Town Hall in the morning, at which a commemorative plaque was presented to the Honvéd party by Malcolm Birch, the mayor. Wolves had given souvenirs, too – sets of cufflinks, embossed with their crest, to each member of the touring group, and a Spode bowl as a memento to the club. József Bozsik, replying to new chairman James Marshall at the dinner, said he hoped their meeting could now become an annual event, adding that his team was already looking forward to welcoming Wolves to Budapest the next year. That game – which, on 9 October 1963, Honvéd would win 2-1 – would be the clubs' last for three decades, however, and by the following season, Wolves would have other things on their mind.

After their close shave in 1961/62, Wanderers had made a fine start to the current campaign, their 11-match unbeaten run defying the critics' suggestions that 'long-ball' had had its day. 'Many people claimed we were finished,' said Ron Flowers, a veteran now at 28, in a quote included in *The Title: The Story of the First Division*. 'I'm confident we have demonstrated that the Wolves style is still the best and most successful.' But by the time of Honvéd's visit, Wolves had slipped from first to eighth: they would recover to finish fifth, but another poor showing in 1963/64 piled the pressure on again. No one was prepared, however, for the way in which the next season would begin.

* * *

On Tuesday, 15 September 1964, the front page of the *Express & Star* was dominated by a story that pushed prime minister Alec Douglas-Home's announcement of a general election to a small column at the side. 'Cullis agrees to go' read the banner headline, the block capitals stretching across the width of the page. After more than 30 years at Molineux, Stan Cullis's dismissal as Wolves manager sent shockwaves around the footballing world.

The decision had been made two days earlier, at a specially convened meeting of the directors at the ground. 'It was unanimously[40] decided to inform the manager, Mr Stanley Cullis, that the board wished to be released from its contract arrangements with him,' the minutes of 17 September recorded. 'This was conveyed by the chairman to Mr Cullis on 14 September 1964, and Mr Cullis consented to the release.

'It was with great regret that this action had to be taken and that his long association with the club had to end.

---

40 Though the absence of director Cliff Everall, who was away on holiday, prompted some questioning of whether the verdict was truly unanimous, he had given his agreement, the record of the meeting confirms.

The board wished to place on record its appreciation of his valued service to the club, as a player 1934–1947, assistant manager 1947/48 and manager since 1948.'

Wolves had lost six of the seven games they had played so far – a 1-1 draw with Leicester City on 2 September having given them their solitary point – but Cullis had only been in charge for two. After being taken ill at his desk on 28 August, club doctor Jack Richmond had ordered him to take a check-up then some time away from his job to rest. After a fortnight by the sea in Eastbourne he had returned, refreshed and ready, he told Ken Jones of the *Daily Mirror*, for the challenge that lay ahead: 'The determination and dedication that have made Cullis one of the game's great managers is still there,' the reporter commented, neither yet knowing what was in store. Later that day, John Ireland – who had replaced James Marshall as Wolves chairman seven weeks earlier – told Cullis of the board's decision, hours before his team was due to play West Ham: a 'happy return' for the manager, said the *Birmingham Post*'s Gron Williams with unintended irony in his report of Wolves' 4-3 win. 'Molineux went wild,' he wrote, 'small boys tried to run across the pitch: it was quite like the old days.' By the time his piece was published, however, the news of Cullis's departure was out. '[It is the] end of a golden era', lamented Cyril Chapman in the next edition of the paper. 'A man generally regarded as the post-war king of managers has lost his throne.'

Ken Jones, whose interview with Cullis had been published only a day earlier, was now left to reflect on the 'cruellest soccer sacking I can recall … The [dismissal], and the way of it, is no credit to Wolves' board: the blow to Cullis must have been bitter after a soccer lifetime spent in the service of this one club. From his home last night he told me, "Football, like many other professions, is a hard world. One has to be tough … Thirty years is a long time. But this is life, and one has to accept it." Cullis was calm. But I detected a note of disillusion. A sad note. He was a different man from the one I had interviewed just a day before: a man who seemed then as determined as ever to fight for the Wolves.'

The fans' disbelief was equally palpable. 'They can't call themselves Wolves any more,' said supporter Dave Roberts, quoted on the same page. 'How can they, now that Cullis has gone?'

'I remember where I was when I heard the news,' Harry Hunt recalled. 'You know these things like the death of Kennedy, when you knew exactly what you were doing at the time? Well, I know what I was doing at the time. I was working over at Pendeford in the factory estate there, and I went in and said, have you heard the news? I told them what had happened. It was the whole front page of the *Daily Mail*: a huge thing, a football story on the front page. But he hadn't been well, and I don't think they gave him a chance.'

'It was very strange,' said Andrew Cullis, remembering the episode in an interview for this book. 'We had television cameras camped outside our house for about three days, and my mother, who didn't like press and so on, didn't allow me or my sister out of the house until they'd gone. It was also a bit strange because the chairman who sacked him, John Ireland, only lived about half a mile away from us up the road.

'But it was a huge shock, because in those days managers weren't sacked like that, and a huge shock to my dad, obviously.'

Ted Farmer, still struggling with injury during Cullis's final days, described them in *The Heartbreak Game*. 'On the brief occasions I saw him, he looked decidedly ill and subdued,' he wrote. 'He locked himself away from all players and staff, thereby having little or no influence on coaching tactics, team talks or possible means of motivation for a rapidly declining team which was sitting on the bottom of Division One.' For Farmer, the chairman did what he had to do, despite the wrath it brought down on his head. 'It was the bravest gamble of Mr Ireland's life,' he said, 'for Mr Cullis was a cult figure in Black Country homes. He was criticised and hounded for making a decision that most of the staff knew was inevitable.'

But whatever the rights and wrongs of the call, there is no doubt it was badly handled, not least in the board's apparent lack of plan as to who his successor might be. By the time former Huddersfield Town and Scotland manager Andy Beattie was appointed as caretaker manager nearly two months later, seven straight losses had left Wolves' relegation to the Second Division all but guaranteed. But while the team would bounce back, the damaging rift with the former manager would take far longer to repair: with Ireland still involved with the club it was not until Sir Jack Hayward's takeover in 1990 that the relationship could properly begin to mend. 'At Christmastime we used to go to the Midlands to stay with my mum and dad and we always went to football matches, but we never went to Wolves,' Andrew recalled. 'We went to Birmingham, West Brom,

Coventry, Leicester and Nottingham, but never Wolves. My wife never asked me at the time why we weren't going to Wolves, but she realised later why that was not going to happen.

'One of the great things for us was when Sir Jack was in charge, and they had a benefit match for him and then the stand named after him. It was a very good healing for my dad, because having given so much of his heart and his life to Wolves, it was a significant moment when he was invited back.'

It gave fans another reason to be grateful to the man who had just rescued the club from an even lower ebb. It would have been a tragedy had Wolves' greatest-ever manager not been reconciled with them again: the man who had brought success of a kind never seen before or since to the town. Three league titles, two FA Cups, and, at a time when the English game needed them most, the jewel in his crown, the floodlit friendly victories played out in front of a chock-full Molineux, whose legacy is felt to this day.

'Wolves won the FA Cup and three league champ-ionships during my 13 years as a Molineux first-team man,' wrote Billy Wright in *One Hundred Caps and All That*. 'But the triumphs of this memorable chapter in Wolves' history I think most people will remember clearest and longest are the "little internationals" against the club elite of Europe and the Soviet Union. I am sure, at least, that those people fortunate enough to be at Molineux when we beat Spartak of Moscow and Honvéd of Budapest in the space of a month towards the end of 1954 will not care to dispute this.

'Molineux stands alone on such nights. A hazy cauldron of unbridled partisanship in which the spectators are the actors no less than the players. The hostile glare of the floodlights, the bracing nip of the night air, the hungry, ever-flowing roar of 55,000 throats, the cigarettes and matches which flicker like darting fireflies up on the big bank ... the result is an atmosphere which is almost overwhelming.

'Hampden and Ninian Park have a flavour of their own on a big-match day, but even those bowls of prejudice must take their place behind Molineux when the people of the Black Country come to town.'

Monday, 3 December 1962: Wolves 1 Honvéd 1

Wolves: Davies; Showell, Thomson; Kirkham, Slater, Flowers; Wharton, Crowe, Murray, Broadbent, Hinton.

Honvéd: Faragó; Lévai, Marosi, Dudás; Perecsi, Kotász; Nagy, Komora, Nógrádi, Tussinger, Vági.

Goalscorers: Wolves – Hinton (87); Honvéd – Nagy (85).

Referee: J. Finney (Hereford).

Attendance: 13,914.

Epilogue

The History Makers

'IT WAS the period of the club's history that established its reputation. The team of the 50s was the one that set the standard, and the fans expected every subsequent Wolves team to reach those heights again. We could feel that sense of expectation, that we want this and we're here to make you do it: it was wonderful in one respect, but quite a lot to carry on our shoulders as well. And we still had some of those players around: Billy Wright, Bert Williams, Johnny Hancocks, Jimmy Mullen, they were all still there and coming to the matches. The history makers.

'So we definitely felt the pressure from what they'd achieved, but we benefitted from it as well. The name of Wolverhampton Wanderers was world-renowned because of that team, and it still is. You go anywhere in the world where people follow football, and they'll know Wolves. Peter Broadbent, Bill Slater, Ron Flowers: the names just trip off the tongue.'

Like the lady who lost her shoes to the Honvéd crowd, Wolves' next generation had some big boots to fill. John Richards was 19 when he made his first-team debut, a little under a year after Joe Gardiner – Cullis's right-hand man through the glory days, now chief scout – had brought him to the Midlands from his native Warrington. His appearance in the 3-3 draw with West Bromwich Albion on 28 February 1970 was the first of a 487-game career in gold and black that would bring a record 194 goals. Later a club director and a chair of the Former Players' Association, he was inducted into Wolves' Hall of Fame in 2010.

'When I moved to Wolverhampton in 1969, the pride in the club was very evident in the way that people spoke about it, even though it had just gone through a difficult period after being relegated,' he continued. 'The players of the 50s were so loved and respected. They still are: you mention their names today and there's a sort of reverence that goes with them.

'It's amazing what football does for people. For the fans, it's their memories. It's a massive part of their lives. I meet people who were at the floodlit games who talk in exactly the same way about them: how it felt to be crammed up against each other, the kids sat on the bit of wall that went round the pitch, watching the game. How there weren't more injuries,' he added, 'I'll never know.'

Today's all-seat experience is a world away from those days, when so many crowded into the ground. But though the times moved on, that special atmosphere kept its edge, and for a big game under lights, most of all.

'The first time it really made me gasp was [on 8 May] 1972 when we played Leeds, two days after they'd won the [FA] Cup Final at Wembley,' said John. 'They needed a draw to win the league. We'd had some big games at Wolves before – local derbies like West Brom, which always made your eyes light up – but this was the first time I'd seen that many people in a crowd. Just getting to the match was incredibly difficult.

'You'd see 35, 40,000 at Molineux, but this time the gate was well over 50,000: it was packed to the rafters, and a good hour before kick-off as well. It was exactly how the former players had described it, when they'd travelled in on the bus with the fans, walked up the street and down the Molineux Alley and seen it absolutely rammed with people. It gave me a real idea of what it must have been like back in those days.

'Wolves fans love a night match, and all because of those 50s games. They love coming out in the dark, seeing the way the lights hit the colours and illuminate the stadium: there's a buzz about it that's different from a regular Saturday game. And it lifted us as players, without a doubt. When you got that atmosphere it gave you a little extra boost as you stepped out of the tunnel and on to the pitch. You were bouncing with the adrenaline and anticipation in the air.

'Goodness knows what it would have been like for the players back then, when they were only just starting to experience it. It must have been absolutely fantastic.'

'I loved playing under the lights: more than I did on a Saturday, to be honest,' said fellow Hall-of-Famer Kenny Hibbitt, whose 574 appearances between 1969 and 1984 – the second-most in the club's history – produced 114 goals. 'We had some massive matches: against Leeds in '72, Liverpool in '76 when they needed to win to win the league and we needed a result to stay up – there were 50,000 there again, it was crazy – and, of course, in the UEFA Cup in '71/72, when we got to the final.

'It's hard to put into words how it felt, coming from Bradford Park Avenue in the old Fourth Division to end up playing in Europe. I just loved it. I absolutely loved it.'

Two decades after the pylons first went up at Molineux, it was that UEFA Cup adventure that came closest to recapturing the magic of Wolves' early floodlit years. Victories over Académica de Coimbra, ADO Den Haag, Carl Zeiss Jena and, in the quarter- and semi-finals, Juventus and Ferencváros inspired a whole new generation of supporters as Wolves showed they could hold their own among the cream of the continent again. 'It was surreal, really. Fantastic,' said Mel Eves, then a 15-year-old pupil at Wolverhampton Grammar School. 'I'd been brought up on the tales of Billy Wright and Bill Slater and the team of the 50s, and although it was only just catching up with all the great teams that had visited back then for a lot of the fans, it was great for somebody like me that hadn't been around to see them. I went to all the home games, stood on the North Bank: it was wonderful.'

Unsurprisingly, it was the meeting with Juventus that really captured their imagination. Thirteen-time winners of the Italian league and runners-up to Leeds United in the final edition of the Inter-Cities Fairs Cup the year before, the pre-tournament favourites had been odds-on to progress, especially against a Wolves side missing two key men in Mike Bailey and Derek Parkin. A 1-1 draw in Turin, however, put Wolves on course for their most famous win under the Molineux lights since Real Madrid 15 years before.

'[We] had a lot to live up to,' said Jim McCalliog, Wolves' captain – and goalscorer – in the first leg at the Stadio Comunale. 'The Wolves teams of the 50s and 60s were fantastic, and the UEFA Cup run of 1972 was our way of trying to emulate what those great sides had done. To get that goal in Turin against Juventus, one of the biggest names in world football, and to come away with a draw meant we could take them back to Molineux where we fancied our chances against anybody. It was a volley and I hit it with my left foot so sweetly, and when you hit them you know if they're going in or not. As soon as I [did], I was on my way to the side and to the crowd because I knew it was heading into the bottom corner.' With minutes remaining, a blinding save from Phil Parkes kept Wolves on level terms: they had failed to go one better than Leeds and get a seventh straight European win in a year, but their jubilant band of supporters among the 45,000 in the ground hardly cared.

Not that some twists and turns didn't still lie ahead. At Molineux a fortnight later, a crowd of 40,421 watched Helmut Haller inspire a late Juventus charge, his penalty putting the *Bianconeri* to within a goal of the semi-final after Danny Hegan and Derek Dougan had given Wolves a 2-0 lead. The equaliser, though, never came: Haller took the plaudits for a magnificent individual display – Hegan, too, after what many judged to be his finest-ever for the club – but Wolves had a new piece of history and the place in the final four. 'Phew, that was close!' read the headline in the *Express & Star* the next day. 'Wolves just edge home.' Nerves had been jangling as those last minutes ticked by, but, in the end, 'just' was enough.

'When I first joined Wolves as a 17-year-old, I would look at all the photographs, the history of the club, and try to take it all in,' said Kenny Hibbitt in *Golden Glow:*

Favourite Wolves Floodlit Matches 1953 to 2021. 'Jimmy Mullen, Hancocks, Broadbent and Slater, Billy Wright, the matches they played in, they inspired me. They made me want to play in those kind of games as well.

'Juventus under lights was unbelievable. I feel that when we beat them, the team came of age. Having competed against one of the world's best sides at the time, I think it took a lot of the fans back to when Wolves beat Spartak and Honvéd. Although all European matches under the lights at Molineux were an occasion, the Juventus one was incredible.'

The fairy-tale ending, however, was not to be. Despite dominating both legs of the final against Tottenham Hotspur – an all-English showdown to settle this first UEFA Cup – Martin Chivers's 88th-minute winner at Molineux proved decisive as a 1-1 draw at White Hart Lane condemned Wolves to a 3-2 aggregate defeat. Bill McGarry's men had gone a step further than Cullis's Cup Winners' Cup semi-finalists, but were returning home empty-handed just the same.

'To play in the UEFA Cup Final was the sort of thing I'd dreamed about, but it was a disappointment in the end,' said Kenny. 'I remember [Spurs manager] Bill Nicholson coming into our dressing room after the game and saying that we had been the better side. A lot of managers would do that – it's an easy thing to say when you've won – but I know it came from his heart. I liked Bill: I thought he was a fantastic manager and 100 per cent honest, and he was right, we didn't deserve to lose. But we did, and, in the end, the result is what it's all about.'

But while the longed-for European title had eluded them, the wider burden of expectation was lightened a little by victory in the League Cup Final in 1974, Hibbitt and Richards with the goals against Manchester City that secured Wolves' first major trophy since the 1960 FA Cup. Six years later – this time against Brian Clough's Nottingham Forest, a few weeks before they retained the European Cup – a goal from Andy Gray won the same competition again, adding silverware to a red-letter season that also brought a sixth-placed finish in the league. Memories of that time are tinged with bitter-sweetness – the financial issues that would take hold of the club would soon begin to emerge – but the League Cup winners of 1974 and 1980 had added their own chapters to the story that had so often been their motivation. Having the chance to spend more time with those that had written it was an extra bonus as, in due course, the next generation took ownership of the famous gold shirt and the legacy it represented.

'I was born in the 50s, so the history of the club is in my DNA,' said Mel Eves, one of the heroes of 1980, who had signed for the club he had always supported on leaving school in 1975. 'We lived in a pub, and the conversation then was all about the great Stan Cullis teams: Billy Wright, Bert Williams, Hancocks, Mullen and the others. My dad took me to Jimmy Mullen's shop on Broad Street to buy my first pair of football boots, in fact: Winit Jupiters, and I got to meet the great man himself.

'It was at Jimmy's funeral [in 1987] that the idea for the Wolves Former Players' Association came about,' he went on. 'Billy Wright and the other lads said that they didn't want to meet only at funerals in the future. Peter Creed, who was at the *Express & Star* at the time, got on well with them all so they asked him to pull it together, and it was his honour to be the first secretary of the association when it was then set up. It was for the lads from the 50s and early 60s at first, but they opened it up to more recent players as time went on. I was invited, along with quite a few others who had played more than 200 games for the club, which was the stipulation at the time.

'It was fantastic to be able to rub shoulders with Billy, Bert Williams and the rest: absolute legends from a Wolves perspective, and such humble men as well. Peter Broadbent, for example, who a lot of people described as the best they'd ever seen: if you didn't know he was a footballer, even, you'd never have guessed. Norman Deeley: scored two goals in the 1960 [FA] Cup Final, could have had a third, but he was just a normal bloke. He'd say, "Well, I just played, didn't I?"

'But there's one evening I'll always remember. I'd gone to Molineux to watch a midweek reserve game, so called in to reception to ask where I should go. I usually went up into the directors' box or to one of the corporate boxes to watch as an ex-player. And Billy Wright was there. He asked where I was watching from and I said I wasn't sure, so he said, "Do you want to come with me?" So we walked all the way round the North Bank to what was then the John Ireland – now the Steve Bull – Stand and went into one of the boxes there. A waitress came – Billy was a director of the club by then – we got some tea and biscuits, and sat there: me and Billy Wright, watching the game.

'You think about the career he had: the first to play 100 games for his country (worldwide, that is, not just in England) as well as all he achieved at Wolves, but he was just like Uncle Bill, having a chat. Occasionally he'd say,

"He's got a chance, he's not bad, him, he's doing well, so-and-so," but he wouldn't ever say something like, "He's OK, but he'll never be as good as Peter Broadbent," for example. He was very humble. If anybody had come in, they wouldn't have had a clue that he was who he was.

'It was very special. I was fortunate to meet Billy on a load of occasions, but that was the time it was just me and him. I couldn't tell you anything about the game, who was playing, even. I was just thrilled to be there with the great man.'

'I had more dealings with Bert Williams than anyone else,' said John Richards, one of the four – along with Kenny Hibbitt, Derek Parkin and Geoff Palmer – to play in both League Cup finals. 'Jimmy Mullen and Ron Flowers, too: they were the people that stayed local. We used to see them at the matches and we'd talk about the [50s] games and things like that.

'Bert just loved that period. They went all over Europe – Hungary, Russia, Austria – and in those days that would have been really something. I never went on an aeroplane until I was 19, 20, so imagine being in the 50s, travelling to all these different countries to play. It must have been incredible.

'But they worked really hard. Bert used to say that Stan was very shrewd. The opposition was up against it when they came to Molineux because he regarded his team as [the fittest] in the world. There was a lot of admiration for him [and] a lot of fear, too. Stan had been brought up by Major Buckley, who ruled with a rod of iron: he had written-down rules that the players had to follow. I don't know if it was exactly the same with Stan, but he certainly didn't mess about. And even after they'd stopped playing, when Stan came along to the occasional event, they still referred to him as Mr Cullis, long after they'd all retired. It was that sort of respect and that sort of generation of people. You respected the people who were in senior positions, and the manager of the club was the most senior position you could get.

'But after he'd stopped it was almost as if he'd said, "Right, that's it. I've had my time, it's done, dusted and gone by." He was very reserved, didn't give much away. When you were trying to ask him questions, he'd say things like, "Yes, he was a good player," or, "Yes, they were tough opposition." I suppose he took the attitude that he preferred to talk nicely about people and other teams and managers, so he would never voice any particularly strong views or opinions. I never heard him criticise anyone, whether that was the opposition or his own players.

'I'm sure there would have been people he didn't get on with or who didn't get on with him, and I've heard from players who described the tough streak he had in him. He didn't hold back from a discipline point of view, that's for sure. He was on top of everyone. If players got injured, they weren't discarded, as such, but they were basically ignored until they were fit to play again. So he was very hard from that point of view.

'But by the time I met him it had been a long time since he'd been at the club, and he was just a total gentleman. I think it's a tribute to him that that was how he was: he set his standard when he was working, but outside of that he was the man he wanted to be.'

In 2009, Stan Cullis, Billy Wright and Ron Flowers were among the six inaugural inductees to the Wolves Hall of Fame, set up that year to honour the most influential figures of the past. Bert Williams, Peter Broadbent, Bill Slater, Jimmy Mullen, Roy Swinbourne, Malcolm Finlayson, Johnny Hancocks, Dennis Wilshaw and Joe Gardiner would later join them, so too the team that beat Honvéd, the men that lit 'the spark', as reads the inscription beneath the commemorative sculpture by artist Luke Perry unveiled at Molineux on 13 December 2024 – the 70th anniversary of the game – 'that ignited European club competition'.

'Every club needs its heroes,' said John. 'They're the players that bring in the youngsters, that the parents tell their sons and daughters about, "I saw Billy Wright, captain of Wolves, captain of England"; "I remember Derek Dougan, and Dave Wagstaffe – Waggy – now, he could put a ball on a sixpence"; "Kenny Hibbitt, he could hit goals from anywhere." It's what football's all about, especially in a place like Wolverhampton, whose fortunes have ebbed and flowed with those of the team. Wolves are very much a part of the city, and their history is why we've got tens of thousands of followers in all different parts of the world. Viking Wolves, Swedish Wolves, Australian Wolves: we've got supporters everywhere.

'And why? It goes back to the 50s, to the floodlit games; to beating Honvéd, to beating Moscow Dynamo. It's that legacy that remains.'

And whatever the future may bring, it is that heritage that will be Wolves' enduring inspiration. Others may have more silverware to show for the decades of European football that followed after, but Wolves will always be its pioneers, the club that made it a reality as they took on – and beat – the very best in the world.

Whether the team will ever scale such peaks again remains to be seen, but one thing, at least, is certain. The legend of the floodlit friendlies will live on, a part of Molineux folklore, of what it is to be a Wolves fan. 'It was like a fairy-tale,' said Michael Taylor. 'Manchester United call their ground the theatre of dreams, but Molineux was that for me. Floodlights, mist, stars in luminous shirts: it was unbelievable.'

That magic is no less potent today. For those like Michael, who were lucky enough to be there, it was an experience they would never forget. For the rest of us, the story of those famous games and the men that played in them will forever cast its spell.

Appendix 1:

The Floodlit Friendlies

*Players listed by position/number of goals scored. *Replaced*

	South Africa 30 September 1953	Celtic 14 October 1953	Racing Club de Avellaneda 10 March 1954	First Vienna 13 October 1954	Maccabi Tel Aviv 28 October 1954	Moscow Spartak 16 November 1954	Honvéd 13 December 1954	Moscow Dynamo 9 November 1955	CCA Bucharest 29 November 1956	MTK Budapest 11 December 1956	Borussia Dortmund 27 March 1957	Valencia 10 April 1957	Real Madrid 17 October 1957	South Africa 29 September 1958	Dinamo Tbilisi 10 November 1960	Honvéd 3 December 1962	Total Appearances	Goals Scored
Bill Baxter		4															1	0
Colin Booth									8/1								1	1
Peter Broadbent	8/1		8	8	8/2	8	8	8	Sub/1	10	10/1	10	8/1		10	10	14	6
Eddie Clamp			6				6					4/1	4	6	4		6	1
Chris Crowe															8		1	0
Fred Davies																1	1	0
Norman Deeley			6/1	10								11	7		11*		5	1
Cliff Durandt														8	Sub/1		2	1
Ted Farmer															9/2		1	2
Malcolm Finlayson									1				1	1	1		4	0
Ron Flowers				4	6/1	6	6		6	6	6	6	6		6	6	11	1
Bill Guttridge		3															1	0
Johnny Hancocks	7	7	7	7	7/2	7/2	7/1	7		Sub							9	5
Gerry Harris									3	3		3	3				4	0
Alan Hinton																11/1	1	1
Harry Hooper									7/1	7	7/1	7					4	2
Des Horne													11/1				1	1
Gwyn Jones														3			1	0
Johnny Kirkham																4	1	0
Mickey Lill										Sub			7				2	0
Bobby Mason		8						8		Sub*			10		7/1		5	1
Tommy McDonald				11/1													1	1
Jimmy Mullen	11/1	11	11/1	11				11/1	11		11		11				8	3
Jimmy Murray							9		10/2	9*	8*/1		9/1	9	8/1	9	8	5
Pat Neil										11/1							1	1
Roy Pritchard	3																1	0
Jack Short	2	2															2	0

	South Africa 30 September 1953	Celtic 14 October 1953	Racing Club de Avellaneda 10 March 1954	First Vienna 13 October 1954	Maccabi Tel Aviv 28 October 1954	Moscow Spartak 16 November 1954	Honvéd 13 December 1954	Moscow Dynamo 9 November 1955	CCA Bucharest 29 November 1956	MTK Budapest 11 December 1956	Borussia Dortmund 27 March 1957	Valencia 10 April 1957	Real Madrid 17 October 1957	South Africa 29 September 1958	Dinamo Tbilisi 10 November 1960	Honvéd 3 December 1962	Total Appearances	Goals Scored
Bill Shorthouse		5	3	3	3	3	3	3									7	0
George Showell										2		2	5	5	3	2	6	0
Nigel Sims		1			1												2	0
Bill Slater	4		4	9	4	4	4	4/1	4	4	4			4	5	5	13	1
Les Smith					11	11											2	0
Ronnie Stockin	10																1	0
Eddie Stuart	5		2	2	2	2	2	2	2		2		2	2	2		12	0
Roy Swinbourne	9/1	9			9/3	9/1	9/2										5	7
Doug Taylor			9/1														1	1
Colin Tether										3							1	0
Bobby G.M. Thomson											8/2						1	2
Bobby A. Thomson																3	1	0
Terry Wharton																7	1	0
Bert Williams	1		1	1		1	1	1		1	1	1					9	0
Dennis Wilshaw		10/2	10		10/1	10/1	10	10	9*			9/1	9	10/1			10	6
Billy Wright	6	6	5	5	5	5	5	5	5	5	5	5					12	0

Guide to positions

1 goalkeeper; 2 right-back; 3 left-back; 4 right-half, 5 centre-half, 6 left-half; 7 outside-right, 8 inside-right, 9 centre-forward, 10 inside-left, 11 outside-left.

Appendix 2

Other Floodlit Matches

Wednesday, 17 October 1951 (friendly, at Whaddon Road): Cheltenham Town 3 Wolves 3

Cheltenham: Nicholls; Allcock, Horder; Rigby, Sherlock, Rushworth; McIlvenny, Cowley, Shiner, Mills, Dean.

Wolves: Parsons; McLean, Pritchard; Flowers, Stuart, Wainwright; Booth, Whitfield, Swinbourne, Neal, Clews.

Goalscorers: Cheltenham – Rigby (pen 11), Dean (80), Cowley (85); Wolves – Neal (23), Allcock (og 55), Swinbourne (56).

Referee: Not recorded.

Attendance: Estimates vary between 4,500 (*Cheltenham Chronicle*) and 8,000 (*Express & Star*).

Fans of Cheltenham Town would remember Whaddon Road's first floodlit game for their team's thrilling comeback, but for Wolves it would go down as a match that helped shape their thoughts on lighting Molineux as well. 'While Mr Stanley Cullis and 62,000 others were watching the popularisation of floodlit football in the marble hall atmosphere of Highbury last night, other representatives of the Molineux elite, including 11 players, were convincing 8,000 people in much humbler surroundings of the future of this new style of entertainment,' wrote Phil Morgan, who clearly liked what he saw. 'It was [a success] in almost every sense: the lighting was adequate, the football was entertaining and the crowd went away quite happy.

'I sought out the view of experienced Angus McLean and Dennis Parsons, because I felt there might be special difficulties for the goalkeeper. McLean said he found little trouble with the powerful lamps, whilst the white ball was easily followed in the air. He said there was the impression sometimes that it came towards him much quicker than he had anticipated. To use a cricket term, it was sometimes "fast off the pitch". Parsons also had this impression of the ball reaching him more quickly than expected. Lights at the side facing towards goal, he said, caused him occasionally to lose sight of the ball for a split second.

'[But] from a spectator's viewpoint, I found no real trouble in following the ball or the players.'

As we have seen, the games at Whaddon Road and Highbury were discussed by Wolves' board at their meeting the following day, when it was agreed to begin the process of bringing floodlit football to Molineux.

* * *

Wednesday, 27 February 1952 (friendly, at Revo Electric ground): Revo FC 1 Wolves 15

Revo: Hodges; Poole, Naroway; Forrest, Stanley, Fellowes; Parkes, Wooldridge, Harris, Smart, Baker.

Wolves: Meeson; Showell, Spencer; Wainwright, Stuart, Russell; Deeley, Price, Pearce, Booth (Cooper HT), Wills.

Goalscorers (times of goals not recorded): Revo – Parkes; Wolves – Deeley (4), Pearce (2), Wills (2), Cooper (2), Price (2), Russell, Booth, Wainwright.

Referee: Not recorded.
Attendance: Not recorded.

A game designed to 'demonstrate a means of floodlighting within the scope of the smaller clubs, and to provide information to representatives of the bigger clubs on what could be done on their grounds', as the *Express & Star* explained – 'part social evening, part sales convention' – saw the Revo Electric Company's Birmingham Works League team put emphatically to the sword. Under Tividale's 40 1,000-watt lamps – set on ten pitchside poles, the lowest 27ft off the ground – Wolves' fourth-string racked up 15 goals through eight different scorers. It was an exhibition from both sides' perspective, you could say.

There was, in fairness, a 'ringer' in Wolves' ranks: Norman Deeley, not yet 19 but already a first-team regular. He would be the stand-out player of the match, scoring four goals and assisting several others with passes and crosses from the wing. One was finished by Colin Booth, who had to be taken to hospital after 25 minutes for stitches to a badly cut eyebrow; Len Cooper replaced him at half-time, and duly added two more. 'The crowd enjoyed the match,' said Morgan, 'and the Revo team took their drubbing in such good part that there was a sincere sort of cheer when, with nine goals against them, they took advantage of [keeper Dave] Meeson's only mistake for Parkes to get their consolation goal.'

But mismatch though it was, the evening more than served its intended purpose: the company's demonstration of what could be accomplished on a relatively modest budget was an important step in opening further eyes to what bigger resources might achieve. '[Those watching] could not fail to be impressed by what they saw,' said Morgan, 'and they could see, quite clearly, although [the misty] conditions were not exactly ideal.

'Plans for the more ambitious proposals allow for many more lamps on poles, or towers up to 70ft above the pitch,' he concluded, 'and having seen the effect of Revo's 40 lamps, it is not hard to visualise the brilliance possible from a full-scale scheme on a big ground.'

* * *

Tuesday, 27 January 1953 (friendly, at Ashton Gate): Bristol City 1 Wolves 4

Bristol City: Cook; Guy, Bailey; Peacock, Roberts, Tovey; Boxley, Atyeo, Rodgers, Williams, Regan.

Wolves: Williams; Short, Pritchard; Baxter, Shorthouse, Wright; Smith, Booth, Swinbourne, Stockin, Mullen.

Goalscorers: Bristol City – Rodgers (26); Wolves – Stockin (12, 14, 88), Smith (81).

Referee: H.A. Roberts (Bristol).

Attendance: 24,319.

Played two days before William France presented to the board his initial plans for floodlighting Molineux, Wolves' match against Bristol City was the first experience of floodlit football for many of their senior players. 'They all found it enjoyable,' Phil Morgan reported, 'although as far as this particular installation is concerned they were generally agreed that the 14 lamps were much too low on their 35ft poles, and tended to provide glare when the ball came in off the wings.'

They didn't have it all their own way – Bert Williams was called into action twice in the opening minutes, while centre-forward Arnold Rodgers got on the scoresheet in the 26th minute to crown a good display – but Wolves were generally untroubled by their third-tier opponents, with Jimmy Mullen, in particular, running the show. 'His skilful left-wing runs were appreciated by everybody,' said Morgan, 'with the exception of the unfortunate right-back [Ivor] Guy.' By the time of Rodgers's goal, the visitors already had two, both coming from Ronnie Stockin in only his second senior appearance for the team. His first, after 11 minutes, was an almost casual sideways flick from Mullen's precise pass: his second came two minutes later, a side-step taking him away from a City defender to leave a simple finish past Tony Cook. The visitors' two-goal advantage was restored when Les Smith cut in from the right to score late in the second half. Stockin completed his hat-trick, and a comfortable victory, with two minutes of the game to go. 'It was in every way a pleasant occasion and in some respects an instructive one for Wolves, who are on the verge of providing their own floodlighting system at Molineux,' said Phil Morgan. 'Wolves did what was expected of them ... They drew one of the biggest crowds of the season, they played some attractive football, and their internationals stood out as they properly should in a 4-1 win.'

* * *

Monday, 23 February 1953 (friendly, at Manor Ground): Headington United 2 Wolves 3

Headington: Ansell; Ramshaw, R. Smith; Crichton, Craig, Hudson; Steel, Yates, Mitchell, Mills, J. Smith.

Wolves: Sims; Orwin* (triallist), Gibbons; Baxter, Russell, Stuart; Broadbent, Stockin, Guttridge, Booth, Hancocks.

Goalscorers (including times of goals, where recorded): Headington – R. Smith (15), Mills; Wolves – Guttridge (30), Hancocks, Stuart.

*As reported in the *Express & Star*: named as Corby by the *Oxford Mail*.

Referee: Not recorded.

Attendance: 10,180.

Southern League side Headington United were beaten but far from disgraced by a Wolves eleven featuring eight players with first-team experience. Buoyed by a run of 17 straight wins, the hosts began the game at a blistering pace, their positivity being rewarded in the 15th minute with the opening goal: Nigel Sims could only parry a shot from Roy Smith, and the right-back drove the rebound into the net. But their hopes of a giant-killing were set back by two Wolves goals before half-time. After Stockin flicked on a Peter Broadbent centre for Bill Guttridge to equalise on the half-hour, Johnny Hancocks fired Wolves into the lead from a throw-in after Headington left him unmarked on the edge of the box.

Hancocks had started the game on the left wing with Broadbent out on the right, but the second half saw them back in their more familiar positions as Stan Cullis reshuffled his pack. Eddie Stuart took over at centre-forward, Guttridge falling back to right-back, while Stockin's move to outside-left allowed Hancocks and Broadbent to switch to outside- and inside-right. It was the hosts who had the best early chance of the half, Harry

Yates driving a shot wide, but it was no real surprise when Wanderers increased their lead, Hancocks's cross being trapped by Stockin for Stuart to meet in his stride.

Headington stuck to their task, a header from Norman Mills giving them a deserved second, but with the effects of their earlier exertions becoming more apparent as the half wore on, Wolves were never really threatened in the end. 'The football provided by the Wolves was often as brilliant as the orange [sic] of their fluorescent shirts, but Headington were eager to show that they are a force to be reckoned with,' said the *Oxford Mail*. 'That they held the Wolves to a single goal was a tribute to the eagerness and determination which they put into their game.'

* * *

Monday, 2 March 1953 (friendly, at Boothferry Park): Hull City 3 Wolves 1

Hull: Bly; Phillips, Jensen; Harris, Berry, Denham; Linaker, Horton, Gerrie, Tarrant, Cripsey.

Wolves: Williams; Gibbons, Pritchard; Wright, Shorthouse, Baxter; Hancocks, Stockin, Swinbourne, Booth, Mullen.

Goalscorers: Hull – Horton (28), Gerrie (65, 88); Wolves – Swinbourne (70).

Referee: W.C. Yates (Hull).

Attendance: 21,034.

Wolves' first floodlit defeat was inflicted at the home of second-tier Hull City, then third from bottom in the league. The visitors were disappointing, creating few clear-cut chances, while the hosts, by way of contrast, excelled. 'All that Wolves did at Hull was to give the City team reason to believe there is hope for them yet so far as threatened relegation to the Third Division is concerned,' wrote Phil Morgan the next day. 'They were well-beaten by a more determined team.'

Having said that, there was more than a touch of fortune in all three of the home side's goals. The first was scored by Ken Horton after the ball rebounded kindly off Williams, who had left his line to challenge winger Johnny Linaker, and the other two by Syd Gerrie, the second after an attempted clearance by Len Gibbons struck him on the foot and went into the net before the Wolves keeper could move. A header from Roy Swinbourne, converting Hancocks's cross, provided a crumb of consolation, but it was a night to forget overall. 'Wolves did not shine under the lights at Hull' said the *Express & Star*'s headline. For the men from Molineux, there wasn't much else to say.

* * *

Tuesday, 10 March 1953 (friendly, at Queen Street): Bilston 2 Wolves 4

Bilston: McGregor; Price, Wright; Foster, Kirkham, Pearson; Elliott, Swift, Cook, Harris, Guest.

Wolves: Parton; Gibbons, Kerr; Bolton, Guttridge, Stuart; Hancocks, Flowers, Pearce, Booth, Clews.

Goalscorers: Bilston – Guest (56), Elliott (88); Wolves – Stuart (48), Pearce (60, 86), Hancocks (71).

Referee: A.E. Westwood (Stratford-upon-Avon).

Attendance: 8,000.

Queen Street's inaugural floodlit game provided plenty of entertainment for a record 8,000-strong crowd. Former

West Brom winger Billy Elliott lined up for the hosts, but Johnny Hancocks was the star of the show, delighting the fans with exhibition-style tricks and some light-hearted moments as well: a murmur of anticipation swept round the whole ground every time he was given the ball.

After a scoreless first half in which Elliott and fellow winger Billy Guest also shone, Eddie Stuart gave Wolves the lead, nodding home Colin Booth's centre soon after half-time. The hosts equalised eight minutes later – through Guest, who headed in Foster's free kick – but the visitors soon restored their advantage after, in a break up the field, Hancocks's shot was only parried by McGregor, and Pearce put the ball into the empty net. After 71 minutes Hancocks drove in from 25 yards, before Pearce scored again to make it four. Elliott's flying header reduced the deficit, but the game was already long-won.

The storm damage that had caused the game to be rearranged from its original date in February could be viewed, said Phil Morgan, as something of a blessing in disguise. 'It meant the provision of much better standards for their lights as well as one or two modifications of the lighting itself: carried out, by the way, by the firm who installed the splendid system at [Newcastle's] St James' Park,' he wrote. With 42 lamps focused on the pitch there was plenty of light; there were plans, too, said chairman Bill Morris, to add more. 'When this is done, Bilston will have a system which will compare favourably with any non-league club in the country,' said Morgan, '[and] if the next three floodlit games already arranged are half as popular as last night's, [the] success of the venture – and the cost – must be assured.'

* * *

Wednesday, 18 March 1953 (friendly, at Cross Keys): Wolves 4 West Bromwich Albion 2

Wolves: Williams; Short, Pritchard; Baxter, Shorthouse, Slater; Hancocks, Stockin, Swinbourne, Wilshaw, Mullen.

Albion: Sanders; Rickaby, Millard; Dudley, Dugdale, Rawlings; Griffin, Allen, Evans, Nicholls, Lee.

Goalscorers: Wolves – Stockin (1, 90), Mullen (46), Sanders (og 70); Albion – Nicholls (57, 68).

Referee: F. Read (Willenhall).

Attendance: Not recorded.

The first floodlit meeting of the Black Country rivals took place in the modest surroundings of the Cross Keys, home of Hednesford Town. 'Imagine taking the Sadlers Wells ballet to a wooden hut in some remote, but ballet-loving, village, and you have an idea of what happened on the Hednesford football ground at the Cross Keys last night,' said Phil Morgan. 'Here was an occasion unique in Hednesford's long football history, for something like £200,000 worth of professional footballers in two of the leading teams in the country went freely to this far from palatial little ground to inaugurate a floodlighting system which had cost the club less than £100.' Putting up the lights had been a real community effort: the ten poles on which the lights were mounted were bought by ten supporters at a cost of £1 each, while the fittings were obtained at a generous discount and installed by some friendly electricians. They were all rewarded with fine weather, and an occasion they wouldn't forget.

In a pre-echo of the next time the two would play under lights for the FA Charity Shield, Wolves first established then lost a dominant two-goal lead. The goals, from Stockin and Mullen, had come in the opening minute of each half, either side of a rare penalty miss by Hancocks five minutes before the break. But back came Albion with two in 11 minutes, both from Johnny Nicholls: the second a real beauty, created from the space he made by selling Bill Shorthouse a dummy before he fired the ball into the net. The Baggies were level for just two minutes, however, as goalkeeper Jimmy Sanders, apparently troubled by the lights, back-handed an innocuous-looking Hancocks cross into his own goal. Stockin completed the scoring with the last kick of the game. A win for Wolves, and for Hednesford's ingenuity, too.

* * *

Monday, 5 October 1953 (Staffordshire Senior Cup first round, at Queen Street): Bilston 0 Wolves 0

Bilston: Mason; Price, Wright; Foster, Wakeman, Pearson; Smith, Tatler, Kirkham, Swift, Whittall.

Wolves: Dwyer; Gibbons, Guttridge; Crook, Stuart, Bolton; Punter, Murray, Bonson, Mason, Cooper.

Referee: Not recorded.

Attendance: Not recorded.

A battling performance from Bilston earned them a replay against Wolves in the first round of the Staffordshire Senior Cup at Queen Street. Outplayed for much of the match, the hosts frequently relied on the heroics of goalkeeper Mason, who denied centre-forward Joe Bonson on several occasions when he had looked odds-on to score. But they gave the visitors some scares, too, Guttridge twice clearing off the line while Noel Dwyer was forced to keep out shots from Kirkham and Swift. The home side had taken a while to settle down, but were holding their own in the game.

And though the white-shirted Wolves came at them again after the interval, it was Bilston who had the clearest chance to win it when Stuart handled midway through the second half. Jack Kirkham's spot kick struck the foot of the post, however, a miss his side would live to regret. It was the home supporters who went away happier, though, after watching their team's creditable all-round display.

Those who could, that is, through the thick fog that had enveloped the ground shortly before the start. 'Behind-the-goal spectators caught only snatches of the play as the lights strove to break through,' said the *Evening Despatch*. 'Fog is an old problem – and a tricky one – and the Wolves players certainly didn't help matters with their white shirts. I thought here was a clear case for Wolves' "Technicolor" shirts.' Falling the day before their trip to Bury, Wolves' rayon kit was presumably unavailable. A colour change for one side or the other would still have been necessary anyway, as Wolves' 'Technicolor' shirts would have clashed with Bilston's tangerine.

* * *

Tuesday, 6 October 1953 (friendly, at Gigg Lane): Bury 3 Wolves 1

Bury: Goram; Griffiths, Massey; Daniel, McLean, Bardsley; Plant, Walton, Fletcher, Kelly, Gleadall.

Wolves: Sims; Clamp, Pritchard; Chatham, Shorthouse,

Baxter; Hancocks, Broadbent, Swinbourne, Wilshaw, Stockin.

Goalscorers: Bury – Fletcher (21), Kelly (79), Plant (82); Wolves – Stockin (40).

Referee: A.E. Ellis (Halifax).

Attendance: 17,272.

In an echo of their defeat at Boothferry Park seven months earlier, Wolves were beaten by the sheer determination of a Second Division side making a special effort in front of their home fans. On a night that began with a pre-match performance from a local brass band and community singing led by the Radcliffe Male Voice Choir, Gigg Lane became the first senior ground in Lancashire to host floodlit football. It was an evening to remember for both the town and the club, which took over £2,000 at the turnstiles from a large and enthusiastic crowd.

Wolves, feeling the absence of Wright and Mullen, never settled down to anything approaching their normal form, relying on the good goalkeeping of Sims to keep them from falling behind. But they still moved the ball quickly and with purpose, and, after Doug Fletcher finally beat Sims in the 21st minute, Stockin's well-placed header sent them in to the break deservedly on level terms.

The second half, though, was Bury's. Wolves began it brightly enough, but the Shakers were soon in control and were 'always the more enterprising, the more aggressive', said 'Ranger' in his report in the *Bury Times*. 'If only Bury could play so well in their league engagements!' Both Walter Kelly and Ken Plant hit the woodwork before the former restored their lead, forcing the ball over the line in a goalmouth scramble. Four minutes later the latter extended it, knocking home a John Walton cross to put the game beyond doubt. But the result notwithstanding, Wolves had again 'played their part in furthering the cause of floodlit football', wrote Phil Morgan, 'and whilst I thought the Bury lighting not so vivid as that at Molineux, there was the same colourful atmosphere and the same spectacular air that puts this type of entertainment in a class by itself.' Former Wolves defender Angus McLean, he added, had had a splendid game at centre-half. '[The] only men in the Wolves side who lived entirely up to their reputations,' he said, 'were Shorthouse, Sims and Hancocks.'

There is an intriguing addition to the story as well, revealed in the board minutes of the clubs. 'A letter from the BBC suggesting the televising of our floodlit match with Wolverhampton Wanderers was discussed, and this was agreed providing the Football League and Wolverhampton Wanderers approve,' reads an entry from the meeting of Bury's directors on 21 July. Six days later the consent of Wolves' board was given. What happened next, though, is unclear: there is no further reference to the matter in the subsequent records of either club, while the minutes of the management committee meetings of the Football League – the last remaining body required to give permission – make no reference to it either. The record of the committee's discussion on 13 September does, however, show that the BBC's request to televise three other floodlit games around the same time – one of them the FA Charity Shield between Arsenal and Blackpool, played the week after the friendly at Gigg Lane – had been approved. Whether the BBC had pulled out, satisfied with the other floodlit fixtures it had secured, is open to speculation. There is certainly no surviving film of the match.

* * *

Wednesday, 28 October 1953 (friendly, at Highfield Road): Coventry City 1 Wolves 0

Coventry: Taylor; Jones, Kirk; Jamieson, McDonnell, Austin; Nutt, Dorman, Brown, Waldock, Johnson.

Wolves: Williams; Short, Stuart; Baxter, Shorthouse, Slater; Stockin, Broadbent (Mason), Swinbourne (Guttridge), Wilshaw, Taylor.

Goalscorer: Jamieson (pen 50).

Referee: G. Pankhurst (Warwick).

Attendance: 18,680.

With Wright and Pritchard unfit, Mullen unwell and Hancocks apparently rested – he didn't take the field despite being named in the eleven released to the press the day before the game, but played against Preston in the league three days later – Wolves had planned to experiment against Coventry at Highfield Road, naming Stuart at left-back in place of Guttridge, who had been deputising for the injured Roy Pritchard in the league. Events, however, overtook them, as further injuries forced a rethink at half-time, and Guttridge ended up resuming his position for the second half of the game.

Highfield Road's biggest crowd of the season had turned out in spite of threatened fog, but they were left disappointed by what was a mediocre match overall. Missing Wright and their wingers in particular, Wolves struggled to get into the game, a situation hardly helped by the knocks sustained by first Swinbourne then Broadbent over the course of the first half. Bobby Mason replaced the latter, with Stuart taking the centre-forward's role. There was little improvement in Wolves' performance, however, and Coventry soon took the lead.

The goal came from a penalty, conceded by Jack Short and converted by Iain Jamieson five minutes after the break. It proved to be the winner, as two glaring misses put the seal on what had been a poor evening for the visiting team. 'How Wolves and the crowd missed the international wingers,' sighed the *Express & Star*.

* * *

Monday, 9 November 1953 (Staffordshire Senior Cup first round replay, at Queen Street): Bilston 1 Wolves 7

Bilston: Harris; Price, Wright; Foster, Kirkham, Pearson; Gandy, Swift, Hicklin, Whittall, Townsend.

Wolves: Dwyer; Guttridge, Clamp; Neal, Russell, Flowers; Howells, Stockin, D. Taylor, J. Taylor, Booth.

Goalscorers (including times of goals, where recorded): Bilston – Clamp (og); Wolves – Howells (3), Stockin (18: first of 3 goals), Booth, D. Taylor (2 goals).

Referee: Not recorded.

Attendance: Not recorded.

More than a month after Wolves and Bilston drew at Queen Street, the replay was finally played – not at Molineux, as it turned out, but at the non-league ground again. Bilston had hoped to play under the lights in Wolverhampton, but their request to do so was denied. '[Wolves'] floodlights were installed only for big attractions,' club chairman James

Baker rather bluntly explained – much to the indignation of counterpart Bill Morris, who felt his team had earned the right to the game – as he offered them Molineux on a Wednesday afternoon instead, a proposal Bilston declined.

It was back to Queen Street, then, for a much stronger Wolves side that showed their superiority from the start. Ron Howells opened the scoring in the third minute, driving a ball from Jack Taylor past Harris in the Bilston goal, before Stockin made it two quarter of an hour later with a fine individual strike. The home side battled hard, getting to the interval with no further damage done, and in the second half could even celebrate a goal, gifted by an error from Eddie Clamp, who hit an attempted back-pass straight into his own net. The lapse was an isolated one, however, as Wolves quickly took control again and further goals came at regular intervals, from Booth, Stockin – who completed his second floodlit hat-trick – and Doug Taylor. 'Playing grand football, the fit Wolves forwards completely swamped the Bilston defence,' said the next day's *Birmingham Gazette*. 'Only the hard-working Harris … and centre-half Kirkham limited the visitors' score.'

Wolves' run in the competition ended at the semi-final stage. After beating West Brom in the (daytime) second round, they lost to eventual winners Aston Villa – for whom Dennis Parsons was in goal – at Villa Park.

* * *

Wednesday, 29 September 1954 (FA Charity Shield, at Molineux): Wolves 4 West Bromwich Albion 4

Wolves: Williams; Guttridge, Shorthouse; Flowers, Russell, Clamp; Hancocks, Broadbent, Swinbourne, Deeley, Wilshaw.

Albion: Sanders; Rickaby, Millard; Dudley (Dugdale 83), Kennedy, Brookes; Griffin, Ryan, Allen, Carter, Lee (Hodgkisson 65).

Goalscorers: Wolves – Swinbourne (12, 65), Deeley (46), Hancocks (73); Albion – Allen (55, 57, 82), Ryan (76).

Referee: G. Gibson (Manchester).

Attendance: 45,035.

Perhaps the greatest match in the history of the Charity Shield – discussed in detail in Chapter 5 – featured an additional moment of controversy, too. Five minutes after Deeley had put Wolves into a 2-0 lead at the start of the second half, referee Gordon Gibson awarded a free kick to Albion on the edge of the Wanderers box. Jimmy Dudley touched the ball and Ronnie Allen drove it home, only for it to be disallowed and Wolves awarded a free kick instead.

'[The referee] told me afterwards that the move would have been in order had Dudley either not touched the ball at all, or had moved it for a distance equal to its circumference,' the *Birmingham Gazette*'s Rex Bellamy explained. 'We think Mr Gibson was wrong,' wrote Phil Morgan. 'His explanation … may be so, but at worst the only penalty for Albion should have been an order for the free kick to be re-taken.

'The FA Referees' Chart is quite clear when in its advice to referees it says, "If, in the opinion of the referee, the ball had not rolled completely over or travelled the distance of its circumference, he must order it to be kicked off properly."

'This was a direct free kick for "hands", from which, of course, a goal could have been scored direct.'

* * *

Wednesday, 18 April 1956 (Football League First Division, at Molineux): Wolves 5 Tottenham Hotspur 1

Wolves: Williams; Stuart, Shorthouse; Slater, Wright, Howells; Broadbent, Booth, Murray, Wilshaw, Mullen.

Tottenham: Reynolds; Norman, Hopkins; Blanchflower, Clarke, Marchi; McClellan, Harmer, Smith, Brooks, Robb.

Goalscorers: Wolves – Murray (36), Wilshaw (38), Slater (pen 45, pen 90), Broadbent (53); Tottenham – Harmer (pen 71).

Referee: J.J. Bean (Glamorgan).

Attendance: 29,890.

Molineux's first floodlit league match ended in an emphatic win for Wolves, who, but for some outstanding goalkeeping from Ron Reynolds, could easily have doubled their score. Though the hosts dominated from the start, it wasn't until the 36th minute that Jimmy Murray found the opening goal, but two minutes later it was two, Dennis Wilshaw holding off the challenge of Danny Blanchflower and Maurice Norman to bundle Booth's cross over the line. On the stroke of half-time Wolves had three, Bill Slater – now the team's penalty taker in succession to Johnny Hancocks – converting a spot kick after Norman's handball. A trio of goals in nine minutes, and Wolves were on their way.

Eight minutes after half-time Peter Broadbent – playing at outside-right (new signing Harry Hooper was not yet eligible to appear) – 'turned on a sixpence', in the words of Phil Morgan, to make it four. Spurs pulled one back from the penalty spot, but, after Wilshaw was tripped, Slater had the final word, calmly dispatching the game's third spot kick only seconds from the end. '[Slater] has brought the science of soccer to the task performed for so long in the cannonball tradition by Hancocks,' wrote Morgan. 'The first kick Slater drove to the goalkeeper's left, the second to his right, and this by a man who, feeling off-colour all day, had taken a half-time stimulant and a nasty knock 14 minutes from the end.'

Playing in their rayon kit, his team-mates were similarly inspired. 'What an effect floodlight has on Wolves!' said Charles Harrold in the *Birmingham Gazette*. 'And how it draws the people! A 30,000 crowd turned up for last night's game, and they saw Wolves in truly "electric" mood, playing as though they were beginning the season, rather than finishing it.'

* * *

Wednesday, 29 August 1956 (Football League First Division, at Molineux): Wolves 5 Luton Town 4

Wolves: Williams; Stuart, Harris; Slater, Wright, Flowers; Hooper, Broadbent, Murray, Booth, Mullen.

Luton: Streten; Dunne, Aherne; Pemberton, Kelly, Shanks; Cullen, Turner, Morton, Pearce, Adam.

Goalscorers: Wolves – Murray (15, 38), Slater (pen 17), Broadbent (27), Mullen (44); Luton – Cullen (7), Turner (9, 30, 65).

Referee: E.S. Oxley (Pontefract).

Attendance: 46,781.

Wolves' first floodlit league game of the 1956/57 season was a match to remember, a true end-to-end thriller played at exhilarating speed. A brace of goals in as many minutes from Mike Cullen and Gordon Turner had dealt the hosts an early double blow, but a header from Murray and a Bill Slater penalty then drew them level after 17. Peter Broadbent put Wanderers in front ten minutes later, beating Town keeper Bernard Streten after running on to Hooper's through ball. Back came Luton with a flying header from Turner, but Wolves restored then extended their advantage, Murray burying a strike from just inside the box before Mullen's shot on the turn made the interval score 5-3. 'By half-time, the crowd were applauding what was probably the most thrilling display they had ever seen in a league match,' said the *Birmingham Gazette* the next day.

There was little let-up in the second half – the clubs had agreed that the lights would be switched on at half-time – but only one more goal, Turner completing his hat-trick with a rising drive that flew past Williams 25 minutes before the end. Though Wolves had the ball in the net on two more occasions, both were disallowed and 5-4 it remained, giving Wolves their second victory of the four-game-old season and ending Luton's three-match winning run. 'Molineux is the place for sensations,' said Bill Holden in the *Daily Mirror*. The 46,781 fans, a home crowd bettered only by the one that would watch Wolves draw with Manchester United the following March, agreed.

* * *

Wednesday, 2 October 1957 (Football League First Division, at Molineux): Wolves 4 Tottenham Hotspur 0
Wolves: Finlayson; Stuart, Harris; Clamp, Wright, Flowers; Deeley, Broadbent, Murray, Wilshaw, Mullen.
Tottenham: Reynolds; Baker, Hopkins; Blanchflower,

Ryden, Iley; Medwin, Harmer, Smith, Stokes, Brooks.
Goalscorers: Murray (12), Flowers (38), Broadbent (52, 59).
Referee: L.J. Hamer (Bristol).
Attendance: 36,024.

Eighteen months after their demolition of Tottenham Hotspur in Molineux's first floodlit league game, Wolves celebrated the completion of their new floodlights with another comprehensive win. While the visitors had their chances – Tommy Harmer, Johnny Brooks and Alf Stokes all missed good opportunities to score – it was the hosts who made theirs count, Jimmy Murray setting the tone in the 12th minute with a fine finish after an exchange of passes with Deeley had cracked open the Tottenham defence. Three minutes later the striker was forced to go off the field after a collision with John Ryden, the Spurs centre-half, but Wolves stayed on the attack, Wilshaw and Broadbent forcing saves from Ron Reynolds and, with Murray now back after treatment, a 25-yard drive from Ron Flowers then extended their lead, the Spurs keeper seemingly deceived by the flight of the ball.

In the second half it got worse for the visitors as a clearance from Finlayson went to Flowers and then Murray, who slipped a pass through for Broadbent to finish. Seven minutes later, with Mullen now the provider, the inside-right chested home number four. 'Stokes missed two marginal chances after the interval,' said the *Daily Herald* the next day. 'Peter Broadbent had two marginal chances and scored them both. Therein lay the difference.'

* * *

Monday, 28 October 1957 (friendly, at Easter Road): Hibernian 2 Wolves 3

Hibernian: Leslie; Hughes, Muir; Turnbull, Paterson, Nicol; Smith, Frye, Baker, Preston, Harrower.

Wolves: Finlayson; Stuart, Jones; Clamp, Wright, Flowers; Deeley, Broadbent, Murray, Mason, Mullen.

Goalscorers: Hibernian – Preston (60), Frye; Wolves – Murray (33, 80), Clamp (74).

Referee: J.A. Mowat (Burnside).

Attendance: 26,000.

'To the famous continental teams who have been taught to respect the Wolves floodlight form can now be added Hibernian, one of the leading Scottish teams,' said Phil Morgan after Wolves became the first visiting side to win under the lights of Easter Road. Their 3-2 victory, repeating the scoreline of their win over Real Madrid 11 days earlier, in no way flattered them. 'The Scots, proud as they are,' said Morgan, 'were among the first to acknowledge Wolves as the better team and ... mark this as one of the finest games seen on the ground for a long time.'

Wolves – 'looking not unlike their opponents of a few nights ago' in their all-white strip – took the lead in the 33rd minute after a fine piece of skill from Murray, who caught a long pass from Broadbent on his left foot, transferred it to his right then guided the ball past Lawrie Leslie in the Hibernian goal. Tam Preston equalised for the hosts on the hour, but the visitors' lead was soon restored, Finlayson setting a move in motion that ended in Clamp's narrow-angled cross-shot from the byline with 74 minutes gone. Hibs equalised for a second time, John Frye driving home following a free kick on the left wing, but Wolves' next turned out to be the winner. It was again scored by Murray, who hooked Mullen's low centre into the net to seal Wanderers' success.

***

Wednesday, 20 November 1957 (friendly, at Stade Émile Versé): RSC Anderlecht 2 Wolves 0

Anderlecht: Week; de Vogelaere, Culot; Hanon, de Koster, Vanderwilt; Schoefs, Lippens, Stockman, Jurion, van den Bosch.

Wolves: Dwyer; Stuart, Harris; Clamp, Wright, Flowers; Deeley, Broadbent, Murray, Thomson (Booth 30), Hooper.

Goalscorers: van den Bosch (14), Lippens* (15).

*Charles Harrold's report in the *News Chronicle* names Anderlecht's second scorer as Jacky Stockman.

Referee: F. Smidts (Antwerp).

Attendance: 38,000.

A near full-strength Wolves – only Finlayson, Mason and Mullen were missing from the side that would play at the Bernabéu three weeks later – were shocked by the Belgian champions, who threw them straight off balance with two goals in the first quarter-hour. Outside-left Jeng van den Bosch had a hand in both, taking advantage of a defensive slip to score the first himself then setting up the diving header from Martin Lippens that doubled the advantage a minute later. Wolves – wearing white, as they had against Hibernian – made some adjustments, switching Broadbent and Deeley and bringing on Colin Booth for Bobby Thomson, and came close several times, Broadbent heading over from Deeley's pass seven minutes before the break and Murray, Deeley and Flowers seeing good efforts saved by Félix Week soon after. Harry Hooper – in his final first-team appearance before his transfer to Birmingham City (he would sign off with a hat-trick in the reserves) – made several good runs, too, but the home defence stood firm, closing out the win that the part-timers deserved. 'Wolves were the team we wanted to beat more than any, for we rated them the top opposition in England,' said Anderlecht coach Bill Gormlie. 'It was not for the want of trying that our boys failed,' Stan Cullis conceded. 'The Belgian team played very well indeed.'

***

Wednesday, 11 December 1957 (friendly, at Estadio Santiago Bernabéu): Real Madrid 2 Wolves 2

Real Madrid: Alonso; Becerril, Santamaría; Atienza, Santisteban, Zárraga; Kopa, Marsal, Di Stéfano, Rial, Gento (Mateos 16).

Wolves: Finlayson; Stuart, Harris; Clamp (Showell 51), Wright, Flowers; Deeley, Broadbent, Murray, Mason, Mullen.

Goalscorers: Real Madrid – Mateos (54), Rial (72); Wolves – Mason (30), Atienza (og 81).

Referee: E Harzig (France).

Attendance: 60,000.

Played in non-stop, driving rain – which had, two hours before kick-off, broken a 17-day drought in the Spanish capital – the return match between Wolves and Real Madrid was, at times, a brutal affair, characterised by tackling that showed the cynical side of the European champions' game. 'I thought the refereeing performance of the French official, [Edouard Harzig], was appalling,' the *News Chronicle*'s Ian Wooldridge complained. 'On five occasions throughout this game he carpeted Spaniards for hideous fouls on Wolverhampton players. Not once did they bother to listen to his reprimands, and not once did Harzoc [sic] call them back.' The worst came a few minutes into the second half, when Eddie Clamp was felled by a clattering challenge from José María Zárraga, the left-half, nowhere near the ball, going in studs-high on his thigh. 'One of the most vicious fouls I have ever seen,' said the *Daily Herald*'s Peter Lorenzo. Clamp tried to carry on after receiving treatment but collapsed, and had to be carried off the field.

Wolves had answered an earlier piece of provocation in the best possible way. In the 30th minute Alfredo Di Stéfano had reacted to a free kick being given against him by picking up the ball and booting it at Clamp, but, from the set piece, Bobby Mason had headed home Mullen's pinpoint cross, Broadbent feeding the winger the ball after a dazzling solo run. But three minutes after the right-half's enforced departure came the equaliser from Enrique Mateos – despite, said both reporters, being clearly offside – before Héctor Rial smashed in a great goal to make it 2-1 with 18 minutes to go. But Wolves never gave up – Harris, Stuart, Wright and Flowers, as well as the previously outstanding Clamp, were the heroes of the night, said Wooldridge – and, on 81 minutes, justice was done when Mullen swung in another high, drooping ball and Ángel Atienza, under pressure from Murray, turned it into his own net. 'The First Division leaders tonight put up one of the bravest shows of any British team abroad by holding, and so nearly taming, [the] European champions,' said Lorenzo in summary. 'Wolves, I am convinced, would have become the first foreign side to beat Real on their own soil in five years but for [the] wicked tackle … which robbed them of one of their toughest defenders.'

* * *

Monday, 6 October 1958 (FA Charity Shield, at Burnden Park): Bolton Wanderers 4 Wolves 1

Bolton: Dean (Hopkinson 20); Hartle, G. Edwards; Hennin, Higgins, M. Edwards; Bannister, Stevens, Lofthouse, Hill, Holden.

Wolves: Finlayson; Stuart, Harris; Flowers, Wright, Clamp; Mannion, Durandt, Murray, Mason, Horne.

Goalscorers: Bolton – Hill (43), Bannister (44), Lofthouse (56, 67); Wolves – Durandt (89).

Referee: A. Holland (Barnsley).

Attendance: 36,029.

The cup winners defeated the title holders in the annual Charity Shield after taking a grip on the game they would never relinquish with two goals just before half-time. There had been a moment of drama for Bolton not long after the 7pm kick-off time when goalkeeper Joe Dean dislocated his left shoulder in an awkward fall – Nat Lofthouse took over while regular keeper Eddie Hopkinson, at the ground as a spectator after being selected to play for the Football League in Glasgow the next day, got ready to take over after being given special permission to do so by the league officials in the ground – but Wolves' inexperienced forward line couldn't take advantage, despite the best efforts of Flowers and Clamp to get them into the game.

There had initially been some promising signs, Murray heading against the post while Gerry Mannion (on his first-team debut) and Cliff Durandt both tested Hopkinson, but the goals, from Fred Hill and Dennis Bannister, knocked the wind from Wolves' sails. Durandt did pull one back in the 89th minute – his first senior goal – but by then Lofthouse had made the match safe with strikes either side of the hour.

The 'Battle of the Wanderers' would be rejoined in daylight on 24 January in the fourth round of the FA Cup. Bolton would come out on top again, Lofthouse with the winner to see the holders through to face Preston and, in due course, Nottingham Forest in the quarter-final of the competition, which they lost 2-1. Forest would go on to lift the cup for a second time.

Lofthouse had also had a spell in goal against Wolves at Molineux in February 1957, when Hopkinson broke a finger on 65 minutes. Though Bolton lost 3-2 the 'Lion of Vienna' kept a clean sheet, even saving a last-minute penalty from Harry Hooper.

* * *

Wednesday, 12 November 1958 (European Cup first round first leg, at Molineux): Wolves 2 Schalke 04 2
Wolves: Sidebottom; Stuart, Harris; Slater, Wright, Flowers; Deeley, Broadbent, Jackson, Mason, Mullen.
Schalke: Loweg; Brocker, Laszig; Borutta, Kreuz, Karnhof; Koslowski, Kördel, Siebert, Jagielski, Klodt.

Goalscorers: Wolves – Broadbent (48, 65); Schalke – Siebert (23), Koslowski (88).
Referee: A. Alsteen (Belgium).
Attendance: 45,767.

'Schalke shake our champions' read the headline in the *News Chronicle* after Wolves were left to regret a string of missed opportunities by a side whose fortitude was rewarded with a 2-2 draw. Penned into their own half for long periods of the game, the Germans were only able to launch spasmodic attacks of their own, but they gave Wolves a lesson in taking their chances by converting two of their efforts on goal – the first in the 23rd minute, from a breakaway move started by Otto Laszig and finished by centre-forward Günter Siebert, swerving away from three defenders and finding the corner of the net. Wolves hit back, Mason, Broadbent, Deeley and Allan Jackson – given his chance in the team after scoring a hat-trick for the reserves – all going close, but still without success, and half-time arrived with the hosts still 1-0 down.

Three minutes after the restart, however, they were level, Deeley flicking a pass back from the byline for Broadbent to tap home, and then, 17 minutes later, they had the lead, Broadbent beating Karl Loweg with a terrific headed goal. It was Willi Koslowski who had the final word, however, collecting a cross from Berni Klodt to strike a killer blow. 'The stout-hearted Germans matched sinew with sinew, sweat with sweat,' wrote John Camkin. 'On this form they will be favourites to end Wolves' first bid for the European Cup.'

* * *

Tuesday, 18 November 1958 (European Cup first round second leg, at Parkstadion): Schalke 04 2 Wolves 1

Schalke: Loweg; Brocker, Laszig; Borutta, Kreuz, Karnhof; Koslowski, Kördel, Siebert, Jagielski, Klodt.

Wolves: Finlayson; Stuart, Harris; Clamp, Wright, Flowers; Deeley, Broadbent, Jackson, Mason, Mullen.

Goalscorers: Schalke – Kördel (12), Siebert (39); Wolves – Jackson (48).

Referee: G. Versyp (Belgium).

Attendance: 43,000.

'Stout hearts were not enough to turn [the] European Cup tide Wolves' way,' rued the *Express & Star*, as Wanderers' maiden European challenge ended in a 2-1 defeat in Gelsenkirchen. The Midlanders did everything but score the goal that would have taken them to a play-off game. Wolves 'touched their best form of the season', wrote Peter Lorenzo, but could find no way through the German lines.

With Malcolm Finlayson now recovered from the shoulder injury that had kept him out at Molineux (21-year-old Geoff Sidebottom had deputised in goal) but with Bill Slater absent – his other duties as a lecturer at Birmingham University had called – Wolves began with clear intent but, as in the first leg, somehow found themselves behind, Kördel pouncing on a loose ball to score with Schalke's first shot of the game. The hosts, unchanged from Molineux, had doubled their lead before half-time – again very much against the run of play – Siebert finding the net for the second time in the round from Helmut Jagielski's through ball. In the 48th minute Wolves at last got one back – Deeley fed the ball to Mason who, in turn, set Jackson up to score – but despite continuing to pepper the Schalke defence, they couldn't get the equalising goal. With minutes left, Jimmy Mullen – who, like Mason, had already hit the post – sent a close-range shot agonisingly wide after more excellent build-up play. 'Desperate, desperate luck,' said Stan Cullis afterwards. 'We should have walked it.' Few disagreed.

* * *

Wednesday, 30 September 1959 (European Cup preliminary round first leg, at Walter Ulbricht Stadion): ASK Vorwärts 2 Wolves 1

Vorwärts: Spickenagel; Kalinke, Kiupel; Krampe, Unger, Reichelt; Wirth, Meyer, Riese, Nöldner, Kohle.

Wolves: Finlayson; Stuart, Harris; Flowers, Showell, Clamp; Lill, Mason, Murray, Broadbent, Deeley.

Goalscorers: Vorwärts – Nöldner (24), Kohle (28); Wolves – Broadbent (16).

Referee: M. van Nuffel (Belgium).

Attendance: 65,000.

A match that began with the entire posse of press photographers dashing to the goal which Wolves were due to attack ended with their written colleagues united in bafflement at how poor the English champions had been. Vorwärts, whose coach Harald Seeger had watched Wolves beat Fulham 9-0 in the league two weeks before, played a nine-man defence, working hard to keep possession while denying their opponents any chance to show their attacking flair. As Wolves struggled to break them down, they often resorted to playing aimless balls up the field more in hope than expectation of reward. Peter Broadbent was an exception, and on 16 minutes, having seen an earlier shot blocked by a wall of defenders, he provided the opening goal, taking a ball dropped by goalkeeper Karl-Heinz Spickenagel two steps to his right and lashing it home. Two minutes later he was through again, but couldn't find his previous power. The East Germans weren't about to give him a fourth opportunity, however, and marked him closely for the rest of the game.

A defensive error gave the hosts the equaliser in the 24th minute, and soon after Wolves were behind, Horst Kohle scoring despite Eddie Stuart's desperate attempt to clear off the line. It stayed 2-1, Wolves frustrated by Vorwärts' time-wasting and hampered by a leg injury that left Stuart a virtual passenger for the final 24 minutes, requiring Deeley to drop back into defence. In the end, however, they only had themselves to blame. '[Wolves] should certainly win the return,' said the *Daily Mirror*'s Bill Holden, 'because they simply cannot play so badly again.'

* * *

Wednesday, 7 October 1959 (European Cup preliminary round second leg, at Molineux): Wolves 2 ASK Vorwärts 0

Wolves: Finlayson; Stuart, Harris; Slater, Showell, Flowers; Lill, Mason, Murray, Broadbent, Deeley.

Vorwärts: Spickenagel; Kalinke, Kiupel; Krampe, Unger, Reichelt; Riese, Meyer, Vogt, Nöldner, Kohle.

Goalscorers: Broadbent (54), Mason (76).

Referee: G. Versyp (Belgium).

Attendance: 55,747.

Wolves put the memories of Berlin behind them with their first European Cup win, but not without some scares, Günter Riese twice going close in the early exchanges as Vorwärts tried to add to their first-leg lead. But soon they were relying on Spickenagel to keep it intact as the hosts settled in to the game, the East German keeper twice saving from Murray, the first from point-blank range. By now it was clear that the visitors were determined to do all they could to hang on – their now-familiar spoiling tactics drew considerable ire from the crowd – but this time Wolves were equal to it: on 54 minutes Spickenagel performed another miracle save, now from Bobby Mason, but he couldn't prevent Peter Broadbent from knocking the rebound over the line; a little over 20 minutes later, Mason gave Wolves the aggregate lead, hammering Murray's centre into the Vorwärts net. It could have been more had a second-half shot from Gerry Harris also been given as a goal. 'It was a foot over the goal line,' said Mickey Lill later. Referee Gerhardt Versyp disagreed.

'They fought,' said Stan Cullis of his men, adding that, tactically, Vorwärts had played into their hands. 'They seemed to have a complex about Ron Flowers,' he said. 'They spent so much time and energy looking after him that they often forgot to attack.'

* * *

Monday, 12 October 1959 (friendly, at Celtic Park): Celtic 0 Wolves 2

Celtic: Fallon; MacKay, Mochan; Smith, Evans, Peacock; Chalmers, McVittie, Lochhead, Divers, Auld.

Wolves: Finlayson; Kelly, Harris; Clamp, Stuart, Kirkham;

Mason, Durandt, Murray, Broadbent, Horne.
Goalscorers: Broadbent (21), Murray (70).
Referee: T. Wharton (Glasgow).
Attendance: 45,000.

Five days after Wolves' victory over Vorwärts, the official opening of the floodlights at Celtic Park saw a repeat of the scoreline of the clubs' first night-time meeting, almost six years to the day before. The Hoops had originally tried to bring Real Madrid to Glasgow, but baulked at their £10,000 guarantee; European Cup runners-up Stade de Reims were also contacted before Wanderers were approached. Wolves provided a dazzling enough display, however, to more than justify the call. Despite having to bring in three reserves at short notice, the men from Molineux unequivocally put Celtic in the shade.

Even without Slater, Showell and Flowers, it was 'football as it should be played' said *The Scotsman*. '[Wolves built each] attack with slide-rule precision … giving Celtic's defence no respite whatsoever.' The visitors took the lead in the 21st minute, Des Horne punishing Duncan MacKay's scuffed clearance with a great ball through to Broadbent, who crashed it in from 18 yards. Celtic battled hard, but often fell into Wolves' offside trap – much to the frustration of the crowd – while Malcolm Finlayson, playing superbly in front of Scotland's selectors, was there to deny them if and when it was sprung. Wolves' second put the seal on the win and completed MacKay's night to forget, as his back-heel went straight to Jimmy Murray, who rounded John Fallon to score. 'It was a grand game to watch at Parkhead last night,' wrote 'Waverley' in the *Daily Record*, 'chiefly because Wolverhampton Wanderers brought to Scotland a team obviously built with great thought. A team of almost complete understanding in defence and attack.'

* * *

Wednesday, 11 November 1959 (European Cup first round first leg, at Stadion Partizan): Red Star Belgrade 1 Wolves 1

Red Star: Beara; Durković, Stojanović; Tasić, Spajić, V. Popović; Šekularac, Zebec, I. Popović, Kostić, Rudinski.

Wolves: Finlayson; Stuart, Harris; Clamp, Showell, Flowers; Deeley, Mason, Murray, Broadbent, Horne.

Goalscorers: Red Star – Kostić (37); Wolves – Deeley (28).

Referee: E.W. Ommerborn (West Germany).

Attendance: 40,000.

A 1-1 draw put Wolves into a strong position for the return leg of their European Cup first round tie, but the result only told part of the story of the match, as Cullis's men battled not only their opponents but what the *Daily Herald*'s Peter Lorenzo described as 'some of the most biased refereeing I have ever seen'. Both goals came in the first half, Deeley opening the scoring with a header in the 28th minute before Bora Kostić found the net from a free kick at the edge of the box eight minutes before half-time. From then on, however, it was a hard watch for the 40,000 fans: an endless series of free kicks, the vast majority given against Wolves by West German official Willi Ommerborn, who lost any semblance of grip on the game. 'He went to pieces in the second half after coping fairly well with the first 45 minutes of what was always a man's match,' said Lorenzo.

'Things got so bad in that travesty of a second half that a Jugoslavian [sic] red shirt had only to touch the ground for a free kick to be awarded against Wolves.' But the visitors comfortably held out to secure the draw on the same ground at which England had lost 5-0 to Yugoslavia in May 1958, a match in which the home side's Vladimir Beara and Dragoslav Šekularac had played. 'Now the [Yugoslav] fans know England can still send out teams with skill and guts,' said Bill Holden, summing up a performance full of both. 'Wolves are the best club team who have played in Belgrade,' said Red Star coach Miljan Miljanić afterwards. 'I do not like their football, but I must at least respect it.'

'And that, I hope,' Phil Morgan added, 'is what other continentals may be taught to say before the season is out.'

* * *

Tuesday, 24 November 1959 (European Cup first round second leg, at Molineux): Wolves 3 Red Star Belgrade 0

Wolves: Finlayson; Stuart, Harris; Clamp, Showell, Flowers; Deeley, Mason, Murray, Broadbent, Horne.

Red Star: Beara; Durković, Stojanović; Tasić, Spajić, V. Popović; Stipić, Maravić, Šekularac, Zebec, Kostić.

Goalscorers: Murray (8), Mason (86, 90).

Referee: E. Asmussen (West Germany).

Attendance: 55,519.

Wolves secured their place in the quarter-final of the European Cup with another determined display, their tough-tackling game denying the Yugoslav champions any chance to settle in to what the newspapers described as their more classical style of play. Wanderers attacked from the off, Deeley and Horne both going close, before they took the lead in the eighth minute, Murray floating in a looping cross from the right which, with Beara focused on the waiting Broadbent rather than the flight of the ball, dipped just inside the angle of crossbar and post and into his goal. Two minutes later Murray could have had a penalty when Ljubisa Spajić tripped him in the box, but Wolves' appeals were waved away. Another good shout, for handball, was also denied later in the game.

Red Star had a penalty appeal refused, too, as the home side's 1-0 lead looked more precarious as the match went on. But on 86 minutes Bobby Mason made it safe, stabbing home a cross from Horne then adding a header in the dying seconds to make the final score 3-0. 'It usually goes hard with teams provoking the Wolves,' said Cyril Chapman in the *Birmingham Post*. 'Fulham were given an overwhelming reception at Molineux after having the temerity to win in London, and now it was the turn of Red Star.'

* * *

Wednesday, 10 February 1960 (European Cup quarterfinal first leg, at Camp Nou): Barcelona 4 Wolves 0

Barcelona: Ramallets; Flotats, Gensana; Gràcia, Segarra, Verges; Martínez, Kubala, Evaristo, Suárez, Villaverde.

Wolves: Finlayson; Stuart, Harris; Clamp, Showell, Flowers; Deeley, Mason, Murray, Broadbent, Horne.

Goalscorers: Villaverde (9, 80), Kubala (16), Evaristo (66).

Referee: G. Versyp (Belgium).

Attendance: 80,000.

'Barcelona need to win by three goals tonight to be safe,' Real Madrid's Emil Östreicher had said before the Spanish champions met Wolves, the former Honvéd coach no doubt mindful of the two-goal lead the Hungarian masters had lost at Molineux six years before. But as it turned out Barça went one better in a performance crowned by the goals of Ramón Villaverde, László Kubala and Evaristo but made by Luis Suárez, who provided the assists for Barcelona's opening brace with mazy dribbles down the wing. 'Twice he drew Wolves' defenders like moths to a candle,' John Camkin marvelled. 'With insolent body swerves and twinkling feet, he slid through the whole pack.' Those first 16 minutes proved to be the decisive section of the match: already 2-0 down, the tie had been snatched out of Wolves' hands, the reporter added, almost before it had begun.

It could have been different had Wolves taken the chances they also had in the early stages of the game, Mason, Deeley and Broadbent all missing opportunities to give the visitors the lead. They would continue to enjoy a good deal of the ball but struggled to cope with the fluidity of Barcelona's play, the forwards switching positions to find space and retain possession while evading Wolves' attempts to close them down. On 66 minutes it was three, Brazilian striker Evaristo finishing off a five-man move, before Villaverde completed the rout with the fourth ten minutes from time. Wolves had had further chances – they hadn't played badly at all – but were simply sunk by the better side. 'We were beaten by a magnificent team,' said Stan Cullis. 'As for the score, I consider it just.'

* * *

Wednesday, 2 March 1960 (European Cup quarter-final second leg, at Molineux): Wolves 2 Barcelona 5

Wolves: Sidebottom; Showell, Harris; Clamp, Slater, Flowers; Deeley, Mason, Murray, Broadbent, Horne.

Barcelona: Ramallets; Olivella, Rodri; Gràcia, Segarra, Gensana; Coll, Kocsis, Martínez, Suárez, Villaverde.

Goalscorers: Wolves – Murray (35), Mason (78); Barcelona – Kocsis (29, 42, 60, 74), Villaverde (79).

Referee: L. van Nuffel (Belgium).

Attendance: 55,535.

Former Honvéd inside-forward Sándor Kocsis returned to haunt Wolves twice over, sending them out of the European Cup while ending their unbeaten home record in floodlit football as well. The hosts were under pressure from the start, Showell blocking a first-minute shot from Eulogio Martínez, while the unmarked Lluís Coll gave Wolves a let-off just before the quarter-hour, blazing his shot wildly over the bar. But though their offside trap was working too, it seemed only a matter of time before it was sprung, and, in the 29th minute, the breakthrough duly came.

Kocsis was the scorer but Martínez made the goal, dribbling the ball down the right wing before whipping it in for the inside-right to knock into the net first-time. But Wolves weren't about to lie down, Deeley and Clamp seeing shots kicked off the line before Murray slashed in the equaliser in the 35th minute: Martínez was there to supply Kocsis again, however, who restored Barça's lead three minutes before half-time.

Two more goals from the Spaniards settled the match beyond doubt: the first, a simple header after Martínez had nodded the ball out of Geoff Sidebottom's hands for Coll to hook back in, completed Kocsis's hat-trick; the next, a slotted finish 14 minutes later, gave him number four. Mason pulled one back, but Ramón Villaverde replied almost immediately, taking a ball from Coll past two defenders before driving powerfully past Sidebottom, back in the team after Malcolm Finlayson injured his shoulder in the first leg three weeks before. 'At the end of it all, the stunned but appreciative 55,000 rewarded the Spanish conquerors with a tremendous roar normally exclusively reserved for Wolves' victory nights,' Peter Lorenzo reported. 'Never was a tribute more deserved.'

* * *

Wednesday, 12 October 1960 (European Cup Winners' Cup first round first leg, at Praterstadion): FK Austria Wien 2 Wolves 0

Wien: Gartner; Fischer, Swoboda; Medveth, Stotz, Paproth; Hirnschrodt, Riegler, Nemec, Fiala, Huschek.

Wolves: Sidebottom; Kelly, Showell; Kirkham, Stuart, Flowers; Mannion, Murray, Farmer, Broadbent, Deeley.

Goalscorers: Riegler (71), Huschek (85).

Referee: A. Dusch (West Germany).

Attendance: 25,135.

It was a strangely familiar story for Wolves at the beginning of their Cup Winners' Cup campaign as, in an echo of their experience in Belgrade the previous year, the contentious decisions of a German referee provided the main talking point of the game. 'Eighteen times Albert Deutsch [sic] whistled for free kicks against Wolves,' wrote Charles

Harrold in the *News Chronicle*: 'I thought only about half that number were justified. But from two of them the Austrians scored.'

The goals came after Wolves had made the early running, Broadbent, Murray, Gerry Mannion and Ted Farmer all hitting the post, Broadbent also the bar, while a second-half header from Ron Flowers was so powerful that it nearly knocked goalkeeper Herbert Gartner over his line. The 71st minute, however, saw Wien take the lead, Hans Riegler driving a free kick on the edge of the area past Wolves' five-man wall. Fourteen minutes later they had another, Werner Huschek taking a ball played forward from another set piece and calmly side-footing it home. But while Dusch was certainly the villain of the piece from the visitors' point of view – while they were repeatedly penalised, pushes and niggling fouls from the Austrian players went almost unnoticed, Harrold observed – Wanderers' lack of bite was a disappointment in a game they could and should have easily won. 'It was sad to see Wolves, lacking the power and punch that swept them to many previous triumphs abroad, failing to tame a team they would have eaten last season,' said John Bromley in the *Daily Herald*. His forecast that the Midlanders were as good as out of the competition, however, was distinctly premature.

* * *

Wednesday, 30 November 1960 (European Cup Winners' Cup first round second leg, at Molineux): Wolves 5 FK Austria Wien 0

Wolves: Sidebottom; Stuart, Harris; Clamp, Slater, Kirkham; Deeley, Mason, Farmer, Broadbent, Durandt.

Wien: Gartner; Löser, Swoboda; Medveth, Stotz, Paproth; Hirnschrodt, Riegler, Nemec, Fiala, Schleger.
Goalscorers: Kirkham (1, 26), Mason (35), Broadbent (70, 72).
Referee: J. Gulde (Switzerland).
Attendance: 31,669.

What a difference seven weeks made. The kind of whirlwind performance Wolves usually kept for the closing stages of their floodlit games saw Wien's first-leg lead swept away inside half an hour. 'Their forwards … waltzed around Austria's slack-marking defence to bombard keeper Gartner,' gushed John Bromley, '[while] behind, Bill Slater, killing the menace of Horst Nemec and his men, made the Viennese attack as dangerous as a bunch of balloons.'

Johnny Kirkham was the hero. The out-of-form Eddie Clamp's replacement at the Praterstadion had been drafted in again after Ron Flowers came down with a heavy cold, and opened the scoring in the first minute, driving a shot from the second of the two corners Wolves had already forced through the hands of Gartner and into the roof of the net. In the 26th minute he made it two, heading in a cross from Durandt, before Mason added number three, intercepting a ball rolled out instead of kicked by the unfortunate keeper and gleefully lobbing it over his head. Ted Farmer had the ball in the net three times either side of half-time, too, only to see the linesman's flag raised for offside. But for all their dominance Wolves had to wait until the 70th minute to finally make the game safe, as Peter Broadbent crowned another fine display with a header from another Durandt cross. Two minutes later he put the seal on the win, picking up a pass from Mason and driving it powerfully home. It wasn't quite the 'real, all-out Wolves', Bill Holden felt, but they had still proved far too good for the Austrian team. Their supporters were hoping for more of the same against Scottish Cup holders Rangers in the semi-final in the spring.

* * *

Wednesday, 29 March 1961 (European Cup Winners' Cup semi-final first leg, at Ibrox Park): Rangers 2 Wolves 0

Rangers: Ritchie; Shearer, Caldow; Davis, Paterson, Baxter; Scott, Wilson, Baillie, Brand, Hume.

Wolves: Finlayson; Stuart, Showell; Clamp, Slater, Flowers; Deeley, Murray, Farmer, Mason, Durandt.

Goalscorers: Scott (34), Brand (84).

Referee: J. Cesare (Italy).

Attendance: 79,229.

Wolves badly missed the injured Peter Broadbent as Rangers took a two-goal lead in the first leg of the semi-final in front of a crowd of almost 80,000 at Ibrox Park. Facing a team with its own injury problems, both before and during the match – after manager Scot Symon was forced to field a makeshift forward line (centre-half Doug Baillie was playing at number 9), right-half Harold Davis pulled a thigh muscle in the 17th minute and was a virtual passenger for the rest of the game – Wolves couldn't take advantage, falling behind to a 34th-minute strike from winger Alex Scott. Rangers had already seen an effort from Baillie headed off the line, and they would continue to besiege the Wolves goal, allowing the visitors to show only occasional glimpses of their customary attacking power.

But just when it looked as if the hosts were going to be restricted to a single goal, a rare error from Eddie Clamp presented them with a second, his attempted cross-field pass being blown off course towards Ralph Brand, who finished from 15 yards. 'It's mighty Rangers!' said the headline in the *Daily Record*, below which 'Waverley' gave his thoughts on what was, in the circumstances, an unexpected win. 'Could any other team in Scotland have accomplished Rangers' great feat last night at Ibrox?' he asked. 'I don't think so.'

* * *

Wednesday, 19 April 1961 (European Cup Winners' Cup semi-final second leg, at Molineux): Wolves 1 Rangers 1

Wolves: Finlayson; Stuart, Showell; Clamp, Slater, Flowers; Deeley, Mason, Murray, Broadbent, Durandt.

Rangers: Ritchie; Shearer, Caldow; Davis, Paterson, Baxter; Wilson, McMillan, Scott, Brand, Hume.

Goalscorers: Wolves – Broadbent (63); Rangers – Scott (45).

Referee: G. Dienst (Switzerland).

Attendance: 45,163.

Rangers secured their place in the final of the first Cup Winners' Cup with a 1-1 draw at Molineux, cheered on by around 10,000 travelling fans. But a string of missed chances left Wolves doubly frustrated that the opportunity for them to do so instead had slipped by. 'As well as Rangers played,' said the *Birmingham Post*, 'Wolves really have only themselves to blame.'

With Broadbent back but Farmer absent, Wolves flew at Rangers from the start, Deeley going close in the opening minute then putting another good chance just wide. A drive from Murray went past the post, too, while Davis cleared a Mason effort off the line; a Wanderers goal seemed inevitable as the pressure on the Scots' defence continued to build. A combination of luck and resilience kept them out, however, and on the stroke of half-time came a stunning blow, as Brand beat Slater and played in Scott, who scored his second goal of the round. Flowers nearly equalised straight away, but Billy Ritchie made a stunning, full-length save. The interval arrived with Wolves one down on the night, three behind overall, and with everything now to do.

Eighteen minutes into the second half they finally got one back, Broadbent volleying Durandt's cross through a ruck of players and into the net. But though the forwards continued to create chances, no more goals came and Rangers held on comfortably for a 3-1 aggregate win, bringing Wolves' challenge to an end. 'Rangers, compact and businesslike, never forgot the advantage of their two-goal lead, and this enabled them to adopt a cool approach, which was in direct contrast to Wolves' frequently over-hurried efforts,' said *The Scotsman*. It was a disappointing conclusion to what would turn out to be Stan Cullis's final European campaign.

Bibliography

Bailey, D., *Magical Magyars: The Rise and Fall of the World's Once Greatest Football Team* (Pitch Publishing Ltd., 2019)

Best, G. (with Collins, R.), *Blessed: The Autobiography* (London: Index Books, 2001)

Clough, M., *The Match of the Century: England, Hungary, and the Game that Changed Football Forever* (Cheltenham: The History Press, 2022)

Corbett, C., *Those Were The Days: Wolverhampton Wanderers 1964–1977* (Kingswinford: Geoffrey Publications, 2007)

Corbett, C. & Gordos, S., *Golden Glow: Favourite Wolves Floodlit Matches 1953 to 2021* (Kingswinford: Geoffrey Publications, 2021)

Cullis, S., *All For The Wolves* (London: Hart-Davis, 1960)

Davies, M. & Gibbons, T., *Training With Wolves: The Untold Story of Wolverhampton Wanderers' Trainer* (Kingswinford: Geoffrey Publications, 2019)

Dolloway, A.S., *Charles Buchan's Wolves 1951–1972* (Mansfield: Max Media Publishing, 2018)

Downing, D., *Passovotchka: Moscow Dynamo in Britain, 1945* (London: Bloomsbury Publishing, 1999)

Edelman, R., *Spartak Moscow: A History of the People's Team in the Workers' State* (New York: Cornell University Press, 2009)

Evans, C.J., *Los Leones: The Unique Story of Athletic Club Bilbao* (Pitch Publishing Ltd., 2024)

Farmer, T., *The Heartbreak Game* (Hillburgh Publishers, 1987)

Flowers, R., *For Wolves and England* (London: Stanley Paul, 1962)

Gaddis, J.L., *The Cold War: A New History* (New York: Penguin Group, 2005)

Giller, N., *Billy Wright: A Hero for All Seasons* (London: Robson Books, 2002)

Glanville, B., *Champions of Europe: The History, Romance and Intrigue of the European Cup* (Enfield: Guinness Publishing, 1991)

Godsell, A., *Europe United: A History of the European Cup/ Champions League* (York: SportsBooks, 2005)

Gordos, S., *Talking With Wolves: An Oral History of Wolverhampton Wanderers* (Derby: Breedon Books, 1998)

Gordos, S., *Old Gold Glory: Wolves League Champions 1953/54* (Cradley Heath: Britespot Publishing Solutions, 2003)

Gordos, S., *Peter Broadbent: A Biography* (Derby: Breedon Books, 2007)

Gordos, S., *Cullis: Club and Country* (Kingswinford: Geoffrey Publications, 2012)

Green, G., *Soccer in the Fifties* (London: Ian Allan Ltd., 1974)

Hamilton, D., *Answered Prayers: England and the 1966 World Cup* (London: riverrun, 2023)

Hayward, P., *England Football: The Biography 1872–2022* (London: Simon & Schuster, 2022)

Hendley, J., *Wolves Greatest Games: One Hundred Pieces of Gold* (Pitch Publishing Ltd., 2012)

Hinton, A. (with Bamforth, C.), *Triumph and Tragedy: The Alan Hinton Story* (Kingswinford: Geoffrey Publications, 2021)

Holden, J., *Stan Cullis: The Iron Manager* (Derby: Breedon Books, 2000)

Instone, D., *Wolves: The Glory Years* (Newport: Thomas Publications, 2005)

Instone, D., *Wolves All Over The World* (Newport: Thomas Publications, 2015)

Lowe, S., *Wolves: Match of My Life* (Pitch Publishing Ltd., 2012)

Matthews, S., *The Way It Was* (London: Headline Book Publishing, 2000)

Matthews, T., *The Wolves: An Encyclopaedia of Wolverhampton Wanderers 1877–1989* (Warley: Paper Plane Publishing, 1989)

Matthews, T., *The Wolves Who's Who* (Cradley Heath: Britespot Publishing Solutions, 2001)

McCalliog, J., *Wembley Wins, Wembley Woes* (Fenwick: Langside Publishing, 2021)

Motson, J. & Rowlinson, J., *The European Cup 1955–1980* (London: Queen Anne Press, 1980)

Murray, S., *The Title: The Story of the First Division* (London: Bloomsbury Sport, 2017)

Plant, S., *They Wore The Shirt: Volume 2* (Independently published, 2019)

Puskás, F., *Captain of Hungary* (London: Cassell & Co., 1955)

Quirke, P.A., *The Major: The Life and Times of Frank Buckley* (Stroud: Tempus Publishing, 2006)

Rafters, F., *Standing on the Shoulders of Giants* (Tolworth: Grosvenor House, 2013)

Scragg, S., *A Tournament Frozen In Time: The Wonderful Randomness of the European Cup Winners' Cup* (Pitch Publishing Ltd., 2019)

Shipley, J., *Wolves Against The World: European Nights 1953–1980* (Stroud: Tempus Publishing, 2003)

Smith, B., *Highbury: The Story of Arsenal Stadium* (Edinburgh: Mainstream Publishing, 2005)

Szöllősi, G., *Puskás: Madrid, The Magyars and the Amazing Adventures of the World's Greatest Goalscorer* (Glasgow: Freight Books, 2015)

Taylor, R. & Ward, W., *Kicking and Screaming: An Oral History of Football in England* (London: Robson Books, 1995)

Taylor, R. & Jamrich, K., *Puskás on Puskás: The Life and Times of a Footballing Legend* (London: Robson Books, 1998)

Williams, B., *The Cat in Wolf's Clothing: A Book of Fond Memories* (Independently published, 2007)

Wilson, J., *Inverting the Pyramid: A History of Football Tactics* (London: Orion, 2008)

Wilson, J., *The Names Heard Long Ago: How the Golden Age of Hungarian Football Shaped the Modern Game* (London: Blink Publishing, 2019)

Wright, B., *Football Is My Passport* (London: Stanley Paul, 1957)

Wright, B., *One Hundred Caps and All That* (London: Robert Hale, 1962)

Documentaries

Wolves: The Champions (BBC Football Focus, 1988)

The Official Video History of Wolverhampton Wanderers (Astrion Video, 1995)

Legends of Soccer: The One and Only Billy Wright (Action Sports International, 1999)

Champions of the World (Aidem Digital, 2016)